PUBLISHING 1-2-3

ENHANCING YOUR LOTUS SPREADSHEETS FOR HIGH-IMPACT PRESENTATIONS

PUBLISHING 1-2-3

ENHANCING YOUR LOTUS SPREADSHEETS FOR HIGH-IMPACT PRESENTATIONS

MARY CAMPBELL

M&T Books
A Division of M&T Publishing, Inc.
501 Galveston Drive
Redwood City, CA 94063

© 1991 by M&T Publishing, Inc.

Printed in the United States of America

All rights reserved. No part of this book may be reproduced or transmitted in any form or by any means, electronic or mechanical, including photocopying, recording, or by any information storage and retrieval system, without prior written permission from the Publisher. Contact the Publisher for information on foreign rights.

Limits of Liability and Disclaimer of Warranty
The Author and Publisher of this book have used their best efforts in preparing this book and the programs contained in it. These efforts include the development, research, and testing of the theories and programs to determine their effectiveness.

The Author and Publisher make no warranty of any kind, expressed or implied, with regard to these programs or the documentation contained in this book. The Author and Publisher shall not be liable in any event for incidental or consequential damages in connection with, or arising out of, the furnishing, performance, or use of these programs.

Library of Congress Cataloging-in-Publication Data

Campbell, Mary-
    Publishing 1-2-3/ Mary Campbell
    p. cm.
    Includes index.
ISBN 1-55851-199-7 (book only)
    1. Lotus 1-2-3 (Computer program) 2. Business Presentations--Graphic methods--Computer programs. 3. Electronic spreadsheets--Publishing. 4. Desktop publishing--Computer programs. I. Title.
HF5548.4.L67C342   1991
650'. 0285' 5369—dc20
                                                                            91-4453
                                                                            CIP

94   93   92   91   4 3 2 1

All products, names, and services are trademarks or registered trademarks of their respective companies.

        Editor: Tova F. Fliegel   **Cover Design:** Lauren Smith Designs
        Layout: TFF

Contents

WHY THIS BOOK IS FOR YOU 1

INTRODUCTION 3
How This Book is Organized 3
How To Use This Book 4

CHAPTER 1: TEN BASIC DESIGN OBJECTIVES 7
Conveying Your Message 8
    Deciding What Is Reasonable 8
    Making a Plan 9
    Reviewing the Final Product 11
    Holding the Readers' Interest 12
Presenting an Appropriate Level of Information for the Audience 12
    Creating a Management Summary Presentation 14
    Highlighting Problems or Showing Exceptions 15
    Creating a Report for Reference 16
Presenting Readable Information 16
    Selecting the Correct Size 17
    Creating Multiple Views of the Same Data 17
Presenting Understandable Data 19
    Using Footnotes 19
    Adding Data to Graphs 19
Properly Organizing the Information 21
    Grouping Related Data Together and Providing Summaries 21
    Using Appropriate Spacing to Group Data 21
Varying the Presentation Method 23
Using Consistency in the Level and Method of Presentation 25
Presenting Information Relative to Your Message 26

Create Several Single-Purpose Reports 26
Eliminate the Clutter from Reports and Graphs 27
Using Emphasis to Highlight Important Information 28
Changing the Appearance 28
Adding Information 28

CHAPTER 2: TWENTY DESIGN ELEMENTS TO HELP MEET OBJECTIVES 31
Changing Page Options 33
Determining the Best Page Layout 33
Using Page Orientation Effectively 36
Placing Page Breaks Appropriately 37
Using the Most Appropriate Line Spacing 37
Using Tabs 39
A CLOSER LOOK: Fonts Come in All Sizes 39
Setting Alignment 42
Using White Space Effectively 43
Using Headers and Footers 43
Using Borders 44
Type Options 45
Learning the New Terminology 46
Selecting a Typeface 47
Selecting a Type Style 48
Type Size 48
Other Enhancements 49
Using Color 49
Using Arrows 50
Using Lines 51
Using Boxes 52
Using Shading 54
Adding Captions 54
Using Labels or Annotation 54
Using Graphs 56
Using Graphics Images 58
Table 2-1: Graph Types and Uses 60

CONTENTS

CHAPTER 3: HARDWARE SUPPORT 61
Understanding Monitors and Graphics Adapters 62
    Basic 1-2-3 Requirements 63
    The Importance of Pixels 64
    Different Types of Monitor Adapters 64
Table 3-1: Display Adapters and Their Resolutions 65
    Different Types of Monitors 66
Understanding the Memory in Your Computer System 67
    1-2-3's Requirements 67
    Additional Memory Needed for Add-ins and Other Programs 68
Understanding Disk Types and Capacities 68
    Disk Types in Popular Use 68
Table 3-2: Computer Requirements of Different 1-2-3 Releases 69
    Capacity for Program and Data Storage 70
Understanding Printers 70
Basic Types of Printers 72
    CHECKLIST: Printer Considerations 73
Printer Capabilities 74
    Fonts 74
    Printer Memory 76
    Additional Features 76
A Closer Look at Hewlett-Packard LaserJet Printers 77
    Using Printer Commands for Printer Features 77
    Hewlett-Packard LaserJet Printer Commands 78
    Adding Printer Commands to a Spreadsheet with Setup Strings .. 79
Table 3-3: Frequently Used Printer Commands for the Hewlett-Packard
    LaserJet 80
    Using Printer Control Codes With Menu Selections in 1-2-3 83
    Using the Printing Menu on the Printer Control Panel 83
Other Output Options 87
    Plotters 88
    Film Recorders 88

CHAPTER 4: BASIC 1-2-3 OPTIONS 91
Differences in 1-2-3 Releases 91
    1-2-3 Release 1A 92

PUBLISHING 1-2-3

- 1-2-3 Release 2/2.01 92
- 1-2-3 Release 2.2 92
- 1-2-3 Release 2.3 92
- 1-2-3 Release 3 93
- 1-2-3 Release 3.1 93
- A Common Feature Set 93

Basic Model-Building Skills 95
Changing the Alignment of Entries 95
- CHECKLIST: Model Construction 95
- A CLOSER LOOK: Changing the Alignment of Existing Label Entries 96
- Using Range Label 96
- Using Worksheet Global Label-Prefix 96

Changing the Appearance of Data 97
- Using Range Format 97

Table 4-1: Formatting Options 99
- Using Global Format 101
- Changing the Global Format 101
- Setting the Global Label Alignment 102
- Formatting a Range of Values 102
- Using the Group Command in Release 3.1 102
- Imbedding Setup Strings 102

Controlling Information at the Top, Bottom, and Sides 105
- Using Borders 105
- A CLOSER LOOK: Adding Borders to Your Printout 106
- Using Titles to Work with Screen Data 107
- Adding a Header 109
- A CLOSER LOOK: Adding Titles 109
- A CLOSER LOOK: Creating a Header 110
- Adding a Footer 110

Separating Data 112
- Adding Lines 112
- Using the Repeating Label Indicator 112
- Using @REPEAT 114
- Using a Compose Sequence 115
- Using @CHAR 117
- Adding Boxes 118

CONTENTS

Using White Space 119
Changing the Margins 119
Advancing to a New Page with Print Printer Page 119
Adding a Page Break to the Worksheet 119
Inserting Rows and Columns 120
Inserting Rows and Columns 120
Labeling Data 122
Using Range Justify 122
Using Worksheet Entries to Name Cells 124
A CLOSER LOOK: Steps for Using Range Justify 125
A CLOSER LOOK: Using Label to Name Cells 126
A CLOSER LOOK: Creating a Table of Range Names 126
Entering Names from the Keyboard 126
Keeping Track of the Names You Use 126
Altering the Amount of Data Presented 128
A CLOSER LOOK: Extracting A Subset of Records 128
Recording Criteria 128
Extracting a Subset of Records 129
Database Statistical Functions 130
Selectively Computing Statistics 131
Table 4-2: Database Statistical Functions 132
Changing The Way Data Is Presented 133
Using Copy and Move 133
Data Tables 134
A CLOSER LOOK: Creating a 1-Way Data Table 134
Creating a 1-Way Command 135
Creating a 2-Way Table 135
Creating a 3-Way Table 136
A CLOSER LOOK: Creating a 2-Way Data Table 137
A CLOSER LOOK: Creating a 3-Way Data Table 138
Worksheet Column Hide 138
Changing the Column Width 138
Using Range Trans 141
Data Sort 142
Changing the Page Orientation 143
A CLOSER LOOK: Sorting Data 143

PUBLISHING 1-2-3

Using Graphs to Convey Your Message 144
    Choosing a Type 144
    35mm Slides 146
    A CLOSER LOOK: Creating A Graph Manually 147
Making Changes Easy with Macros 148
    Using the Macro Recorder in Release 2.3 152

CHAPTER 5: USING WYSIWYG WITH 1-2-3 155
    A CLOSER LOOK: Steps For Attaching the Wysiwyg Add-In 156
Installing and Attaching Wysiwyg 156
    The Installation Process 156
    Attaching the Add-In 156
    Activating the Wysiwyg Menu 157
Printing in Wysiwyg 157
Summary of Steps For Printing 158
Table 5-1: Format Indicators and Wysiwyg Formatting Commands 160
Changing Page Layout Options with Wysiwyg 161
    CHECKLIST: Layout Options 161
    Setting the Page Size 163
    Setting the Margins 163
    Using the Preview Feature 163
    Using the Compression Feature 166
    Selective Printing 166
    Creating a Library of Page Layouts 170
Changing the Page Orientation 170
Adding Headers and Footers 171
    A CLOSER LOOK: A Few Quick Steps For Adding a Header or Footer ... 171
Adding Borders 172
Adding Page Breaks 173
Line Spacing 174
Changing the Type 175
    Selecting a Different Typeface 175
    A CLOSER LOOK: Changing the Font of a Worksheet Range 176
    Selecting a Different Type Style 179
    A CLOSER LOOK: Point Sizes 179
    Adding Arrows and Other Symbols 181

CONTENTS

Table 5-2: Wysiwyg Formatting Commands and Formatting Sequences 183
Using Color Effectively 184
Adding Lines and Boxes 186
Using Shading 187
Using Captions, Labels and Other Explanatory Text 188
    Using Text Ranges 188
Table 5-3: Keys to Use While Editing A Text Range 190
Working With Graphs 190
    A CLOSER LOOK: Adding Graphics to A Worksheet 191
    Adding a Graphic to a Worksheet 193
    Creating a Graphic With Wysiwyg 197
    A CLOSER LOOK: Transferring and Copying Graphics 200
Table 5-4: Objects You Can Add in a Text Graph 201

CHAPTER 6: USING ALLWAYS WITH 1-2-3 203

Installing and Attaching Allways 203
    The Installation Process 204
    A CLOSER LOOK: Steps For Installing Allways 204
    Attaching Allways 205
    Activating Allways 205
    A CLOSER LOOK: Steps For Attaching the Allways Add-in 205
Printing in Allways 207
    Changing Page Layout Options With Allways 209
    Setting the Page Size 209
    Summary of Steps For Printing 209
    CHECKLIST : Layout Options 210
    Setting the Margins 210
    Selective Printing 210
    Creating a Library of Page Layouts 212
Changing the Page Orientation 212
    A CLOSER LOOK: A Few Quick Steps For Adding a Header or Footer 214
Adding Headers and Footers 214
Adding Borders 216
Adding Page Breaks 216
Line Spacing 216
Changing the Type 218

Selecting a Different Typeface 219
    A CLOSER LOOK: Changing the Font of a Worksheet Range 219
Selecting a Different Type Style 223
    Using Accelerator Keys to Apply Formats 224
Using Color Effectively 224
Table 6-1: Allways Accelerator Keys 225
Adding Lines and Boxes 226
Using Shading 228
Using Captions, Labels and Other Explanatory Text 229
    Using Text Ranges 230
    Label Justification in Allways 231
    Column Widths in Allways 232
Working With Graphs 232
    Adding Graphs to A Worksheet 233
    A CLOSER LOOK: Adding a Graphic to a Worksheet 233
Changing A Graph's Appearance 235

CHAPTER 7: MOVING BEYOND THE PRINT FEATURES IN 1-2-3 241
Using Bitstream Fonts 242
    A CLOSER LOOK: Bitstream Fonts 242
Using 25 Cartridges in One 242
Table 7-1: Bitstream Font Collections 243
P.D.Queue 244
    Using P.D.Queue to Print 244
    Working With the Print Spooler 245
    A CLOSER LOOK: P.D.Queue 245
JetSet 247
    Selecting a Range to Print 247
    Using JetSet's Print Options 247
    Changing Fonts 248
    A CLOSER LOOK: JetSet 249
    JetSet's Special Printer Control Codes 250
Sideways 250
    Installing Sideways 250
    Selecting a Print Range 251
    Using Other Sideways Options 251

CONTENTS

Using Sideways with a Laser Printer 253
A CLOSER LOOK: Sideways 253

CHAPTER 8: BRINGING 1-2-3 DATA INTO YOUR WORD PROCESSOR 255
Opportunities for Combining 1-2-3 Data with Documents 255
    CHECKLIST: Word Processing Features Desirable for Use with 1-2-3 256
    CHECKLIST: Before Leaving 1-2-3 257
    Adding Projected and Actual Costs to a Letter 258
    Producing a Newsletter 259
    Creating a Financial Spreadsheet with the Addition of Graphics 261
    Options for Saving 1-2-3 Data for Use with a Word Processor 262
    Creating ASCII Files with /Print File 263
    Steps for Creating an ASCII File 264
    Saving to a Worksheet File 267
    Saving Entire Worksheets for Import 268
    Saving Ranges within a Worksheet for Importing 268
    Hiding Columns 270
    Using Range Names in Worksheets to Access Parts of Files 272
    Saving a Graph to a .PIC File 272
    Using the Translate Utility to Create a .DIF or .DBF File 273
Importing Data Into A WordPerfect Document 277
    Importing ASCII Text 278
    A CLOSER LOOK: Importing ASCII Text 278
    A CLOSER LOOK: Importing ASCII Text Using Function List 279
    Importing A .WKS Or .WK1 File 280
    A CLOSER LOOK: Using WordPerfect's Print View Document Mode 281
    Bringing Worksheet Data Files In As Text Using WordPerfect 282
    Bringing Worksheet Data Files In As Tables Using WordPerfect 284
    Editing The Formatting Of Tables After Importing 287
    Creating A Formatted Document With Imported Data 287
    Formatting a Document with Imported Data 292
    Using The Landscape Option To Increase The Width Of The Page 297
    A CLOSER LOOK: Changing Page Size or Orientation within
    WordPerfect 298
Linking Spreadsheet Data to a Document 298
    Considerations For Linking Files 298

Linking With WordPerfect 299
Bringing 1-2-3 .PIC Files into Your Documents 302
    Using .PIC Files In WordPerfect 302
Using Names and Addresses in a 1-2-3 Database to Create a Mail Merge List .. 308
    Creating A WordPerfect Secondary Merge File From A 1-2-3 .DIF File 308
    Creating The Primary Merge File 310
    Performing The Merge 312
Using 1-2-3's Database Features To Select Records To Be Merged 313

CHAPTER 9: USING OTHER GRAPHICS PRODUCTS TO ENHANCE 1-2-3 OUTPUT 315

Exploring Graphics Products 316
Using Harvard Graphics 317
CHECKLIST: Selecting a Graphics Package 318
    Using Chart Galleries 319
Harvard Graphics Slide-show Features 320
Enhancing 1-2-3 Data 320
Using Lotus Freelance 321
    Creating a Template or Backdrop 321
    Creating Text Charts 321
    A CLOSER LOOK: A Proportional Pie Chart with Harvard Graphics 321
    Using the Features of GrandView 323
    Creating a Presentation 323
    Enhancing 1-2-3 Materials 323
    A CLOSER LOOK: The Freelance Igloo Presentation 327
Using DrawPerfect 328
    Objects in DrawPerfect 328
    Other DrawPerfect Features 329
    A CLOSER LOOK: Bob's Stock Chart with DrawPerfect 330
    Enhancing 1-2-3 Graphs 330
Using CorelDRAW 332
    Using Text Creatively 332
    A CLOSER LOOK: Willy's Wild & Wavy with CorelDRAW 335
    Modifying Clip Art 336
    Modifying a 1-2-3 Graph 336
Using 1-2-3 Add-ins to Enhance 1-2-3 Graphs 336

CONTENTS

Using 2D-Graphics 337
    Working With Different Types of Graphs 337
    Selecting a Mode 337
    Compatibility with 1-2-3 338
    Using 2D-Graphics with 1-2-3 Data 338
Using 3D-Graphics 338
    Selecting a Graph Type 339
    The Z-Scale 341
    Other Enhancements 341
    Using 3D-Graphics Options Instead of 1-2-3 343

APPENDIX A: LICS CODES 345

APPENDIX B: LMBCS CODES 351

APPENDIX C: VENDOR CONTACTS 361

INDEX 363

Acknowledgments

Every book I have ever written has seemed like a team effort since there are so many individuals that play a vital role. Individuals that work with me on a regular basis, industry experts, software developers, and the many individuals at the publisher all help to shape a book. This book is no exception. In fact, since it provides information not just on 1-2-3 but other auxiliary products, it has seemed like even more of a team effort.

I would like to personally than just a few of the individuals who contributed so much to this effort:

Gabrielle Lawrence for her help with many different facets of this project.

Martha Studnika, whose WordPerfect expertise helped make the word processing chapter an excellent and comprehensive reference.

David R. Campbell, Jr., whose artistic talents, helped on many of the graphic examples. David also helped by capturing most of the screens for the book.

Tova Fliegel, M&T Books, for her help with everything from editing, art work, and manuscript design. Tova's contribution was equivalent to mine and helped insure a quality product.

Alexandra Trevalyan, Allison Parker, Steve Ormsby, Mary Beth Rettger, and the many others at Lotus who are always such a pleasure to work with.

Brenda McLaughlin, M&T Books, for her idea to do this book and her patience in waiting for 1-2-3 Release 2.3.

Paul Eddington at WordPerfect for providing the latest copy of DrawPerfect quickly.

Jane Baier at Intex for providing assistance with their many 1-2-3 add-ins.

Jennifer Poulsen at Corel Systems and Michael Cuthbertson at SymSoft for providing access to their software.

Christie Gersich at Microsoft for providing help with Microsoft Windows.

Nancy Fischer at Funk Software for her assistance with their products.

Why This Book Is For You

This book is designed for users of 1-2-3 who want to learn techniques for making their 1-2-3 output look its best. If you are interested in improving the information content and appearance of your printed reports and graphs, you will find techniques to help you in this book. The book assumes you already know 1-2-3 basics and gets right to the techniques that you can use to improve any model.

You can use this book no matter what release of 1-2-3 you are using. Although it focuses on new features in 1-2-3 Release 2.3, there are also techniques specialized for 1-2-3 Release 3 and 3.1 as well as many options that are part of 1-2-3 Release 2.01.

In addition to 1-2-3, the book covers techniques in the add-ins Allways and Wysiwyg. The two add-ins were shipped with some releases of 1-2-3 but can be purchased separately if you are still using 1-2-3 Release 2.01.

You will also learn about techniques that require a graphics package or a word processing package. You can adopt the ideas presented no matter which packages you use.

If you already know how to make cell entries, you are ready to use the techniques in this book to improve your 1-2-3 models. The "Closer Look" boxes within the chapters will provide enough detail to insure your success.

INTRODUCTION

How This Book Is Organized

This book is organized into nine chapters and three appendices. The organization of the chapters and appendices follows:

Chapter 1 covers design objectives. Ten basic objectives are used to organize the overall objectives for producing 1-2-3 output.

Chapter 2 discusses basic techniques for implementing these objectives. These techniques are organized into page layout changes, type changes, and other miscellaneous options.

Chapter 3 discusses hardware. It provides information on how hardware selection can affect the output options and quality.

Chapter 4 discusses the options available for improving your output from within the framework of 1-2-3 itself. All you need to invoke these options is a copy of any release of 1-2-3.

Chapter 5 covers the Wysiwyg add-in provided with Releases 2.3 and 3.1. Not only will you see what you are getting on the screen but you will have the ability to vary fonts, print graphs, and otherwise improve your output with this add-in.

Chapter 6 covers the Allways add-in provided with 1-2-3 2.2 and some of the later versions of 1-2-3 Release 2.01. Multiple fonts, page layout options, and color can all be used to improve your output.

PUBLISHING 1-2-3

Chapter 7 covers options available with add-ins that enhance 1-2-3's print features.

Chapter 8 covers options for integrating 1-2-3 data in word processing documents. WordPerfect is used for all of the illustrations since it is the most popular word processing program available today.

Chapter 9 covers the use of graphics products with 1-2-3 data. Harvard Graphics, Lotus Freelance, CorelDraw, and DrawPerfect are used to provide illustrations of actual enhancements to 1-2-3 data.

Appendix A provides a list of the LICS codes used to provide access to special characters in the 1-2-3 Release 2 family of products.

Appendix B provides a list of the LMBCS codes used to provide access to the special characters used with the 1-2-3 Release 3 family of products.

Appendix C is a list of the vendors whose products are covered in this book. It provides quick access to information about the add-ins or products covered if you are not aware of a computer dealer near you where you can take a closer look at these products.

How To Use This Book

You will want to start with Chapter 1 and proceed sequentially through the first four chapters of this book to insure that you are getting the most that 1-2-3 can offer.

After Chapter 4, you will need to take a look at whether you have Allways or Wysiwyg available as an add-in product and choose either Chapter 5 or 6. If you do not have either, read Chapter 5 since it will allow you to decide whether the new Wysiwyg features are sufficiently useful to warrant paying the upgrade fee for the new release.

INTRODUCTION

You can decide on the remaining chapter depending on the types of improvements you are hoping to make to your output. Each of the remaining chapters warrants at least a quick read even if you have not decided to make the types of change discussed since they might provide new ideas that you had not considered.

CHAPTER 1

Ten Basic Design Objectives

As you create 1-2-3 worksheets and graphs your first objective is accuracy: You want to compute formulas correctly and record that information properly. Once you are familiar with the basics of the package you will find that it is easy to meet this objective. As you begin to share your 1-2-3 information with others, you need to expand your objectives beyond the basic tenet of accuracy. You need to consider the manner in which your spreadsheets and graphs are constructed since their design can help you convey your message. Although the same data can be presented in many ways, you want a design that will allow the user to get your full message quickly.

This chapter will discuss ten basic design objectives. These objectives cover some very basic groundwork and will guide your decisions as you create worksheets and graphs with 1-2-3. A before-and-after 1-2-3 example is provided for most objectives to show how a few simple changes can improve the design of your worksheet. Each of the examples in this chapter was created using 1-2-3 Release 2.3. Most examples can be created with any version of 1-2-3, although one of the graph types and some of the formatting is only available with Release 2.3 or 3. Some screens will look different since the graphic features of 1-2-3 Release 2.3's Wysiwyg were in effect.

Later in the book, you will see the application of 1-2-3 Release 3; other add-in tools, such as Allways and Wysiwyg; graphics packages, and word processing programs that enhance your design and help deliver the information. This chapter will show that even very basic changes can help you improve your worksheet presentations.

PUBLISHING 1-2-3

The Ten Basic Design Objectives

The ten basic design objectives are:

- Conveying your message
- Holding the reader's interest
- Presenting an appropriate level of information for the audience
- Presenting readable information
- Presenting understandable data
- Organizing the information to make it more easily understood
- Varying the presentation method
- Using consistency in the level and method of presentation
- Presenting information relative to your message
- Using emphasis to highlight important information

Conveying Your Message

After accuracy, the single most important objective is to convey your message to the readers of your 1-2-3 worksheets and graphs. In a sense, each of the other design objectives are subordinate to this idea since each must help support it.

Deciding What Is Reasonable

Since you understand the data you have created in 1-2-3, you might expect others to assimilate all of the details more quickly than is reasonable. But these individuals do not have day-to-day interaction with the data and potentially the tasks and activities that the data represents. You need to decide how much you can reasonably expect your audience to absorb in a given period of time. Although you might like to make them instant experts on the topic, that scenario is unlikely. If you present too much information, your readers may not retain what is most important.

Your purposes would be better served if you effectively communicated a few key points that your audience can retain. The number of areas you decide to cover and the level of detail you present will depend on the background of these individuals and the amount of time available to them.

TEN BASIC DESIGN OBJECTIVES

One common mistake is to assume that, after studying the data, members of the audience will reach the same conclusion that you did. With less background than you, they may not spend sufficient time with the data to draw any conclusion, let alone the one that you want them to. A better approach would be to spell out the result of your analysis and provide a sufficient level of detail for your audience to examine the validity of your conclusions. If your objective is to show that your division is leading the company in sales and has been the major factor in the increased profitability of the company, you need to include these projections as part of your presentation and supply the necessary detail to prove your theory.

A spreadsheet like the one in Figure 1-1, shown on the following page, is unlikely to make your point. Although all the data is there, the worksheet does not explicitly state the conclusion. Retitling the model, changing the order of the data presented to a high-to-low sorted sequence, adding a contribution-to-profit column, using bold to highlight your division's sales and sales per employee make the message much clearer. Figure 1-2 shows the new worksheet. Figure 1-3 shows a graphic image that again highlights the performance of your division. We created a subtotal for several of the lower-performing foreign subsidiaries to keep to a minimum the number of divisions presented. To improve the graph, you might want to use a second-level graph title of 'U.S. West Leads in Sales'.

Making a Plan

Although it may seem basic, the first result of your analysis of the data, time and readers' level of contact with the information should be to decide what message you want to convey. You need to clearly define and spell out this message to yourself before you can hope to convey it to others.

Decide how much time you will have to present your message. If you have five minutes at a sales meeting, a series of graphs may be the best medium for distributing your information. If you need to fax printed copies to many locations, a short text summary with supporting numbers may be the best presentation method.

PUBLISHING 1-2-3

Figure 1-1 (r.) is unlikely to make your point. However, the revamped worksheet, shown in Figure 1-2 (below) is much clearer. The worksheet model has been retitled, data is presented in a high-to-low sequence, a contribution-to-profit column has been added, and bold highlights the division's sales per employee. But most clear, is the way the information is presented in Figure 1-3 (opposite).

TEN BASIC DESIGN OBJECTIVES

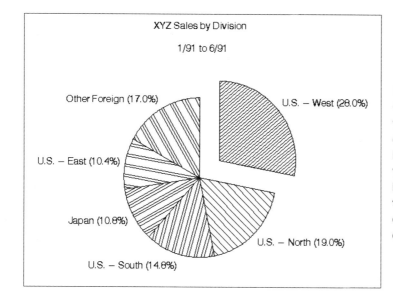

Figure 1-3: Creating graphs with your 1-2-3 data is often the best way to get your point across. It is instantly clear that the western division leads the company in sales.

Reviewing the Final Product

Once you have created your presentation materials, step back and take an objective look at them. If it's an important presentation, you might want to ask someone else to take a look, too. Someone else's perspective may help you fine-tune the materials. If you do not have a second opinion, ask yourself the following questions as you review each screen or section of the presentation. You will also see how you might have answered these questions for Figures 1-1 through 1-3:

- **Is the message that I want to convey spelled out clearly?**

In Figure 1-1, this was not the case. The message was buried within the data.

- **Could the material be interpreted differently from what I intended?**

The data presented in Figure 1-1 could be interpreted to indicate that there were many divisions within the company or that sales of the various divisions varied greatly. Neither conclusion would convey your message to the audience.

- **Can I make changes to prevent misinterpretation?**

Both Figure 1-2 and 1-3 present the message that you are trying to convey more clearly.

- **How can I improve the material to enhance the message's impact?**

Depending on the format of the presentation, you might show your conclusion then a graphic illustration of the result. This creates a quick visual impression of your message.

Holding the Readers' Interest

You can prepare an excellent worksheet design or an impressive graphics presentation and still lose the readers. They will never get your message if they stop looking at your material or tune out your presentation. Variety, organization and some of the other design objectives discussed later in this chapter will help you structure material that makes it easy and interesting to follow your ideas.

Presenting an Appropriate Level of Information for the Audience

For every presentation you need to decide whether to present detail or some level of summary information. To create material at the appropriate level, you must focus on the audience's needs and level of understanding. Also, when creating your material, consider how much time your readers will have to review the information. If you need to provide sales information to branch managers, division heads, and the company president, you will need several different reports that vary in their level of detail.

TEN BASIC DESIGN OBJECTIVES

A potential report distribution schedule might be:

Level	Reports Received
President	Company summary
	Summary by division
	Summary by branch
	Industry competitive analysis
	Trend report at the company level
Division Head	Company summary
	Summary by division
	Summary by branch
	Branch detail for branches in the division
	Competitive industry analysis
	Trend report at the company and division levels
Branch Manager	Detail branch data
	Branch trends
	Competitive analysis with a sample branch in the same industry

PUBLISHING 1-2-3

Creating a Management Summary Presentation

If you are preparing a report or presentation for management you will want to include a summary. You can have detailed information available in the event that the summary evokes a need to look closer at certain specifics, but you should present the management summary first. Some of the methods you might use to organize information in a summary fashion are:

- Product summaries (sales, costs, profits by product)
- Company unit summaries (totals by group, region, or division)
- Actual versus projections at a summary level by product or division
- Summary trends (current month versus last month, same month last year, etc.)
- Summary components as a percentage of the whole
- Summary numbers versus industry averages or a specific competitor or product

Figure 1-4 shows a worksheet that contains detailed sales transactions. Although this supporting detail is needed for other uses, it is too detailed to be useful to upper management. It would be better to show some summary statistics for the day's sales.

```
A1:                                                              READY
         A         B         C          D          E         F    G    H
  1                        Cleveland Sales Data
  2                        January 23, 1991
  3
  4  Dealer    Model     Color          Price Customer  Payment
  5  East      Prancer   Blue         $9,875 Gremler   Credit
  6  West      Donner    Red         $12,300 Stein    Credit
  7  East      Prancer   Green       $10,100 Kaylor   Credit
  8  West      Prancer   Bronze       $9,595 Thomas   Cash
  9  West      Prancer   White        $9,985 Dressler Cash
 10  West      Donner    Black       $14,500 York     Credit
 11  West      Prancer   Blue        $10,800 Larkin   Credit
 12  East      Prancer   Gold         $9,990 Garrett  Cash
 13  West      Prancer   Red         $10,250 Parish   Credit
 14  East      Donner    Red         $12,567 Norris   Credit
 15  East      Prancer   White        $9,980 Wendall  Credit
 16  West      Prancer   Black       $10,115 Javis    Cash
 17  East      Prancer   Silver      $10,110 Parker   Credit
 18  West      Donner    Blue        $14,990 Boyd     Cash
 19  West      Prancer   Brown       $10,320 Smith    Credit
 20  East      Donner    Silver      $15,100 Triplor  Cash
14-Mar-91  12:07 PM                                               NUM
```

TEN BASIC DESIGN OBJECTIVES

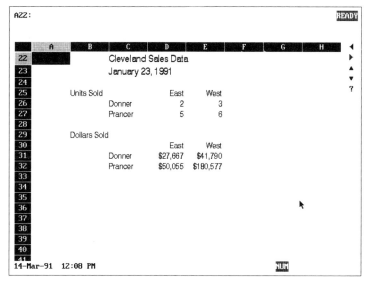

Figure 1-5 shows another report created by referencing the data in a 1-2-3 database with the database statistic functions @DCOUNT, @DSUM, and @DAVG. These functions are easy to use and allow you to define criteria for which data to include in any computation.

Highlighting Problems or Showing Exceptions

Although showing all the detail is seldom the best way to present information, there are times when it is better to display detailed individual records rather than to present a summary. If you are attempting to highlight a problem area or focus attention on problems located in an audit of the detail, you do not want solely to summarize your findings. You need to present the exception or problem data in detail. With 1-2-3, you can use the Data Query Extract command to pull out records from a 1-2-3 database. Figure 1-6, shown on the following page, shows invoice entries with an incorrect total. The Data Query Extract command was used to locate invoices where the total differs from the computation of quantity times price plus freight by more than .01. This method revealed two incorrect invoices. You can print the excerpted area as a report or review it on screen to locate incorrect records.

15

PUBLISHING 1-2-3

```
A13: (H) @ABS(G2-(D2*E2+F2))>0.01                          READY

      A           B           C              D       E         F         G       H
 1  Invoice     Date        Item            Price  Quantity  Freight    Total
 2  C32145    15-Feb-91  Desk - 7A        $297.99     2       $35.00   $595.98
 3  C98712    17-Feb-91  Chair - 33C       $79.95     8       $50.00   $689.60
 4  C99876    17-Feb-91  Clock - 99B       $67.49     7       $10.00   $482.43
 5  D12432    17-Feb-91  Ribbon - 17Z       $9.89     5        $5.00    $49.45
 6  D12587    17-Feb-91  Basket - 88G      $19.95     6       $15.00   $134.70
 7  D12765    17-Feb-91  Pen - 65R          $2.95    19        $4.00    $60.05
 8  D12876    18-Feb-91  Ladder - 75F      $39.95     4       $40.00   $199.80
 9  D15643    19-Feb-91  Bookcase - T      $45.94     8       $32.00   $399.52
10
11
12
13
14
15  Invoices with discrepancies
16  Invoice       Total
17  C32145       $595.98
18  D12432        $49.45
19
20
14-Mar-91  12:09 PM                                                   NUM
```

Figure 1-6: You can use the Data Query Extract Command to list incorrect entries, such as the invoice with the incorrect total shown here.

Creating a Report for Reference

If you do not have 1-2-3 up and running, you may need a detailed report containing every record and field in your worksheet. You will find the completeness of this type of report essential since you cannot pre-plan what data you will need. For example, a clerk must be able to look up serial numbers even when his or her computer system is not operational.

Presenting Readable Information

The information that you present should be clear in its meaning and appear in a readable format. Using type that is too small causes the audience to squint. A type size appropriate for a closeup look may be entirely too small for a group attempting to read a graph positioned overhead at the front of the room. The visual capabilities of the audience may be another factor. If you supply handouts in a very small type size, an

TEN BASIC DESIGN OBJECTIVES

audience of teenagers may not have a problem but middle-aged individuals, beginning to have problems with their vision, may find your data impossible to read.

The layout of the information on a page can also affect its readability. The use of white space can help make it easier to read. See Figures 1-7 and 1-8 on the following page for some simple examples of the difference that readability can make.

Selecting the Correct Size

Text entries and graphs that are appropriate for single individuals to review will not be the correct size for display at the front of a group meeting room. If it is not possible to enlarge the text or graph images sufficiently, you might consider supplying handouts to the participants for reference. You can also direct participants to the handouts at key points in your presentation.

Creating Multiple Views of the Same Data

Another way to make your information more readable is to limit the amount of data on a page or graph. Consider creating several graphs or tables with part of the information in each. You might create a separate graph or table for each department, product, or division rather than showing the data for all of them on one page or slide. You can insert page breaks anywhere in a worksheet to insure that each new section of a worksheet is shown on its own page.

You can use the features of 1-2-3 to selectively print sections of a worksheet. With Releases 3 and above, you can select multiple ranges at one time. With other releases you can still achieve the same results but you will need to invoke "print" several times. With the Data Query Extract command, you can select any subset of the records.

PUBLISHING 1-2-3

Figure 1-7 (r.) shows a spreadsheet that was created without regard to making the information readable. There is virtually no space between columns or sections. But with a few simple changes, you can improve readability.

```
                Dallas  Boston  San FraAtlantaChicagoTotals
1989 Sales      66570   63065   73395   67260   70915   341205
Product A       5090    6435    5155    4255    4685    25620
Product B       36520   26740   36975   38120   30805   169160
Product C       24960   29890   31265   24885   35425   146425
1990 Sales      65950   62825   80805   61810   72360   343750
Product A       11560   13460   16205   10530   12195   63950
Product B       37540   25635   39955   38215   32625   173970
Product C       16850   23730   24645   13065   27540   105830
1991 Sales      77270   66720   88710   69120   86565   388385
Product A       32580   26620   37855   27525   38460   163040
Product B       34295   29970   42425   37215   31420   175325
Product C       10395   10130   8430    4380    16685   50020
% Growth 1989-901990-91
Product A 149.61%154.95%
Product B 2.84% 0.78%
Product C -27.72%-52.74%
```

```
                Dallas   Boston  San Fran  Atlanta  Chicago  Totals

1989 Sales
  Product A     5,090    6,435    5,155    4,255    4,685   25,620
  Product B    36,520   26,740   36,975   38,120   30,805  169,160
  Product C    24,960   29,890   31,265   24,885   35,425  146,425
  Total 1989
  Sales        66,570   63,065   73,395   67,260   70,915  341,205

1990 Sales
  Product A    11,560   13,460   16,205   10,530   12,195   63,950
  Product B    37,540   25,635   39,955   38,215   32,625  173,970
  Product C    16,850   23,730   24,645   13,065   27,540  105,830
  Total 1990
  Sales        65,950   62,825   80,805   61,810   72,360  343,750

1991 Sales
  Product A    32,580   26,620   37,855   27,525   38,460  163,040
  Product B    34,295   29,970   42,425   37,215   31,420  175,325
  Product C    10,395   10,130    8,430    4,380   16,685   50,020
               77,270   66,720   88,710   69,120   86,565  388,385

% Growth        1989-90           1990-91

  Product A    149.61%           154.95%
  Product B      2.84%             0.78%
  Product C    -27.72%           -52.74%
```

Figure 1-8 (l.) shows the same spreadsheet with simple changes, such as wider columns, blank rows added in appropriate locations, indented subheadings, and commas in four-digit numbers—all of which greatly improve readability.

TEN BASIC DESIGN OBJECTIVES

Presenting Understandable Data

There are a number of factors to consider when determining if your data is understandable. It must be presented in clear language. And clarity comes not only from using the same language, but from using the appropriate language. If the average audience member reads at the 5th grade level, presenting college level material would seem as foreign as speaking a foreign tongue. Assessing your audience's comprehension level will help ensure that its members really grasp the information.

Another common error lies in translating technical knowledge to a lay audience. Because the presenter understands the field so well, he or she does not translate the spreadsheet or graph labels, leaving at least some terms obscure. When the audience does not understand key terms, it is unlikely to derive any information from your report or graph. See Figures 1-9 and 1-10 on the following page for a demonstration of how very simple changes can make information much more understandable.

Using Footnotes

Footnotes can often be added to printed graphs to clarify the data or to show how it was obtained. The data in Figure 1-10 might be even more understandable, if it indicated that the numbers represent the number of cans sold. Additionally, using colored labels to show sales for each different type of soup might also be helpful. You might use colors to indicate marketing patterns in different chains with the same average sales or different color labels to flag sales on different days.

Adding Data to Graphs

Graphs can be an effective way to present numeric data since they facilitate comparisons between data values. To make the graph understandable you must at least:

- Use a graph title
- Add x-axis labels for graph types using the x axis
- Add legends when multiple series of data are shown on a graph
- Add data labels when it is important to provide the exact value of a data point

PUBLISHING 1-2-3

Figure 1-9 (r.) shows data recorded as part of a marketing survey that noted the sales of four different kinds of soup when labels of four different colors were used. Looking at the numbers, you cannot discern what types of soup or what color labels are being reported. Figure 1-10 (below) shows the same data with new labels that are understandable to the average reader.

```
Market Study
                    Product Labeling
               A         B         C         D
Product A     105       43        12        78
Product B      58       76       143        92
Product C      13       32         0         5
Product D     125      148        65        25
```

```
                    Market Study
         Number of Cans of Soup Sold in Hometown, USA
                     Jan 1 - Jan 31, 1991

                        Product Labeling
                Red      Green     Blue     Black
Tomato         105        43        12        78
Clam Chowder    58        76       143        92
Vegetable       13        32         0         5
Minestrone     125       148        65        25
```

Figure 1-10: Heading labels were added to the sheet to show that the survey concerns soup sales in the month of January 1991. Labels also reflect the kinds of soup sold.

TEN BASIC DESIGN OBJECTIVES

Properly Organizing the Information

Information that is randomly arranged on the page will take much longer to decipher. The first step most readers will need to take is grouping related facts together in their minds. Only then can they draw conclusions about the information. Depending on the amount of information you have included, there may be too many separate facts to make this organization possible. It is also likely that some facts will be overlooked. At a minimum, time that could be better spent on other activities is spent mentally sorting through and organizing information

Grouping Related Data Together and Providing Summaries

If you are presenting worksheet data about several products, individuals, or company units, you will want to group together like information. The Data Sort command will handle this task if you are listing detailed entries that have one field you can use to sort for grouping. If you are constructing a summary sheet you will need to structure your entries to provide the needed organization.

Using Appropriate Spacing to Group Data

The addition of appropriate spacing can add organization to a worksheet. Figure 1-11 on the following page shows a worksheet that contains a variety of scattered entries. Grouping similar information provides the more organized version shown in Figure 1-12, also following. In addition to spacing you can create dividing lines on a worksheet with special symbols such as an asterisk (*). With 1-2-3's Wysiwyg features, you can draw lines and boxes with menu commands.

PUBLISHING 1-2-3

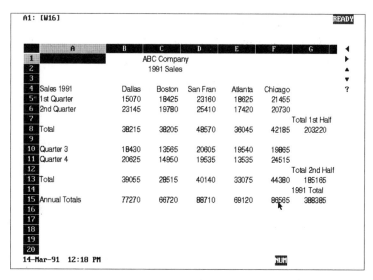

Figure 1-11 (r.): A worksheet with scattered entries. Figure 1-12 (below): Grouping data makes the information much clearer.

Varying the Presentation Method

If your presentation consists of page after page of numbers or even bar graphs, you will begin to lose the audience's interest. If you are using graphs to present your data, you should vary the graph types. Incorporating bar graphs, mixed graphs, and pie graphs adds interest. You can add variety in other ways as well. If your printer supports different fonts, you can show the heading and bottom totals in a different font. White space breaks the monotony of entries in cell after cell of a spreadsheet. Indenting the beginning of labels can help to organize a financial worksheet by levels and can improve readability.

Using graphs for part of a presentation and summary statistics for another part can be helpful. If you are creating a longer report that shows both text and graphics on the same page, you can use the features of Allways, Wysiwyg, or your word processor to add to the visual appeal of the material. Figure 1-13 on the following page shows a series of bar graphs that have been added to a 1-2-3 worksheet with Release 2.3's Wysiwyg features. Choosing the same type of graph for all of data may not be most appropriate. Different graph types add variety to the presentation and also allow you to display your data in the most fitting format. Figure 1-14 shows the same data presented in different types of graphs.

PUBLISHING 1-2-3

Figure 1-13 (r.) shows several bar graphs to represent information. Figure 1-14 (below) shows how you can add interest to the information by varying the graph types.

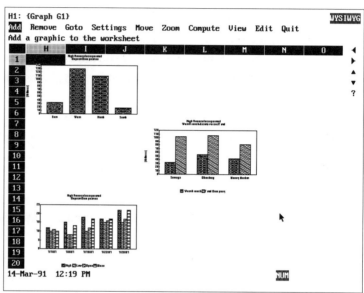

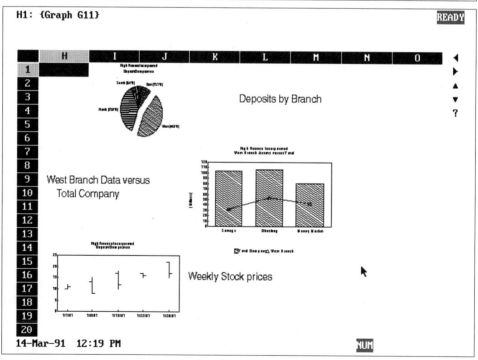

TEN BASIC DESIGN OBJECTIVES

Using Consistency in the Level and Method of Presentation

An inconsistent approach to presenting information makes data difficult to understand. Your readers will have to unnecessarily spend time equating two sets of terminology or labels. If you are going to label one section of a report 'Sales 1991', the next section should be labeled 'Sales 1992,' not '1992 Sales'. The categories used for grouping data in different sections of a report should be identical.

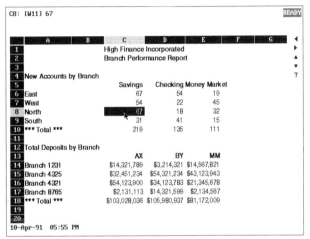

Figure 1-15 (l.) has inconsistent labels whereas Figure 1-16 (below) is consistent.

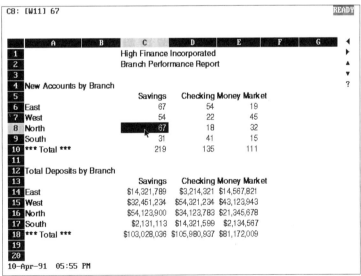

Although variations are important, when you are showing similar information, consistency should override the desire to avoid monotony. If you are using a bar graph to show sales by product in region 1, it would be inappropriate to show region 2 sales with a line graph. Readers would have to make an unnecessary mental shift to use the data in the line graph after viewing the other data in a bar graph. The size of the two graphs should also be the same to maintain consistency in presenting data from both regions.

Although variety is important, it must be tempered with enough consistency to make each piece of a presentation seem like a planned part of the whole. As an example you might use a pie graph to show the breakdown of sales by product for the first region. It would be appropriate to use a pie graph to present the same information for regions 2 and 3, even though you might want to use other graph types in the presentation. You can reserve these other graph types for presenting the change from year to year, for example. Consistency is also important as you create labels for different parts of a presentation. If you have a worksheet for several divisions within a company, it is best to create subsequent sheets by copying the labels from the first sheet. Not only does this process save time but it also means that the labels will be in the same order and have identical spelling.

Presenting Information Relative to Your Message

There is a tendency to provide as much information on a report or graph as possible. But readers usually only have so much time to analyze and understand the information. Presenting information that neither supports nor helps to define your message can distract a reader from the important message and lower the possibility that you will be heard.

Create Several Single-Purpose Reports

Although it may seem easier to create one general-purpose report that everyone can use, you run the risk of including too many elements, making a report difficult to use. Create several small summary reports that clearly present the important data and

TEN BASIC DESIGN OBJECTIVES

limit the number of elements presented. You can pare your distribution list for each report.

Eliminate the Clutter from Reports and Graphs

Each field included on a report should be evaluated in terms of necessity. Just because information is available does not mean that it should be printed. The Data Query Extract command will allow you to easily pull needed fields from a larger base of information. You can select these fields from some or all of the records in your database. Figure 1-17 presents a worksheet that lists contest winners from a sales promotion. This worksheet design can be improved by limiting the fields that show the total for employee salaries and the number of employees in the branch. Neither of these entries adds necessary data.

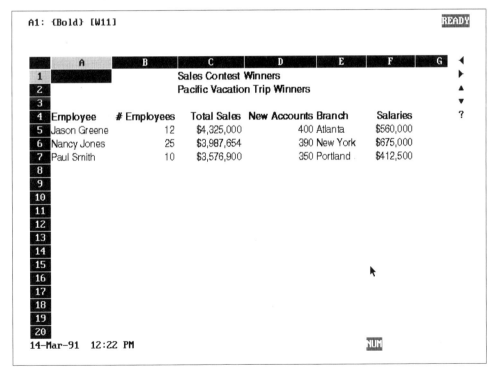

Figure 1-17: A worksheet that can be improved by paring information.

Using Emphasis to Highlight Important Information

If you speak in a monotone when making a presentation listeners are not able to discern what is important in your remarks. If no feeling comes from your statements, everything is assumed to be of the same importance. Adding intonation and emphasis to your voice maintains reader interest and allows you to draw attention to important information. Likewise, you must add emphasis to important printed information to ensure that the reader's attention is directed to it. You might highlight part of the data such as the increase in sales, the reduction in headcount, or the lowered expenses. Other information may be available upon closer examination but it would not be the focal point of the report or graph.

Changing the Appearance

You might use boldface type, underlining, or even additional spacing to highlight printed text. You can use color or hatchmark patterns on graphs to add emphasis; and you can also vary the order in which data is presented. Figure 1-18 on the opposite page shows a basic pie chart. Although your section is labeled, the graph is not particularly interesting. Hatchmark patterns were added in Figure 1-19 and a piece of a pie chart was exploded. The exploded piece shows the largest expenditure of departmental funds.

Adding Information

Notes and arrows are another way to direct attention to a particular area of a graph, but these additions will require that you enhance 1-2-3's basic graph capabilities with another package. When your data is presented in a pie graph, exploding a piece of the pie may be one more alternative that draws attention to one section.

TEN BASIC DESIGN OBJECTIVES

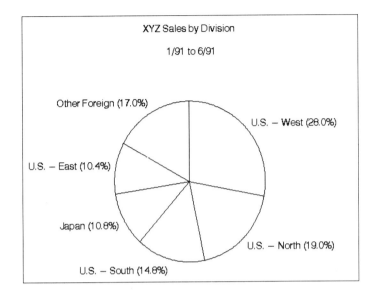

**Figure 1-18 (l.) : A basic pie chart.
Figure 1-19 (below):** The same pie chart has been exploded and hatchmarks have been added for more dramatic emphasis.

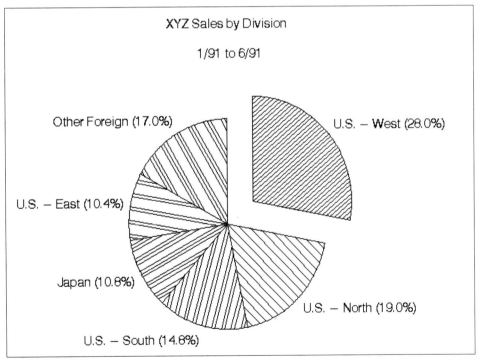

CHAPTER 2

Twenty Design Elements to Help Meet Your Objectives

In Chapter 1 you read about ten different design objectives. In this chapter you will take a look at some of the design elements that can help you meet these objectives. Although each of these objectives is illustrated with 1-2-3 worksheet data or 1-2-3 graphs, this chapter does not focus on the keystroke solutions. Rather, it is an opportunity to focus on design itself. There are numerous examples of "little things" that can make a big difference in whether your audience gets the message you are trying to convey with your 1-2-3 data. In later chapters, you will have the opportunity to explore 1-2-3, its add-in packages, and other popular software that can help you meet these objectives.

The design elements discussed in this chapter are organized into three sections. The "page change" design elements provide a chance to affect the visual impression conveyed by the overall page. Design elements included in this section are listed on the following page.

PUBLISHING 1-2-3

Among the "page change" design elements discussed in this chapter are:

- Page layout
- Page orientation
- Page breaks
- Line spacing
- Tabs
- White space
- Headers and footers
- Borders

Type design elements are also discussed in this chapter. They are important to the appearance of your output but focus more on the micro level in the appearance, style, and size of characters. Type elements discussed in this chapter are:

- Typeface
- Type style
- Type size
- Weight, or the thickness of the characters

Other design elements you will learn about are:

- Color
- Arrows
- Lines
- Boxes
- Shading
- Captions
- Labels
- Graphs
- Graphic Images

TWENTY DESIGN ELEMENTS TO HELP MEET OBJECTIVES

Changing Page Options

You can change the appearance of the printed page by altering its length and the amount of white space on it. You can change the length of the page, the size of the margins, the height of rows, the number of rows of print in an inch of the page length, and the size of the characters printed on the page. A quick look at these options will provide an idea of how simple changes can dramatically affect the appearance of your data.

Determining the Best Page Layout

Page layout can refer to the basic layout of a page in your printout. The term, page layout, is also used to refer to the exact layout of different pieces of information on the page. In this section page layout will refer to the overall look of a page.

Sixty-six lines of text can be printed on a sheet of 8 1/2-by-11 paper if the text is printed on every line from the top to the bottom of the page. Using a standard font that prints 10 characters per inch, you can print as many as 85 characters from the left edge to the right edge of the paper. 1-2-3 provides a default layout that leaves some of this space unused.

In 1-2-3's default page layout, four characters are reserved at the left edge of the paper for a left margin and text prints over only as far as 76 allowing the rest of the right side as margin space. The top of the page allows for a two-line top margin, a line for a header and a blank line on either side of the header for a total of five lines reserved. The bottom allows for another five lines with one available for use as a footer.

If you are using a laser printer it is possible that a half inch at the top and bottom of the page cannot be used. This allows an automatic extra half-inch at the top and bottom of every page providing a maximum of 60 lines. You can reduce the top and bottom margin settings to 0 to recover two lines at the top and two lines at the bottom.

PUBLISHING 1-2-3

You can also edit the page length and the side margins. All changes are made through the /Print Printer Options command. Figure 2-1 shows the default layout provided by 1-2-3 before any changes are made.

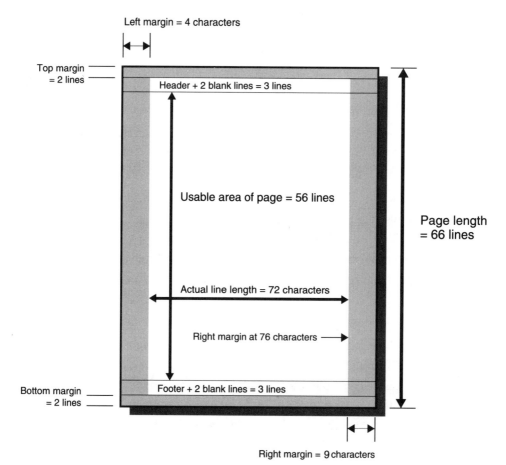

Figure 2-1: The default layout in 1-2-3.

The selection of a good page layout depends on the amount of data that you want to present and your objectives. If you want to pack as much as possible into the display, you might eliminate or minimize the margin settings. You can also change the page length if you would prefer to use shorter or longer sheets of paper for your printing.

TWENTY DESIGN ELEMENTS TO HELP MEET OBJECTIVES

Figure 2-2 shows two tables printed on one sheet of paper. Note the improved appearance in the first table when it is placed on the sheet by itself as shown in Figure 2-3 on the following page. The increase in the left and top margins insure that the data is placed more toward the center of the page. The second chart would appear on another page that looks similar to the first.

```
                         ABC Company
                         Price Schedule
         Product         Quantity Purchased

                    1        10        50       100

         AX-695    $0.39    $3.78    $18.34    $35.90
         AX-377   $ 0.41    $4.03    $19.51    $38.20
         AX-498    $0.94    $9.25    $44.85    $87.81
         AX-255    $1.25   $12.21    $59.16   $115.83
         AX-505    $2.43   $23.83   $115.52   $226.17
         AX-042    $2.49   $24.40   $118.28   $231.57
         AX-723    $2.99   $29.30   $142.03   $278.07
         AX-120    $3.25   $31.85   $154.38   $302.25
         AX-880    $4.56   $44.69   $216.59   $424.06
         AX-874    $4.63   $45.42   $220.13   $430.99
         AX-948    $7.12   $69.79   $338.25   $662.25
         AX-499    $7.21   $70.62   $412.28   $670.14
         AX-364    $8.68   $85.03   $412.13   $806.91
         AX-952   $10.84  $106.23   $514.90  $1008.12
         AX-082   $10.93  $107.11   $519.18  $1016.49
         AX-852   $11.41  $111.83   $542.03  $1061.24
         AX-887   $11.50  $112.69   $546.19  $1069.39
         AX-830   $12.45  $122.01   $591.38  $1157.85
         AX-201   $13.05  $127.89   $619.88  $1213.65
         AX-791   $14.12  $138.39   $670.76  $1313.27
         AX-161   $14.20  $139.18   $674.58  $1320.76
         AX-294   $16.50  $161.73   $783.89  $1534.77
         AX-439   $16.57  $162.38   $787.07  $1541.00
         AX-602   $18.37  $179.99   $872.41  $1708.09
         AX-589   $18.41  $180.46   $874.70  $1712.57
         AX-509   $19.09  $187.11   $906.92  $1775.65
         AX-133   $19.13  $187.47   $908.65  $1779.04
         AX-946   $19.89  $194.96   $944.95  $1850.10
         Miles    Weight (Lbs)             Shipping Cost Schedule
         Domestic    10       50       100     1000     5000
         0-100     $15.50   $ 50.38   $77.50   $465.00  $1162.50
         100-200   $18.00   $58.50    $90.00   $540.00  $1350.00
         200-350   $20.50   $66.63   $102.50   $615.00  $1537.50
         350-500   $23.00   $74.75   $115.00   $690.00  $1725.00
         500-750   $25.50   $82.88   $127.50   $765.00  $1912.50
         750-1000  $28.00   $91.00   $140.00   $840.00  $2100.00
         1000-1300 $30.50   $99.13   $152.50   $915.00  $2287.50
         1300-1600 $33.00  $107.25   $165.00   $990.00  $2475.00
         1600-1900 $35.50  $115.38   $177.50  $1065.00  $2662.50
         1900-2500 $38.00  $123.50   $190.00  $1140.00  $2850.00
         2500 up   $40.50  $131.63   $202.50  $1215.00  $3037.50
         International
         Germany   $35.00   $3.75    $192.50   $225.00   $375.00
         France    $33.00  $107.25   $181.50  $1155.00  $4125.00
```

Figure 2-2: Bunching up tables is unpleasing to the eye.

PUBLISHING 1-2-3

```
                        ABC Company
                       Price Schedule
     Product          Quantity Purchased

                    1       10       50       100

     AX-695       $0.39    $3.78    $18.34    $35.90
     AX-377       $ 0.41   $4.03    $19.51    $38.20
     AX-498       $0.94    $9.25    $44.85    $87.81
     AX-255       $1.25    $12.21   $59.16    $115.83
     AX-505       $2.43    $23.83   $115.52   $226.17
     AX-042       $2.49    $24.40   $118.28   $231.57
     AX-723       $2.99    $29.30   $142.03   $278.07
     AX-120       $3.25    $31.85   $154.38   $302.25
     AX-880       $4.56    $44.69   $216.59   $424.06
     AX-874       $4.63    $45.42   $220.13   $430.99
     AX-948       $7.12    $69.79   $338.25   $662.25
     AX-499       $7.21    $70.62   $412.28   $670.14
     AX-364       $8.68    $85.03   $412.13   $806.91
     AX-952       $10.84   $106.23  $514.90   $1008.12
     AX-082       $10.93   $107.11  $519.18   $1016.49
     AX-852       $11.41   $111.83  $542.03   $1061.24
     AX-887       $11.50   $112.69  $546.19   $1069.39
     AX-830       $12.45   $122.01  $591.38   $1157.85
     AX-201       $13.05   $127.89  $619.88   $1213.65
     AX-791       $14.12   $138.39  $670.76   $1313.27
     AX-161       $14.20   $139.18  $674.58   $1320.76
     AX-294       $16.50   $161.73  $783.89   $1534.77
     AX-439       $16.57   $162.38  $787.07   $1541.00
     AX-602       $18.37   $179.99  $872.41   $1708.09
     AX-589       $18.41   $180.46  $874.70   $1712.57
     AX-509       $19.09   $187.11  $906.92   $1775.65
     AX-133       $19.13   $187.47  $908.65   $1779.04
     AX-946       $19.89   $194.96  $944.95   $1850.10
```

Figure 2-3: Limiting the amount of information on a page can dramatically improve appearance. Compare this example to the layout depicted in Figure 2-2.

Using Page Orientation Effectively

Most printers purchased today automatically support two different orientations for the way information is placed on a page. It is possible to use the default Portrait layout that writes lines across the 8-1/2" page width. If you switch to a Landscape orientation, the printout is printed across the 11" width. These capabilities assume that your printer supports both landscape and portrait orientations.

TWENTY DESIGN ELEMENTS TO HELP MEET OBJECTIVES

Placing Page Breaks Appropriately

Once you layout the page definition, 1-2-3 automatically inserts page breaks when a page is full. The placement of these page breaks might not be ideal for your data. You can choose to insert a page break indicator in Release 2.01 and above. You can also create a page break at any location by printing more than one range and issuing the Print Printer Page command between ranges.

Using the Most Appropriate Line Spacing

If you print a worksheet on most printers with the default settings you will get six lines of printed output to the inch. Although this default output is adequate for most of what you will do, you may want to explore other options. You can make changes directly to some printers with menu selections or you can send a setup string with the message to your printer before you start printing. If you are using Release 2.2, 2.3, or 3.1, you can change the height of one or more rows. You would use the Allways or Wysiwyg add-in to make this type of change. As an example, doubling the row height without additional changes will make the spreadsheet appear as if it is printed with double spacing since the size of the characters remains the same. A double-spaced listing of spreadsheet formulas would allow you to note space changes on the printout. Figure 2-4 on the following page shows data printed eight lines to the inch on an HP Laserjet Series III. A setup string of \027&l8D was used to set the printer although this string will vary based on the model number that you used. You can change the spacing between the lines made through adjustments in the row heights or use another setup string. Figure 2-5 shows the same entries printed with a setup string of \027&4D to set the printer to display four lines to the inch.

You can also change the font with the releases listed. You will learn much more about fonts later in the chapter. For now, it is important to know that the height of rows will automatically be adjusted for you as you choose fonts with larger point sizes with Allways or Wysiwyg. As long as you print the worksheet with the Wysiwyg or Allways add-ins, the number of rows and characters that 1-2-3 attempts to print on a page will be automatically adjusted based on the point size of the font selected. The "Closer Look" box labelled "Fonts Come in All Sizes" shows some possiblilities.

PUBLISHING 1-2-3

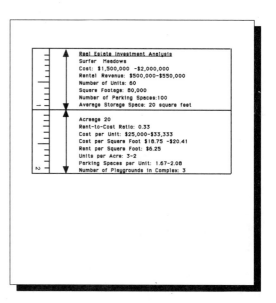

Figure 2-4 (r.): Data printed eight lines to the inch on an HP Laserjet Series III with a setup string of \027&l8D. Figure 2-5 (below) shows the same entries printed with a setup string of \027&4D to set the printer to display four lines to the inch.

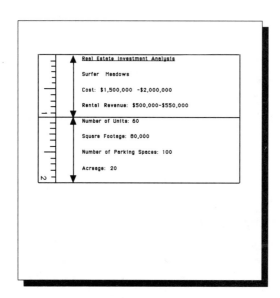

TWENTY DESIGN ELEMENTS TO HELP MEET OBJECTIVES

In releases of 1-2-3 prior to 2.3, your only option for making changes to the spacing between rows was to use a setup string or menu buttons on the printer itself. Depending on the printer model you might have chosen a different number of lines per inch or a different size font. Choosing a different font changes the size of the characters whereas a different number of lines per inch leaves the character size the same and affects only the distance between each row of printed text. 1-2-3 does not automatically adjust for changes made through the printer. If you set your printer to eight lines per inch, 1-2-3 will still be using a page length of 66 lines. This means that page breaks will not match the actual end of the paper and you will not take advantage of the expanded capacity of the page. You would need to use /Print Printer Options Page-Length and set the length to 88 lines if your frame of reference is the 11-inch page that would hold 66 lines when the print was six lines to the inch. If you had already changed your page length to 60 for six lines to the inch output with a device like a laser printer that cannot print from edge to edge of a page, 80 would be the appropriate setting.

Using Tabs

Indenting subtopics or categories from the main topic or category can help to organize information for your reader. If you look at the account entries in Figure 2-6, it is not immediately obvious that there are main account headings and subaccounts beneath them. The data in Figure 2-7 makes this much clearer since the indentation defines the relationships.

A CLOSER LOOK

Fonts Come in All Sizes

This is Bodoni, 10 point.
This is Bodoni, 12 pt.
This is Bodoni, 14 pt.
This is Bodoni, 16 pt.

This is ITC Century bold, 10 pt.
This is ITC Century bold, 12 pt.
This is ITC Century bold, 14 pt.
This is ITC Century bold, 16 pt.

This is Helvetica, 10 pt.
This is Helvetica, 12 pt.
This is Helvetica, 14 pt.
This is Helvetica, 16 pt.

PUBLISHING 1-2-3

Unfortunately, 1-2-3 does not make it easy to achieve this indentation. 1-2-3 does not use the TAB key to indent entries within a cell. If you want each entry indented by two positions, you need to press the space bar twice before entering a label entry. If you decide after entering all of the account names that you want to indent you can edit each label entry that should be indented, press HOME followed by RIGHT ARROW then press the space bar twice before you press ENTER. If you need this type of feature on a regular basis you can store the needed keystrokes in a 1-2-3 macro that might look like this:

\t {EDIT}{HOME}{RIGHT} ~

Note that there are two spaces between the entry that represents press the RIGHT ARROW key and the tilde (~) that indicates that ENTER was pressed. Any time you want to indent the text you would run the macro \t after positioning the cell pointer on the label you want to indent.

If you import your data into a word processor you can use the TAB key to separate the entries into columns the desired distance apart. In fact, you will want to use a TAB rather than spaces in the event that you print the data with a proportional font. Using TAB will insure that columns after the first column line up properly whereas spaces will cause the column to misalign unless you are using a proportional font.

TWENTY DESIGN ELEMENTS TO HELP MEET OBJECTIVES

ABC Company
Balance Sheet
As of 31 Dec, 91

Assets		Liabilities	
Cash	$13,564	Notes Payable	$40,000
Notes Receivable	$3,000	Accts. Payable	$4,390
Accts. Receivable	$6,439	Salaries Payable	$15,040
Inventory	$2,942	Interest Payable	$1,500
Land	$75,000	Total Liabilities	$60,930
Accum. Depreciation	$1,500		
Building	$68,000	Owner's Equity	
Accum. Depreciation	$3,050	John Doe, Capital	$103,465
		Total Liabilities	
Total Assets	$164,395	& Owner's Equity	$164,395

In Figure 2-6 (above), it is difficult to make out the relationship of each item to its larger category. However, in Figure 2-7 (below), a few indentations and some boldfacing makes these relationships almost instantly apparent.

ABC Company
Balance Sheet
As of 31 Dec, 91

Assets		**Liabilities**	
Cash	$13,564	Notes Payable	$40,000
Notes Receivable	$3,000	Accts. Payable	$4,390
Accts. Receivable	$6,439	Salaries Payable	$15,040
Inventory	$2,942	Interest Payable	$1,500
Land	$75,000	Total Liabilities	$60,930
Accum. Depreciation	$1,500		
Building	$68,000	**Owner's Equity**	
Accum. Depreciation	$3,050	John Doe, Capital	$103,465
		Total Liabilities	
Total Assets	**$164,395**	**& Owner's Equity**	**$164,395**

PUBLISHING 1-2-3

Setting Alignment

In 1-2-3, entries within cells can be aligned with the cell borders. For label entries you can use the default left alignment or choose right or center alignment for the labels. For values, alignment is with the right edge of a cell. Entries containing decimals can be aligned with the decimal point as well as the right edge of the cell by specifying a fixed number of decimal places. It is not possible to change the alignment of numbers within 1-2-3 to any alignment other than right.

The normal screen display in 1-2-3 uses a monospace font in which every character on the screen requires the same amount of space. This means that the fifth letter in each label entry within a column will always align with the fifth letter of other entries as long as left alignment is used. When you switch to a WYSIWYG display as provided by Allways and Wysiwyg add-ins, the fonts available to you include many proportional fonts where each letter uses a different amount of space. You will notice in the first column of Figure 2-8 that the part numbers do not align even though they have the same number of characters. This is because a proportional font is used.

Part Number	Item	Price
AB-214-I11	Bubble Bath	2.85
MX-383-M33	Sponge	1.53
KL-208-G21	Rubber Ducky	3.95
IJ-191-L10	Soap (Bar)	0.98
UY-863-O06	Soap (Liquid)	1.39
RX-128-F83	Bath Mat	6.89

Figure 2-8: The part numbers do not align due to the use of a proportional font.

TWENTY DESIGN ELEMENTS TO HELP MEET OBJECTIVES

Using White Space Effectively

The white space included on a page is just as important as the data. The space helps create a pleasing visual appearance. It can also serve to divide individual pieces of information making it much more readable. The problem with the earlier printing of the two tables of 1-2-3 information on one sheet of paper as shown in Figure 2-2 was that there was no white space on the page. The page was dense and difficult to read. Once the tables were separated on two pages, the white space made the information much easier to read.

Using Headers and Footers

Headers and footers offer important identifying information that will make it easier to work with the data in a report. If pages in a report become separated it is easy to tell where an individual page came from. Header and footer information can also be used to indicate the source of the data on a report, how current the information is and any other information that you feel is important. The header shown at the bottom of the page provides the name and department of the individual who created the report as well as the date of distribution. The footer at the bottom of the same page provides a page number. Once defined in 1-2-3, each page will contain this same information even though you only enter it once. The effort required to use headers and footers is minimal yet those elements can make your information convey a much more professional image than the same data presented without headers or footers. In 1-2-3 both headers and footers are limited to a single line. If you need multiple lines at the top of every page you will have to define the rows as border rows and 1-2-3 will print them immediately before your data on each page.

A sample footer might read:

David Campbell   Accounting Department   23-Feb

PUBLISHING 1-2-3

Using Borders

The Borders option in the 1-2-3 /Print Printer Options menu allows you to print multiple pages of output with several lines or columns of identifying information at the top or left side of each page. This option is an ideal solution when you want to create a multiple- line heading. You can also use Borders when the worksheet data that you want to print is too wide to fit on a single page and, to have your information be meaningful, you need the identifying information on the left of the worksheet entries printed on each page. Figure 2-9 shows small section of the second page of a report printed without Borders. The same data when printed with Borders looks like Figure 2-10.

**Figure 2-9:
Mysterious
worksheet entries
lack borders.**

```
01-Feb    142.00    1,105.80    77.41    66.35
02-Feb    128.00    1,051.31    73.59    63.08
03-Feb     56.00      441.59    30.91    26.50
04-Feb     93.00      710.43    49.73    42.63
05-Feb     53.00      484.58    33.92    29.07
06-Feb     81.00      653.44    45.74    39.21
07-Feb     87.00      707.08    49.50    42.42
08-Feb     81.00      657.82    46.05    39.47
09-Feb     77.00      653.99    45.78    39.24
10-Feb     54.00      425.72    29.80    25.54
```

TWENTY DESIGN ELEMENTS TO HELP MEET OBJECTIVES

```
Date     Units Sold    Sales      Tax    Shipping
01-Feb     142.00    1,105.80    77.41    66.35
02-Feb     128.00    1,051.31    73.59    63.08
03-Feb      56.00      441.59    30.91    26.50
04-Feb      93.00      710.43    49.73    42.63
05-Feb      53.00      484.58    33.92    29.07
06-Feb      81.00      653.44    45.74    39.21
07-Feb      87.00      707.08    49.50    42.42
08-Feb      81.00      657.82    46.05    39.47
09-Feb      77.00      653.99    45.78    39.24
10-Feb      54.00      425.72    29.80    25.54
```

Figure 2-10: Borders help to identify information.

Type Options

Not too many years ago unless you were going to a typesetter or printer, the only choice you had to make in presenting financial information was whether to use a pica or elite typewriter for the output. Even with the advent of the PC, not much was available by way of variation. The first generation of laser printers introduced the Courier typeface family with easy variations in size and style for the face built into sets of characters called fonts. The sidebar earlier in this section shows you a few of the variety of fonts that are readily available today. The intelligent laser printer was capable of producing everything from bold, and italic to several sizes of Courier type.

PUBLISHING 1-2-3

The latest laser printers have numerous fonts built-in. In addition, you can purchase font cartridges that plug into the laser printer and provide the ability to create documents in another font set. Another popular option is to purchase soft fonts (soft meaning that they are provided on diskette). These fonts are loaded onto a hard disk and sent to the printer when the printer is turned on at the beginning of each session.

Now that your personal computer provides the desktop publishing features that were formerly only available from a printer, you will need to learn a few new skills if you want to create the sharpest looking documents possible.

Learning the New Terminology

With the introduction of desktop publishing to the PC there is no longer a need to produce each document using the same typeface or character design. Fonts containing a complete set of characters are available in many designs. In most cases the font set includes the entire alphabet in both upper and lower case, all the special symbols on the keyboard, and other special characters such as mathematical symbols or foreign characters. Some font sets seem formal, others have a lively flair, and still others such as Gothic or Century Schoolbook are reminiscent of times gone by. 1-2-3 Release 2.3 provides a font set composed of dingbats or typographical design elements. This font set is named Xsymbol. A font set creates all its characters in a specific size. Often an entire font family is available to provide the same typeface in different sizes and with different type style options such as boldface.

All fonts can be categorized in two basic groups. A font is either a serif font with embellishments on the lines that make up the characters or a sans serif font—without any embellishments. The serif fonts vary greatly from those with some very minor little stubs at the ends of lines to those fonts, such as script fonts, that have very noticeable additions to the lines that make up the characters.

The size of the font that you select will be measured in points. A point equals approximately 1/72 of an inch. Points are used to measure the height of a capital letter

TWENTY DESIGN ELEMENTS TO HELP MEET OBJECTIVES

in the font set to determine the size of the font. Another important measurement term is "pica." A pica is used to measure line length. One pica is equal to 12 points with six picas fitting in one inch.

The printing term "leading" (pronounced ledding) refers to the amount of space between lines. The term came from the days when strips of lead were used a separators between lines of type. Today you determine leading by row height with the add-ins that provide WYSIWYG features.

Selecting a Typeface

Your selection of a typeface can add impact to your message. The most important factors in making a good selection are the content of your document, the audience your material is intended for, and your personal preferences. Although there are choices that would obviously be poor such as the selection of Script or Gothic for a financial report, there are hundreds of fonts that would be acceptable. Choosing from among the many acceptable choices is subjective. The "Closer Look" box along the side of this section provides a glimpse at a few of the many typefaces from which you can select.

At times you will want to select multiple type faces. You can choose multiple fonts from the same font family without a problem since the typeface is the same but the size or style is different. This would allow you to use large headline characters and smaller characters in the body of the worksheet area. Another option is to vary typefaces. If you choose to vary typefaces, you should attempt to combine a serif font with a sans serif font. The combination of serif and sans serif will add contrast to your document. If you choose two serif fonts you might have conflict rather than contrast. To learn more about the art and science of typography you might look at a few of the titles available at your local branch library.

PUBLISHING 1-2-3

Selecting a Type Style

Type styles are variations within one font family. The typeface remains basically the same design while the width, weight, or angle of the characters changes. You might have a font family that offers a light, medium, heavy, and bold style for the same typeface. The typeface might also be offered in italic, bold italic, and light italic. The width of the characters might be regular, condensed, or extended. Draw programs such as CorelDRAW, allow you to manipulate text as graphics using fill patterns, rotation, outlining, skewing, and setting the text to a path as options for making creative changes to the text.

Type Size

Within a font family you are likely to find sizes ranging from a small 4- or 6-point size to 24-point or larger. A 6-point font might be appropriate for a footnote. The main body of your document will normally be created in a font size somewhere between 9 and 14 points, usually 10 or 11 points. Headings at the top of a page might be presented in a font size between 18 and 24 points depending on which size you selected for the main portion of the data.

It is important to choose a size suited to your purpose and audience. A group of readers in their mid-forties or older will often be farsighted and need larger type if their glasses are not readily available. If you are distributing a report to be read in the office, a smaller size might be acceptable. Literature available for reading by passers-by in a mall should be large as this group is unlikely to get your message if they have to put on their reading glasses to see your message.

The size of the space that you have available will also affect the font size somewhat. You do not want to choose a font that is so large that it looks as if your message will barely fit on the page. Likewise, a font that is so small that it seems lost in a vast area of white space is also inappropriate.

TWENTY DESIGN ELEMENTS TO HELP MEET OBJECTIVES

Other Enhancements

Although page layout and typeface changes are the two most common tricks used to vary the appearance of output, there are many other changes that you can make. Expand your horizons as you take a look at the remaining design elements in this section.

Using Color

Color can be an effective attention getter. Recent studies have also indicated that color can have subtle psychological effects.

When you think of using color with your 1-2-3 worksheets and graphs, you must have a way of using this color in your final output. A macro run screen shown on a color monitor can effectively use the colors that you choose. Likewise, 35-mm slides created from captured screens and data printed on a color output device such as a color printer or plotter will utilize the colors on the screen. Although color will make an attractive display with which to work, without these options color will not affect your final output.

Releases 3 and 3.1 of 1-2-3 are the only ones for which there is a color option for 1-2-3 cell entries. With these releases, you can change the color with which negative numbers are shown. Other than this limited color application, you must look to the add-ins to enhance your output with color. Another option for any 1-2-3 user is to use colored paper for output. A fine quality ecru or grey watermark bond may distinguish your printed output from the same information printed on standard white bond.

The Wysiwyg and Allways add-ins have many options for changing the color of various screen components. Both add-ins have features for changing the color of the background or text for the entire worksheet or a range as well as the cell pointer. In addition, Wysiwyg has many additional color options including using different colors for the grid, the frame, negative values, lines, shadow effects, and unprotected cells.

PUBLISHING 1-2-3

The color insert section in the middle of the book shows some of the color features of Wysiwyg when used with 1-2-3 Release 3.1.

Using Arrows

Arrows provide an easy way to direct a reader's attention to a particular piece of information. Arrows can be added to a 1-2-3 worksheet to draw attention to a profit increase or an over-expenditure. They can also be added to graphs along with a note. Figure 2-11 provides an example of an arrow added to a 1-2-3 graph with one of the graphics packages discussed in Chapter 9.

To add an arrow to the worksheet you will either need to use the Wysiwyg features of 1-2-3 Release 2.3 or 3.1. With any release of 1-2-3, you can print the data to a file then import it into your word processor. You can then add a graphic image for the arrow to the file and print it from the word processing software. Figure 2-12 shows

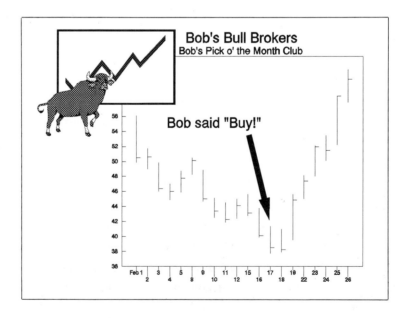

Figure 2-11: Arrows added to a 1-2-3 graph using an add-in.

50

TWENTY DESIGN ELEMENTS TO HELP MEET OBJECTIVES

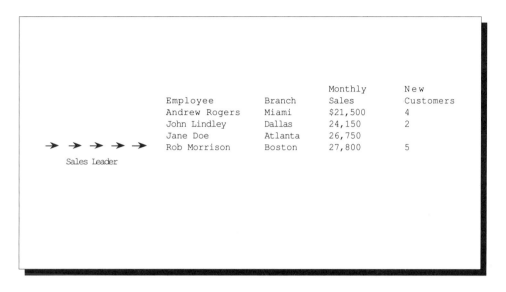

Figure 2-12: Arrows created in 1-2-3's Xsymbol font emphasize key points.

some arrows added to a 1-2-3 Release 2.3 worksheet. These arrows were created by entering lowercase a's and using the Xsymbols font to display the entry as dingbats. Appendix B provides a list of the Xsymbol characters that correlate to each of your keyboard characters.

Using Lines

Underlining an entry can draw attention to the information. It is more subtle than a box and is useful for highlighting a total or other important information. Unfortunately, underlining is not possible in 1-2-3 itself since you can only make one entry in a cell. As soon as you type the underline symbol, you cannot place another entry in that cell without destroying the underline entries.

The Wysiwyg and Allways add-in packages allow you to create lines around a cell without affecting the contents of the cell. You can outline the entire cell as you did with boxes. You can also choose to use the bottom frame of the cell to create an entry that appears like underlining. Figure 2-13 provides an example of underlining that is used

PUBLISHING 1-2-3

to indicate that a total will follow as well as double underlining highlighting the grand total.

Using Boxes

Boxes set off data from the rest of the text. You might use a box around a total line to draw attention to this piece of information. If you have instructions for how to perform a specific task. Boxes can be drawn in any release of 1-2-3. Using releases without the Wysiwyg and Allways add-ins requires that you use labels to build the lines comprising the box. Features such as @REPEAT and the \ repeating label can make the task easier. You can even use special ASCII symbols not available from the keyboard with the @CHAR function.

If you have Wysiwyg, you can use the Lines command to draw boxes. Figure 2-15 shows an input form with boxes drawn around each of the areas where data entry is expected. You can choose the Outline option to draw individual boxes with single lines. You can also use Wysiwyg's double or wide line feature to outline a range of cells.

The weight that you use in the lines can make a dramatic visual difference. The various fonts discussed earlier differ in terms of line weight as well as other style elements. When you are drawing lines and boxes on your own, you can use a variety of characters with which to draw your box. These can vary from the underline or dash to a much more dramatic special character. To give the lines a look with a heavier weight you can also use the bold option to darken. Dark and heavy lines contrast nicely with a lighter look and draw attention to the area where a heavier appearance is shown.

With Wysiwyg and Allways you can change the weight of lines used to draw boxes from normal to wide or double. Figure 2-16 shows several boxes on the screen using several different weight options.

TWENTY DESIGN ELEMENTS TO HELP MEET OBJECTIVES

```
                    ABC Company
                  Income Statement
               For Year Ended 31 Dec, 1991

Revenue                              $154,750

Less Expenses
Salaries Expense         $64,500
Utilities Expense          5,400
Rent Expense              14,900
Telephone Expense          1,150
Office Supplies Expense      543
Total Expenses                         86,493

Net Profit                            $68,257
```

Figure 2-13 (l.) demonstrates the simple use of lines for emphasis. Figure 2-14 (below) shows how boxes can be used as information holders.

Name:
Address:
City: State: Zip:

PUBLISHING 1-2-3

Using Shading

Shading is a grey scale pattern that can be used to add emphasis to information. Where color output is not an option, shading is the only variation beyond standard black or white screen entries that is available to you. Although 1-2-3 itself has no shading options the Wysiwyg and Allways add-ins support shading. Word processing packages with graphic support often provide the ability to shade the background of a box or other area that you can use for imported 1-2-3 data or other information. You can use Wysiwyg's shading option to highlight a total as shown in Figure 2-16.

Adding Captions

Captions can be used with tables or graph that are included with other information. Just as the figure in this book have descriptive captions you will want to use captions when you insert data from 1-2-3 into a word processing document.

If you include a graph in a word processing document, the graph is likely to have titles. You will not want the caption at the bottom to duplicate the information in the titles, instead you might want to have it provide the reason for the graph's inclusion. For example, the title might read: ABC Sales Performance and the caption might read increase in Product 1 sales over the last year dramatically increased profits. The caption assists in conveying the graph's message to your audience.

Using Labels or Annotation

Labels and other annotations can draw attention to important information and provide descriptive information. You can use notes at the side of a spreadsheet printout to provide important explanations. You might box these comments as shown in Figure 2-17 shows captions added to a balance sheet to draw attention to specific account balances.

TWENTY DESIGN ELEMENTS TO HELP MEET OBJECTIVES

This is a box drawn with the outline option.

This is a box drawn with the double outline option.

This is a box drawn with the wide outline option.

Figure 2-15 (l.) shows boxes drawn using several different weight options.

Figure 2-16 (r.): Shading can add the appropriate emphasis.

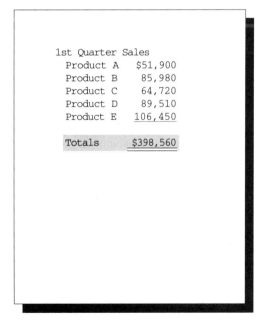

PUBLISHING 1-2-3

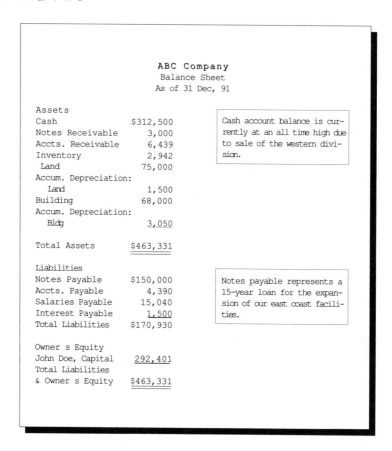

Figure 2-17: The captions added to this balance sheet demonstrate another attention-getting technique.

Using Graphs

Graphs can create a mental picture of the information that you want to convey quickly. Rather than having to pore over hundreds of numbers to make an interpretation, graphs can often convey the same information without requiring the audience to perform a detailed or complicated analysis of your information. The graph essentially paints a picture of what the numbers are saying. When you look at the numbers and graph in Figures 2-18 and 2-19, it is easy to see why the message comes across clearer and more quickly when you present the graph.

TWENTY DESIGN ELEMENTS TO HELP MEET OBJECTIVES

```
ABC Company
Sales
         Product A    Product B    Product C    Product D
1988     46,060       83,450       102,930      154,300
1989     53,080       76,060       104,060      164,820
1990     63,890       85,950       110,430      168,760
1991     69,290       93,930       120,710      169,080
1992     76,610       99,760       129,980      180,930
```

Figures 2-18 (above) and 2-19 (below) contain the same data but how it is displayed makes all the difference.

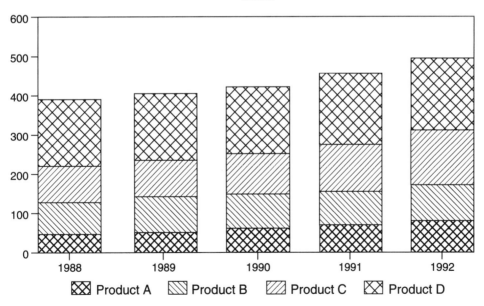

57

PUBLISHING 1-2-3

There are so many different types of graphs that you can usually find one that meets your needs. Depending on the type of information that you have to convey and the message that you are presenting you can find a graph type that meets your needs. Table 2-1 provides a list of some common graph types along with instances where each type might make the best choice.

Grid lines can be an important addition to your graphs. It can be difficult to accurately assess the exact values shown on bar and line graphs. Although your eyes can follow across to the Y axis, it is still difficult to make an accurate determination of the value associated with the point on a line or the top of a bar. Figure 2-20 shows a line graph with both vertical and horizontal grid lines. This makes it easy to follow the point to the value of either axis.

If you were creating a vertical bar graph you would only use a horizontal grid line. Pie charts do not use grid lines.

Using Graphics Images

Graphics images can serve as attention getters. They can be the difference between someone taking a closer look at your numbers or graph or bypassing that information as just one of many papers that cross their desk each day. Figure 2-21 shows worksheet data that has been printed on a page along with a clip art image. The visual appeal is much more striking than the same information without the clip art.

Although 1-2-3 itself does not have any clip art images that are part of the package, you can use a graphics package or a word processing package that supports graphics to add these graphic images to your 1-2-3 data. The final printout will be created using the print features of the other package rather than those of 1-2-3. You will learn how to utilize the features in some of these other packages in Chapter 9.

TWENTY DESIGN ELEMENTS TO HELP MEET OBJECTIVES

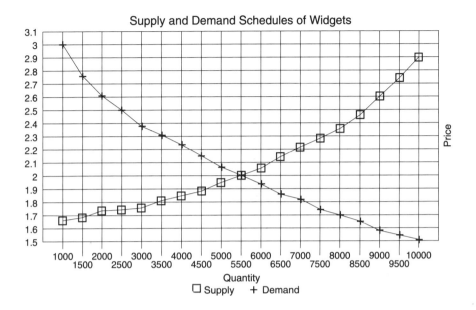

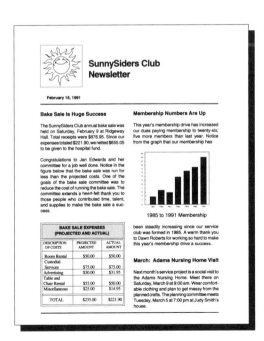

Figure 2-20 (above): An easy-to-follow line graph with both horizontal and vertical axes. Figure 2-21 (l.): Worksheet data is enhanced with clip art and a bar graph in this newsletter format.

PUBLISHING 1-2-3

Table 2-1
Graph Types and Uses

Type	Used to show
100%	Bar Components of a whole over time
Area	Changes in volume or quantity over time
Bar	Comparison between series or trends over time
HLCO	Changes over many time periods especially where it is important to show changes in minimum and maximum values as with stock or bond prices
Line	Trends and comparisons between series
Mixed	Changes over time for multiple series especially where one or more series are a component of the whole
Pie	Components of a whole
Stacked Bar	Components of a whole over time
XY	Correlation between pairs of values in two series

CHAPTER 3

Hardware Support

You can run 1-2-3 on almost any personal computer made today. The basic features of 1-2-3 work on all computers and will calculate all your formulas correctly. The configuration of your system will affect the appearance of the output on your screen and in hard copy, and may limit your use of add-in software.

Your monitor will affect your ability to see graphs on screen and will affect the clarity of other information. Early monitors have an especially big impact on your display since even those that have graphics capabilities supply limited details and only a few colors.

Just as your monitor affects your display, your printer or plotter affect your output. To print both text and graphics, you need a printer that will support both. Output quality varies dramatically from the draft quality produced on a dot matrix printer designed for speed to the high-resolution graphics image produced by a laser printer. Plotter devices, which create color transparencies, vary in terms of their quality and the number of different pens that you can use with them. Although 1-2-3 does not directly support output to film, you can use supplemental software to capture 1-2-3 information on a film recorder for the production of 35-mm slides.

Although there is no need for you to become a hardware technician to produce great output, you will want to understand some hardware basics. This will allow you to understand the capabilities and limitations of the various machines you might have in your office.

PUBLISHING 1-2-3

Understanding Monitors and Graphics Adapters

A monitor is nothing more than a screen that the computer uses to display information. Various computer systems support a wide variety of monitors. The data that you see on a monitor can be one of two types: text or graphics. All monitors will display text. To display graphics, a monitor must be connected with a graphics adapter card in your computer.

The Allways or Wysiwyg add-in screens default to graphics although they will display on a text screen. However, in a text screen, these add-ins will not show the data as it will appear when printed. Likewise, 1-2-3 Release 3 worksheets default to a graphics screen, but you can display only the basic information if you have a text screen. Graphics resolution is measured in pixels—dots of light evenly spaced in a grid pattern on the screen. Each dot can be turned on or off and, on a color screen, can be assigned any color.

Text screens place all of their information in rows and columns. These screens are created by the program telling the computer the character and color that it wants in each column and row of the display. The only differences you will find in text screens are whether the monitor can display colors, the clarity of the characters displayed, and the number of rows that can appear on the screen. Since the column and row positions are predefined, text screens are more quickly refreshed with new information than graphics screens are.

Graphics screens are screens that a program draws with a pattern of pixels. The quality of these graphics displays is as good as the graphics adapter and monitor you use. This will depend on the number of pixels in the grid that makes up the screen. Table 3-1, following, shows the number of pixels in some of the popular monitor/adapters available today.

HARDWARE SUPPORT

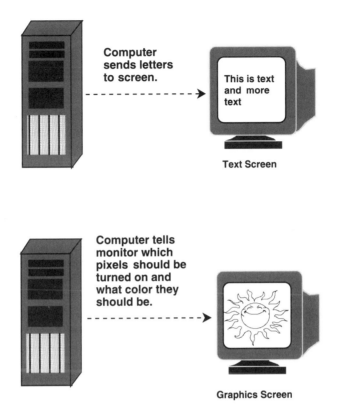

Figure 3-1: How text and graphics screens work.

Basic 1-2-3 Requirements

With 1-2-3 you can use any type of monitor—color or monochrome, displaying graphics or not. If your monitor cannot display graphics, you can still create graphs although you will not see how the graphs appear until you print. When you install 1-2-3, you need to pick out a screen display because while 1-2-3 can check which display adapter card is connected, it cannot tell if the monitor attached to the back of the display card matches it.

A monitor with features above the bare minimum may make it easier for you to work with 1-2-3. For example, if you have a color monitor, you can take advantage

PUBLISHING 1-2-3

of 1-2-3's colors to differentiate parts of the screen and series in a graph. Also, having higher resolution display equipment means that graphics screens will look better. If you have a graphics monitor, Allways and Wysiwyg screens will display data as it will appear when you print. A poor quality monitor will not have a negative effect on your printed output: The quality of your output will be limited only by your printer's limitations. A graph that is displayed with a lower resolution CGA monitor will print the same as one displayed on a VGA monitor if the same printer is used for both. If you select a Hewlett-Packard LaserJet Series III printer, the output will appear significantly better than the CGA screen image appears.

The Importance of Pixels

The resolution of screen displays is measured by the number of pixels that make up the screen. Each pixel is one dot of light. In color monitors, this is created by combining red, green and blue at different intensities to create different colors. For example, a VGA monitor can display 600-by-480 pixels. The higher the number of pixels, the more detailed the display. As an example, Figure 3-2, which follows, shows half of a screen using a CGA display and half of a screen using a VGA display. You can easily see the difference. The difference between display adapters and their accompanying monitors is measured by the number of pixels that fit across and down the screen.

Different Types of Monitor Adapters

A graphics adapter card is hardware that converts the computer's image of what currently should appear on the screen into signals that the screen can understand for displaying the images. CGA, EGA and VGA are acronyms that have been assigned to the various graphics adapters. They represent Color Graphics Adapter, Enhanced Graphics Adapter, and Virtual Graphics Adapter, respectively. Each new generation of monitors has gained in ability to draw sharper images on screen.

Many of the common display adapters are listed in Table 3-1 along with their resolution in pixels. With several display adapter types, you can have different

HARDWARE SUPPORT

resolutions depending on the number of colors on the screen. When you purchase your system, the information that accompanies the computer or the display adapter card will indicate the display adapter card you have. This is the selection you usually make in the 1-2-3 Install program for selecting your graphics screen. Later versions of the 1-2-3 installation program test the hardware in the computer to determine the correct display adapter. Usually, you only need to change this information when you know it is wrong or you have a monitor that does not match the display adapter.

Table 3-1
Display Adapters and Their Resolutions

Display Adapter	Resolution
MDA	720-by-350, monochrome
CGA	640-by-200, monochrome; 320-by-200, four colors; 160-by-200, 16 colors
MCGA	640-by-480, monochrome; 320-by-200, 256 colors
EGA	640-by-350, 16 colors; fits 43 lines on text screens
VGA	640-by-480, 16 colors; 320-by-200, 256 colors; fits 50 lines on text screens
Hercules	720-by-348, 16 colors
8514/A	1024-by-768, 256 colors

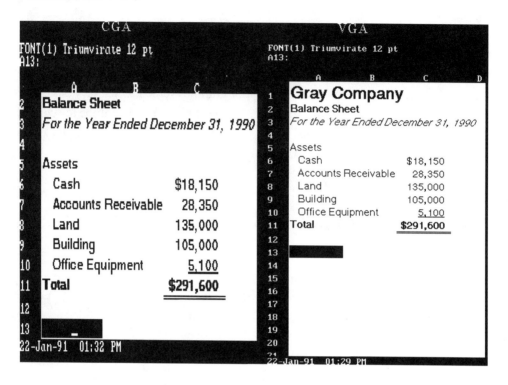

Figure 3-2: The left side displays a CGA screen with noticeably lower resolution than the VGA screen on the right.

Different Types of Monitors

A monitor receives information from your computer's graphics adapter and displays it on the machine. It does not require any input from you once it is set up. The only time your monitor will affect how you use 1-2-3 is when the installation option that you select does not match your adapter card. For example, if you are using a monocolor VGA display with a VGA adapter card, you will need to select a monochrome display when installing 1-2-3. This may also be the case with liquid crystal displays on laptops although you may want to experiment to select the display you like best. Selecting color by mistake may cause your screen to appear blank when you start the program.

HARDWARE SUPPORT

Understanding the Memory in Your Computer System

Your computer has several different types of memory that it uses for running programs. Each type of memory has advantages and disadvantages. When you use 1-2-3, as well as other programs, you need a minimum amount of memory to run and store data. All computers have conventional memory. Conventional memory is the memory up to 640K that DOS can use to store DOS programs, other application programs and your data. This type of memory was initially all that the computer had. Many newer computers actually have 1 MB of conventional RAM although DOS can only use 640K of it.

Another type of memory is expanded memory. Expanded memory was the first attempt made to increase a computer's storage ability beyond the memory available in the memory chips on the motherboard or main board of the machine. Since this type of memory has been available for some time, many programs, including 1-2-3, can use it. You may be surprised to learn that doubling memory by adding expanded memory will not double the size of the spreadsheet that you can create with 1-2-3. This phenomenon occurs because 1-2-3 places pointers in conventional memory that enable you to access the cell entries stored in expanded memory. Your use of expanded memory, then, is limited by the number of pointers 1-2-3 can store in conventional memory.

The third and newest type of memory is extended memory. This memory, which is as fast as conventional memory, is added to conventional memory in the computer's hardware. Since this memory is still relatively new, not all programs can use it effectively.

1-2-3's Requirements

1-2-3 has several hardware requirements. One requirement is that the hardware have sufficient memory to load 1-2-3. But you want your memory to exceed this minimum so that you may create and use reasonably sized spreadsheets. If you have

PUBLISHING 1-2-3

expanded memory, 1-2-3 will use it (except for Release 1A). If you have extended memory, 1-2-3 Release 3 can use it to store your data. The varying amounts of conventional memory required by each release of 1-2-3 are listed in Table 3-2.

Another requirement 1-2-3 makes of your computer is disk storage. If you install 1-2-3 on a hard disk, the information that comes with the 1-2-3 disks must also be put on your hard disk. The amount of hard disk storage required for the different releases is listed in Table 3-2 on the following page.

Additional Memory Needed for Add-ins and Other Programs

In addition to 1-2-3's basic memory and disk space requirements, 1-2-3 add-ins also require memory and disk storage. For example, Allways requires an additional 128K of RAM and 1.2 MB of hard disk space. Also, using some add-ins, such as Allways and Wysiwyg, requires you to use 1-2-3 with a hard disk. To use Wysiwyg with 1- 2-3 Release 2.3, you need 512K RAM and 6 MB of disk space. The basic 1-2-3, 2.3 program only requires 1.7 MB and Wysiwyg only requires another 700K but you are likely to want the additional features such as PrintGraph and the other add-ins that require additional memory. To use Wysiwyg with 1-2-3 Release 3.1, you need 1 MB RAM and 5 MB of disk space for 1-2-3 and Wysiwyg.

Understanding Disk Types and Capacities

Disks are an ideal media for data storage because they can store a lot of information in a small area. For example, you can fit a 180-page text file on one low density 5-1/4 inch disk. Besides storing your data, disks also store your programs. Disks come in a variety of sizes and capacities.

Disk Types in Popular Use

A computer uses two basic types of disks. You are probably most familiar with floppy disks since they are removable. These come in different sizes and capacities. These disks are used for data storage, backup copies, program disks and as a method of transferring data from one computer to another. Floppy disks usually come in 5-1/4 inch and 3-1/2 inch sizes. Both can be regular or high density.

HARDWARE SUPPORT

Table 3-2
Computer Requirements of Different 1-2-3 Releases

1-2-3 Release	Requirements	
	Conventional Memory	**Hard Disk Space**
1A	192K	< 1 MB
2.0	1256K	< 1 MB
2.2	384K	1.7 MB
2.3	320K	6 MB
3.0	1 MB	3 MB
3.1	1 MB	5 MB

The second type of disk is a hard disk. The majority of hard disks are built into your machine and cannot be seen. Hard disk drives require less physical space than they did in the past while, at the same time, they offer increased capacity. For example, the same hard disk drive size that would have held 5 or 10 MB in the early 1980's can now store 120 MB. Because you cannot see hard disks, their protective cases often have a light that goes on to indicate that the computer is reading or writing data to the hard disk. Hard disks are also faster than floppies. Part of the reason is that the hard disk is always spinning while a floppy disk only spins in its jacket when you read or write from it. A hard disk can store the same information as many floppy disks. For example, a 120-MB hard drive stores the equivalent of over three hundred 5-1/4 inch disks.

You can add additional external hard disks to further increase storage capacity if you have a large number of programs or a large quantity of data to store. You can also link all of your systems within a network and use a large external hard disk called a file server for the storage of programs and data.

PUBLISHING 1-2-3

In 1-2-3, you can run the earlier releases on floppy disks but you must run later versions on a hard disk. As programs became more complex, they became bigger so with a program like 1-2-3 Release 3, you *must* run it on a hard disk. Even though 1-2-3 2.2 will run off a floppy disk, you will not be able to use the features of Allways unless you have a hard disk. And even with releases that can run on a floppy disk, you may still want to run them off a hard disk to improve speed. Also, on a hard disk, you can create files that exceed the capacity of the floppy disk.

Since neither disk type is permanently error-free, you should always backup your important data. With a hard disk, when you backup your 1-2-3 data, put the disks away from the computer since a disaster that damages your hard disk will also damage any nearby floppies.

Capacity for Program and Data Storage

A 5-1/4" double sided/double density floppy disk can store 360K. The same size disk in a high density format can store 1.2 MB of data or program information. The 3-1/2" disks can either store 720K or 1.44 MB of information depending on whether your disks come formatted. To take advantage of the high density disk capacity, you must use a disk designed for the higher capacity as well as format it using a high density disk drive.

Understanding Printers

When you prepare a spreadsheet to use as part of a presentation, you are likely to use your printer to create your final output. There is a great variety of printer types and printer features. When you print from 1-2-3, you can create a quick printout of your data or you can add embellishments (provided your printer supports them). Printing with Wysiwyg or Allways adds sophistication not available in 1-2-3. 1-2-3 sends to the printer only setup strings, spaces, blank lines, and the characters in the range you print. When you print with Wysiwyg or Allways, the information sent to the printer is more specific and more extensive. For example, printing a page in 1-2-3 sends about 5K of information to the printer while printing the same page with Wysiwyg sends

HARDWARE SUPPORT

13K. Further, with 1-2-3 Release 2 and above you can send setup strings to the printer although you cannot change the string in the middle of a line. With Allways and Wysiwyg not only can you change the setup string for print features, but you can also print text and graphics on the same page. Printing graphics using PrintGraph or the graphics features of Allways and Wysiwyg may send as much as 500K of information to the printer per page. Heavy graphics output, then, takes longer. Also, since the information is printer-specific, you must select the correct printer during installation of the software. Selecting the wrong printer means sending the wrong codes to the printer. Also, selecting the wrong printer may mean the printer features you thought were available really are not. Worse, when you attempt to print with incorrect codes, you can get unpredictable results, such as page after page of blank paper spewing from the printer.

Printer problems also occur when you are using a new printer with an old version of 1-2-3. You must remember to select an older model of the printer you are using. For example, if you are using 1-2-3 Release 2.2 with Allways and printing to a Hewlett-Packard LaserJet Series III, you must select the Hewlett-Packard LaserJet Series II printer. Thus, with Allways, some of the Hewlett-Packard LaserJet Series III features will not be available.

Printing can occur as either a foreground or background operation. When you print in the foreground, all of the computer's resources are devoted to printing. This means you cannot use the computer for other applications until printing is complete. All releases below 3.0 automatically use foreground printing. Background printing allows you to use the computer for other things while you print. Release 2.3 has background printing as an option and Releases 3.0 and higher do it automatically. Background printing requires more resources since 1-2-3, or the program performing the background printing, must temporarily store the print data in memory or in a temporary disk file. When you print in the background, you can continue to use the application. Also in background printing, since the computing power is shared between printing and the application you are using, the application in the foreground will behave more slowly than is usual until the background printing is complete.

PUBLISHING 1-2-3

Basic Types of Printers

You will use one of three basic types of printers. Printers in common use today are daisy wheel, dot matrix and laser. Each has different features. Daisy wheel printers use a printwheel that spins until it finds the appropriate character. Then it strikes the character and continues onto the next one. This is just like a typewriter except a daisy wheel is faster than a typist.

The daisy wheel printer has several drawbacks. First, it can only print the characters on the printwheel so that if you use different fonts, you must switch the printwheel at each font change. Second, a daisy wheel printer cannot print graphs. Third, this method is slower than the others since the wheel must spin to the proper location of each character. Daisy wheel printers are usually reserved for high-quality output.

The second type of printer is the dot matrix. A dot matrix printer uses a grid of dots that can be printed in any location. That means this type of printer can print any characters and graphs. For example, Figure 3-3 shows the dot pattern that makes up an A printed by a nine-pin dot matrix. However, the output of a dot matrix printer is not as precise as that of a daisy wheel printer. A dot matrix prints, prints a row of characters at a time. The number of pins a dot matrix printer has is important since the more pins the more dots per inch and the better the results.

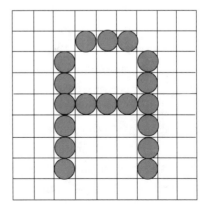

Figure 3-3: A nine-pin dot matrix printer makes this pattern when it prints an A.

72

✔ CHECKLIST

Printer Considerations

Your printer is your second largest equipment expenditure exceeded only by the cost of the system unit. Consider the following items before making a purchase.

THROUGHPUT
- ✔ Number of pages printed per minute.
- ✔ Time to print a text page versus a graphics page.
- ✔ Number of pages normally printed per day: Will it accommodate our needs during work hours?

NOISE
- ✔ Not disruptive—particularly if using several printers in one area.

FEATURES
- ✔ Uses multiple internal fonts.
- ✔ Supports both portrait and landscape modes.
- ✔ Supports various quality levels for text and graphics.
- ✔ Supports the use of all the form types used, including envelopes.
- ✔ Uses an available serial or parallel port.

EXPANDABILITY
- ✔ Accepts additional memory.
- ✔ Memory requirements for printing a combined text/graphics page: How much will it need?
- ✔ Accepts additional cartridges and soft fonts.

MAINTENANCE
- ✔ Can be serviced locally.
- ✔ Has extended warranty and good performance record.
- ✔ Requires little periodic maintenance.
- ✔ Low-cost daily maintenance, e.g. toner cartridges.

SOFTWARE SUPPORT
- ✔ Appears on list of hardware products supported.
- ✔ If emulates a popular printer brand, is it 100% compatible?

COST
- ✔ Fits within the budget.
- ✔ What is the cost of accessories and additional equipment?
- ✔ Price negotiable—perhaps at time of system purchase.

PUBLISHING 1-2-3

The third type of printer is the laser printer which has the best features of all. Laser printers print smaller dots than the dot matrix printers so their images are more clear. Laser printers can often print 150 and 300 dots-per-inch so the detail is like that of the daisy wheel. Laser printers can print text and graphics and they are the fastest. For example, the Hewlett-Packard LaserJet Series III can print eight pages of text per minute. Also, the laser printer is the quietest type of printer and often has many different fonts that allow you to change the style of characters. The only disadvantage of laser printers is price.

Printer Capabilities

A printer can do more than just print your data. A printer may be able to use different size paper, provide multiple fonts and print your data quickly.

Fonts

A printer can have three types of fonts or character styles. A font is a complete set of characters in a specific typeface and size. Fonts can be internal fonts, cartridges and soft fonts. Internal fonts are the fonts that are permanently programmed into the computer. When you print a spreadsheet using the /Print Printer command or you print a text file; the computer only needs to tell the printer the internal font to use and then the characters to print. You can transmit codes to the printer to select a font or use the menu available on some printer models. Most printers have one internal font but you can also use printers that have multiple internal fonts. For example, the Hewlett-Packard LaserJet Series III printer has 68 internal fonts.

Cartridges are hardware components that you add to your printer to provide more built-in fonts. Once these cartridges are installed in special printer slots, you can access them by sending a printer command.

The third type of fonts are soft fonts. These include the fonts provided by Allways or Wysiwyg. Rather than these being part of the printer's hardware, these fonts are created by telling the printer how each character should appear. Sometimes these soft fonts are loaded into the printer's memory to be automatically available. Other types

HARDWARE SUPPORT

of soft fonts, like those provided by Allways or Wysiwyg, are generated as you print the document. For example, when you print a worksheet that uses Allways fonts, the computer creates an image of each character sent to the printer. These take longer to print. Soft fonts also use part of your hard disk and must be loaded into RAM, leaving less memory and disk space for other applications. The advantage of soft fonts is the wide range available.

Fonts are either bitmapped or scalable and can be provided by either the software or the hardware. Bitmapped fonts are defined by where the printer places dots to produce the character. For example, Figure 3-3 shows how a printer defines an A. Bitmapped fonts are only available in pre-defined sizes. The fonts that Allways or Wysiwyg add-ins provide are bitmapped. Scalable fonts are defined by the outline of the shape of the character. For example, Figure 3-4 shows how the letter A might be defined. These fonts can be expanded and contracted to many sizes. PrintGraph fonts are scalable and since these must be scaled for size, they take longer to print than bitmapped fonts do.

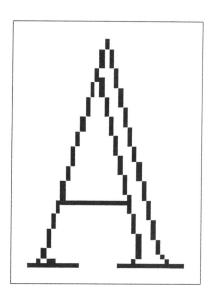

Figure 3-4: The letter A produced by a scalable font.

PUBLISHING 1-2-3

Printer Memory

A printer contains memory for storing the data it is about to print. Printers store data in a buffer area since the computer can prepare information faster than the printer can actually print. As the printer prints your data, the computer then releases more information from the buffer to be printed. The buffer size determines how much information the computer can send to the printer before it has to wait until the printer is ready to accept more. Remember that with some applications, such as 1-2-3 Releases 2.3 and above, printing is done in the background so you can continue to use the application while the computer devotes part of its resources to printing. If 1-2-3 does not print in the background, you must wait until the computer finishes sending information to the printer before you can continue using 1-2-3. You may be able to add more memory to your printer to enlarge the printer buffer. For example, you can add up to 4 MB of additional memory to a Hewlett-Packard Series III printer. This means that the computer can send an additional 4 MB of printer information and the additional memory reduces your waiting time for printing in the foreground.

Additional Features

Printers can contain a wide variety of features besides fonts and memory. These features include the paper feeding mechanism, its speed, and its ability to print sideways—or in landscape mode. Some features are more important than others. For example, a laser printer can produce great output but the expense is not always justifiable.

Printers can accept paper in several ways. A printer may expect you to insert each sheet into the printer or it can use a continuous feeding mechanism so it can print many pages unattended. Printers can also use different sizes of paper. For example, the Hewlett-Packard LaserJet Series III, can accept four sizes of paper and four sizes of envelopes.

An important printer feature is speed. If you print many pages, you will not want a slow printer while, if you only print a few pages, a slow printer that offers other features may suit your needs.

HARDWARE SUPPORT

Another useful printer feature is the ability to print sideways, so to speak, also called landscape mode. Most printers print in portrait mode which means using an 8-1/2"-by-11" sheet of paper so that the page is longer than it is wide. If you need to print a wide spreadsheet range, you may want to rotate the output. Some printers let you switch between portrait and landscape mode by simply sending a command. Other printers need special utilities or cannot do it at all.

A Closer Look at the Hewlett-Packard LaserJet Printers

Hewlett-Packard LaserJet printers are one of the most popular laser printers since they offer so many features. These printers have been consistently improved so that the LaserJet Series III provides the best features yet. Using this printer as an example, this section describes how you can access a printer's features. These features include using setup strings, menus and the control panel on the front of the printer. If you have an earlier model Hewlett-Packard LaserJet, many of the features described below are also available. If you are not using a Hewlett-Packard printer, you will still want to review this section since printers possess similar features even if specific commands vary. When you use a Hewlett-Packard LaserJet printer, the printer requires a one-sixth inch margin on all sides. You also want to use the /Worksheet Global Default Printer Pg-Length command to change the default page length from 66 to 60. And you should use the /Print menu commands to advance the paper rather than using the printer buttons since the latter method will not update 1-2-3's internal line count.

Using Printer Commands for Printer Features

A Hewlett-Packard LaserJet Series III printer understands many instructions that go beyond signifying specific characters to print or where to print dots to create a graph. A printer accepts printer commands to activate features such as boldface, fonts, and rotating the output. You can add printer codes yourself or have an application add them for you. When you use the latter method for adding printer commands, the application will convert its codes for printer features into the appropriate printer commands before it prints your data. Each printer uses different printer commands to activate its features. This is why you need to select the printer before you print. With 1-2-3, you can either provide the printer commands yourself or through setup strings.

PUBLISHING 1-2-3

With Wysiwyg, Allways or Release 3 of 1-2-3, you can select menu commands and 1-2-3 or the add-ins will add the printer commands for you.

Hewlett-Packard LaserJet Printer Commands

For the Hewlett-Packard LaserJet Series III printer, printer commands are created by entering a specific set of characters or values. For example, to boldface text, the computer sends ESC and (s3B to the printer. Printer commands start with ESC and are followed by one or more characters or values. Printer commands can be sent using the characters, the decimal value of the characters, or the hexadecimal value of the characters. For example, to boldface the print command is ESC(s3B, 027 040 115 051 066, or 1B 28 73 33 42. In 1-2-3, you can use characters or the decimal values separated by backslashes. Since upper and lower case letters convert into different values, the printer codes are case sensitive.

Printer commands always end in an uppercase letter. However, if you combine printer commands, only the last letter of the last printer command is uppercase. Printer commands are combined by replacing the uppercase letter of the first printer command with the lowercase letter and removing ESC before the second. For example, the printer command to boldface italicized text is ESC(s3b, ESC(s1S or combined ESC(s3b(s1S. Printer commands are often combined when you change fonts since you may need to change other printer settings at the same time. Table 3-3 lists many of the printer commands that you may want to use and samples of their results. When a printer command includes #, you need to replace it with an appropriate number. For example, the printer command ESC &l6D prints six lines per inch and the command ESC &l8D prints eight lines per inch. You will want to check your printer manual for other printer features. The printer commands activate features that continue until they are deactivated. For example, when the printer starts boldfacing text, the printer continues to boldface all text until the printer receives a command to stop boldfacing or to reset itself. The reset function deactivates all printer features and returns to the defaults. You may want to include this printer command at the beginning of a 1-2-3 session so you remove any changes made by other applications. You do not want to include this printer command at other locations when you print your spreadsheet.

HARDWARE SUPPORT

Adding Printer Commands to a Spreadsheet with Setup Strings

1-2-3 calls printer commands setup strings because you are using strings, or sets of characters, to set the printer. You can enter setup strings with the /Print Printer Options Setup or /Worksheet Global Default Printer Setup commands. You can also enter setup strings directly in the spreadsheet. When you enter printer commands as setup strings, you will enter the ESC character as \027. This is necessary because if you press ESC, 1-2-3 acts on that keystroke rather than including it in the setup string. When you add a setup string with the /Worksheet Global Default Printer Setup command, the setup string is sent to the printer every time you start printing. This command is often used to reset the printer from other applications so, using the Hewlett-Packard LaserJet Series III as an example, you would enter \027E at this command's prompt. When you add setup strings to a spreadsheet using the /Print Printer Options Setup command, the effect of the printer command applies to the entire printed spreadsheet. When you add printer commands in the middle of a spreadsheet, they apply from the point of the printer command until the printer feature is deactivated.

To enter a printer command in a spreadsheet row, move to the row where you want the printer command. Select /Worksheet Insert Row and in the new row, enter !! and the printer command. For example, you can add printer commands to boldface rows 1 through 3 for the spreadsheet in Figure 3-5 by moving to A1 and selecting /Worksheet Insert Row. In column A of the new row, enter !!**\027s3B**. Next, move to A5 and select /Worksheet Insert Row. In column A of the new row, enter !!**\027s0B**. When you print a spreadsheet containing printer commands in the first column of the range it is printing, 1-2-3 sends the printer codes to the printer but does not send any other information in that row to the printer. This means that you can use the remainder of the row to document the printer command as shown in Figure 3-6.

Using setup strings to add printer commands has a few advantages and disadvantages. An advantage of using setup strings with the /Worksheet Global Default Printer Setup command, the /Print Printer Options Setup command, or directly in the spreadsheet, is that you can enter printer commands this way for any 1-2-3 release.

Table 3-3
Frequently Used Printer Commands for the Hewlett-Packard LaserJet

Effect	Printer Command	Example
Reset	ESC E	Returns printer to default settings
Number of Copies	ESC &l#x Replace # with number of copies	Prints one or more copies of each page
Portrait Orientation	ESC &l0O	Regular text
Landscape Orientation	ESC &l1O	Prints text sideways
Reverse Portrait Orientation	ESC &l2O	Prints text upside down
Reverse Landscape Orientation	ESC &l3O	Prints text reversed sideways (270° rotation)
Lines Per Inch	ESC &l#D Replace # with 1, 2, 3, 4, 6, 8, 12, 16, 24, or 48 for lines per inch	ESC&l3 will print three lines to the inch

HARDWARE SUPPORT

Table 3-3, continued
Frequently Used Printer Commands for the Hewlett-Packard LaserJet

Effect	Printer Command	Example
Proportional Spacing	ESC(s1P	This is proportional
Fixed Spacing	ESC(s0P	`This is fixed`
Regular Pitch	ESC&k0S	This is 10 point pitch
Compressed Pitch	ESC&k2S	This is 16.5 point pitch
Elite Pitch	ESC&k4S	This is 12 point pitch
Italic	ESC(s1S	*This is italicized*
End Italic	ESC(s0S	This is not italicized
Bold	ESC(s3B	**This is bold**
Different bold level	ESC(s#B Replace # with a number between -7 and 7; the higher the number, the darker the characters	ESC(s-7B creates light text

Table 3-3, continued
Frequently Used Printer Commands for the Hewlett-Packard LaserJet

Effect	Printer Command	Example
Courier typeface	ESC(s3T	This is Courier
Times typeface	ESC(s4148T	This is Times
Line Printer	ESC(s0T	This is Line Printer
Underline (no spaces)	ESC&d3D	This underlining does not underline spaces
Underline (spaces)	ESC&d0D	This underlining includes spaces
Stop Underline	ESC&d@	This stops underlining

You can use setup strings to change printer features in between rows although you cannot enter them to change printer features in the middle of a row. The disadvantage of using setup strings to activate printer features is that you must know the printer command for the feature you want. Also, if you change the printer you use, you must change the setup string. Using printer features by entering the printer commands is not intended when working with add-ins such as Wysiwyg and Allways since these often have menu commands that will provide the features you want.

HARDWARE SUPPORT

Using Printer Control Codes With Menu Selections in 1-2-3

Depending on the release of 1-2-3 or the add-in you are using, you can also add printer features for your spreadsheet using menu selections. For example, the /Print Printer Options Advanced Layout Line-Spacing Compressed command in Release 3 adds the printer command ESC&l8D when you print the spreadsheet using a Hewlett-Packard LaserJet Series III printer. Wysiwyg and Allways provide more commands that use your printer's features. Examples of these types of commands are the Format Font command used by both which selects the font of a range. The features of these two add-ins are covered in other chapters but you now know that when you select printer features using the add-in commands, that the add-in includes the appropriate printer command. Since printing with 1-2-3 and printing with an add-in are separate, you must issue commands from the add-in to access the add-in's features.

Like using setup strings for printer features, using menu commands has advantages and disadvantages. The biggest advantage of menu commands for printer features is that you do not need to know the printer command for the feature you want. If you change the printer, 1-2-3 or the add-in changes the printer commands to match the selected printer. Also, making changes with menu commands means that 1-2-3 or the add-in can adjust the other parts of the printout for the change. For example, if you use the /Print Printer Options Advanced Layout Line-Spacing Compressed command, 1-2-3 automatically adjusts the number of lines on the page to fit more lines on the same sized page. However, not all releases of 1-2-3 include the menu commands to activate printer features. Also, your printer may have features that are not accessible through the menu. For example, if you want to select the paper source used by a Hewlett-Packard LaserJet Series III, you must use a setup strings since there is no menu command for this printer feature. With Wysiwyg and Allways, you can use menu commands and other add-in features to change printer features in the middle of a row.

Using the Printing Menu on the Printer Control Panel

Another option for changing how the Hewlett-Packard LaserJet Series III prints your spreadsheet or other text is to use the printer control panel. When the Ready and

PUBLISHING 1-2-3

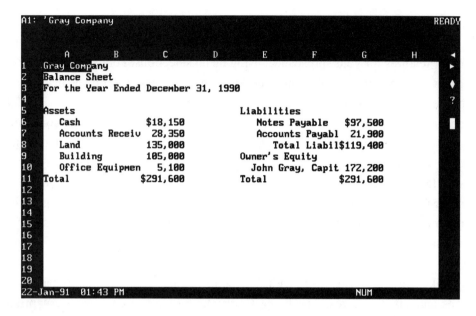

Figure 3-5 (above): Adding printer commands to boldface rows.

Figure 3-6 (below): Using your spreadsheet rows to document printer commands.

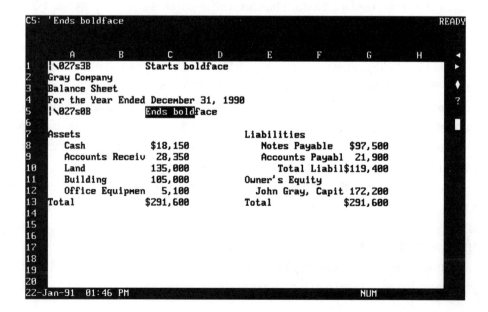

HARDWARE SUPPORT

the On Line button lights are on, the printer is ready to accept information. The Ready light flashes when the printer is currently receiving information. The Hewlett-Packard LaserJet Series III printer has a menu built into the control panel that you can use to select different settings and configuration. You can use this in place of setup strings. The Hewlett-Packard LaserJet Series III printer control panel lets you select the number of copies, the font and its size, the paper, orientation, number of lines on the page, manual feed setting, and symbol set. All of the menu and other control panel options are available after you press the On Line button to turn the light off.

One of the quickest and useful ways you can use the printer control panel is to display a sample of the fonts you can use with your printer. To list the fonts available, press the button labeled Print Fonts. The left and right font cartridge information depends on the cartridges you have installed. From Hewlett-Packard's hard copy of the font list, you can see the font source (left, right or internal), the font number, the symbol set it can use, whether its fixed or proportional, the font size, style, height, name, orientation, a sample and the printer command to create it. You can use this information both when you use the printer control panel to change the output and when you want to add the printer command codes as part of your printed output.

To use the printer control panel to change the print settings, you use the menu which will appear when you press the Menu button. When you press Menu, the 00 READY changes to COPIES = 1 *. The menu displays one option at a time. For each option in the printer menu option, you can press the + and - keys to cycle through your selections. The * indicates the choice for the option that is currently selected. When the choice you want for the option is displayed, press the Enter button and the * will appear next to your choice. Each time you press the Menu button, the display cycles through the different menu options, When you are ready to print, press On Line. As an example of using the menu, suppose you want to print a spreadsheet range containing text in column A using the Times font. To make this change, first press On Line, next press the Menu key twice to change 00 READY to FONT SOURCE. Unless the current setting is I, press + until I appears and then press ENTER. Next, press MENU again for FONT NUMBER. Press + until 10 appears and then press

85

PUBLISHING 1-2-3

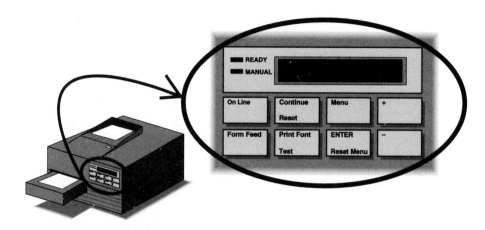

Figure 3-7: The HP LaserJet Series III control panel.

ENTER. Since this is a scalable font, you can select the size of the font you want. Press Menu to display PT. SIZE=12.00, press + until 20.00 appears and press ENTER. Next, press Menu three times to display, FORM and press - until 40 appears. This changes the number of lines per inch the printer prints so that 40 lines appear on the entire page. Since this finishes the changes you want to make, press On Line. Before you print using the /Print Printer Go command in 1-2-3, you will want to press the On Line button so the printer is ready to accept information. Figure 3-8 shows output created with these settings. Later when you want to remove all of these settings, you can select the On Line button and hold down the Enter/Reset Menu button until 09 MENU RESET appears in the display. All of the control panel button options that appear in another color are activated by holding down the button.

Like using setup strings or menu commands for printer features, using the printer control panel has advantages and disadvantages. The biggest advantage of menu commands for printer features is that once you learn how to do it, it is easy to do subsequent times. Some disadvantages, are the changes you make must apply to the entire document rather than a portion. The control panel menu does not let you use all

Gray Company
Balance Sheet
For the Year Ended December 31, 1990

Assets
  Cash
  Accounts Receivable
  Land
  Building
  Office Equipment
Total

Figure 3-8: Output using specific settings, including the Times typeface.

of the printer features available. Also, changes that you make to the printer control panel are overridden by printer commands sent by the computer. Also, using the printer control panel does not have 1-2-3 adjust how the spreadsheet is printed to match your selections. For example, if you change the font to 20-point Times, you must also change the number of lines on the page so that the lines do not run into each other. Another problem occurs when you are using proportional fonts since the spreadsheet columns will not align on your printout. When you use the Allways or Wysiwyg add-in, these software packages process the output so the columns will align.

Other Output Options

Besides using printers to create output for your data, you have other options. These options include plotters and film recorders. You can also capture text and graphic screen images of 1-2-3 data with screen capture program such as INSET or Hot Shot Graphics. You can use these captured images for the creation of a slide show, inclusion in a document created with a desktop publishing package, or to send the image to a slide service for developing. These special output options may not be used as frequently as a printer but they allow you to accomplish tasks that would not be possible otherwise.

Plotters

Plotters are frequently used to create color output and transparencies. A plotter uses individual pens of different colors to draw lines on a page in any shape. Plotters are especially useful for transparencies since you can use special transparency pens that adhere to the transparency better than the ink. Plotters are often used with 1-2-3 to print graphs. For example, you may want to use a printer to print the spreadsheet data and a plotter to print the graphs created with the spreadsheet data in color. Plotters are seldom used for printing pages of text data since it is an inefficient use of them. Plotters vary in the number of pens that are used at one time. There are single pen plotters as well as 2-, 4-, 6-, and 8-pen plotters. If you are using more colors than there are pens, the plotter will assign the pens to color numbers. This way the software will stop for a pen change as each new color is used in the event that you want to use a greater variety of colors than the number of pens available at once. 1-2-3 supports the direct transfer of its output to most of the popular plotters. In addition, the supplemental graphics products that can import 1-2-3 data or graph files can also produce their output on a plotter.

Film Recorders

Another type of output device is a film recorder. A film recorder takes output from the screen and transfers it to camera film to produce slides. Although 1-2-3 does not interface directly with these devices you can transfer your 1-2-3 graphics output to one of the graphics software programs discussed in Chapter 9 and send it directly to a film recorder. You can choose options in these packages that allow you to interface with film recorders such as the Polaroid Palette, PalettePlus, or PTI ImageMaker. You can select the type of film that you want to use with the recorder and even access special hardware fonts that might be built into the features of your recorder. Some graphics products will write their output into a film recorder format and store it as a file that can

HARDWARE SUPPORT

be sent to a slide service. As an example, Harvard Graphics is set up for the Autographix Slide Service. The package includes a booklet on Autographix to describe the services they offer.

CHAPTER 4

Basic 1-2-3 Options

No matter which release of 1-2-3 you are using, you have a number of features available for help in creating professional looking worksheet presentations and graphs. Although this book will show you how to use add-ins and special products oriented toward the latest releases of 1-2-3, you will want to be certain that you are getting the maximum mileage from the basic product.

This chapter is not designed to teach you how to use the basics of 1-2-3 cell entries and formulas. The approach assumes that you have already mastered these techniques. Rather, this chapter focuses on 1-2-3 commands that you can use to improve the appearance of worksheets and graphs without leaving the package. As a starting point, the chapter offers a brief overview of 1-2-3 releases and their differences.

Differences in 1-2-3 Releases

Earlier releases of 1-2-3 offer only a subset of the features offered by the most recent releases. The original Release 1.0 was upgraded several times before the product was split into two different families of product. Release 3 was the first offering in a new 1-2-3 product family that would only work on a 286 or 386 machine with at least 1 MB of memory. This release was subsequently updated to Release 3.1 in the summer of 1990. Release 2.3 is the latest offering in the original product family designed to run on almost any computer including the older model 8088 machines. The sections which follow highlight some of the major new enhancements offered with each new release of 1-2-3.

PUBLISHING 1-2-3

1-2-3 Release 1A

The basic feature set of 1-2-3 Release 1A is much smaller than current releases. In addition to fewer menu options there are no add-ins such as Wysiwyg, a smaller set of built-in functions, and fewer cells into which to enter your data. Despite the differences, the same basic structure is evident when you look at a Release 1A screen.

1-2-3 Release 2/2.01

Although Release 2.01 was replaced with updated versions, there are still a large number of users working with this release. Since it includes almost every one of the commands discussed in this chapter you will be able to identify with all the features and can take the time to duplicate the features presented if you want. If you would like to work with the Wysiwyg or Allways features set, you have to purchase these add-ins separately.

1-2-3 Release 2.2

1-2-3 Release 2.2 was the first release of 1-2-3 to offer settings sheets that allowed you to review all of your selections from menus requiring multiple selections such as Print or Graph. Another major new feature of 1-2-3 Release 2.2 was the inclusion of the Allways add-in that added spreadsheet publishing features such as font selections and the ability to place text and graphs on the same page. Although Allways was available as a separate product for Release 2.01 and was shipped with 2.01 in the months before 2.2's introduction, not many users were aware of its existence. Release 2.2 changed the expectation level of large groups of users in terms of the quality of output that could be produced with the package. Once attached to 1-2-3, the Allways menu was only a keystroke away and allowed a user to make a variety of changes to the appearance of the spreadsheet. Setup strings were not needed to invoke special print features since they could be selected from the Allways menu.

1-2-3 Release 2.3

Release 2.3 offers new graph types including mixed graphs and high-low-close-open (HLCO) graphs for charting stocks. Full support for the use of a mouse makes 2.3 equally accessible by mouse and keyboard users. Allways was replaced with the

BASIC 1-2-3 OPTIONS

Impress Wysiwyg technology, which handles spreadsheet publishing and enhancement features and provides a clear, crisp screen image as shown in Figure 4-1. The many new formatting features and graphics additions that you select appear on the screen as shown in Figure 4-2. An auditor add-in, a file viewer add-in, a new macro add-in, a tutor add-in, new graph types, and background printing also provide new options.

1-2-3 Release 3

The major difference between 1-2-3 Release 3 and earlier releases is its ability to work with multiple sheets in one spreadsheet file (up to 256 in total). You can also have multiple sheets in memory at once with the combined total not to exceed 256. Background printing, integrated features for printing graphs, and new graph types are among other features.

1-2-3 Release 3.1

The main change in 1-2-3 Release 3.1 was the inclusion of the Wysiwyg add-in. The letters stand for What You See Is What You Get, a commonly used industry term. Once the add-in is installed, selecting boldface and special fonts will immediately change the appearance of your work on-screen—assuming you are working with a graphics monitor. Graphs can be added to any location on the worksheet and will display on the screen along with text. Many new spreadsheet publishing options are part of this package.

A Common Feature Set

Although later releases have features that were not available in the first release of 1-2-3, you will find that many of the features covered in this chapter are included in all releases. Although you may not be able to utilize all the techniques presented if you are working with a copy of 1-2-3 Release 1A, you will still benefit from reviewing some of the techniques employed in this chapter to improve the appearance of worksheets and graphs. Options that are only available with a specific release are appropriately labeled.

PUBLISHING 1-2-3

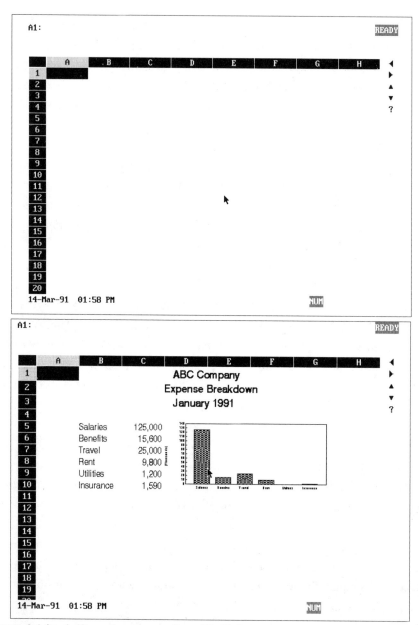

Figure 4-1 (top): The crisp screen image in Release 2.3's Wysiwyg add-in. Figure 4-2 shows the addition of a graph and different text attributes to a Wysiwyg screen.

Basic Model-Building Skills

You are more likely to create models that present your data attractively if you use an organized approach to model creation. Starting with a plan and following a few common-sense guidelines can help. You will want to look at the "Checklist for Model Construction" to ensure that you are starting correctly. Many of these options are discussed in more detail in this chapter along with additional techniques that will help you use 1-2-3's basic features to their fullest.

Changing the Alignment of Entries

Value entries are always right-aligned within cells. This means that anytime you enter a number, formula, or @function, the entry will be right-aligned. A heading for a column of value entries normally consists of a label entry. Although you can use any alignment that you wish for these label entries, the default is left-alignment. This means that the label is preceded by an apostrophe ('). To right align a label, precede the entry with a double quote (") and to center align a label use a caret (^). Using the default left-alignment for label entries can cause a label intended as a heading for a column of values to look as though it does not belong with the values beneath it. This situation is shown in Figure 4-3 where wide columns accentuate the problem in the Units and Price columns. 1-2-3 offers two commands to change the alignment of label entries depending on whether you want to alter the alignment of an existing range of labels or alter all labels that have not as yet been entered. You can look at the details on Range Label and Worksheet Global Label-Prefix to see

---

BASIC 1-2-3 OPTIONS

✓CHECKLIST

Model Construction

✓ Sketch Model on a scrap of paper.
✓ Perform Global Label-Prefix change if the majority of label entries should be other than left-aligned.
✓ Enter framework of labels.
✓ Enter numeric values.
✓ Enter formulas for one set of data.
✓ Verify formula results.
✓ Select Global Format if appropriate.
✓ Allow formatting of individual ranges to override global setting.
✓ Adjust labels with Range Label.
✓ Copy labels and formulas to other appropriate locations.
✓ Create a subset or summary of data if needed.
✓ Create graphs if appropriate.

PUBLISHING 1-2-3

A CLOSER LOOK

Changing the Alignment of Existing Label Entries

1. Move the cell pointer to the first label in the range.

2. Select Range Label.

3. Select the desired label alignment from Left, Right, and Center.

4. Select the range that you want to affect and press ENTER. You can also pre-select the range before invoking the command. This can be a time-saver if you are using a mouse and want to perform several changes to a range.

---

how you can improve your worksheet design with correctly aligned labels.

Using Range Label

The Range Label command will change the alignment of a range of existing label entries. The command performs the same task as individually editing each entry and altering the label prefix that controls the alignment of the command. It is much faster than editing since it changes the alignment of all the labels in the range at one time. All you need to do is specify the range of labels that you want to change and the desired alignment as shown by the steps in a "Closer Look: Changing the Alignment of Existing Labels." The labels in Figure 4-3 can be changed to right alignment to better match the number beneath them with these steps:

1. Select Range Label.
2. Select Right.
3. Select B3..C3 and press ENTER.

The resulting entries now look like Figure 4-4 and appear to match with the value entries.

Using Worksheet Global Label-Prefix

The Worksheet Global Label-Prefix command changes the default label alignment character. Any new cell entry that 1-2-3 interprets as a label entry will automatically have the default label prefix added as its first character. The "Closer Look" box summarizes the steps for using Worksheet Global Label Prefix.

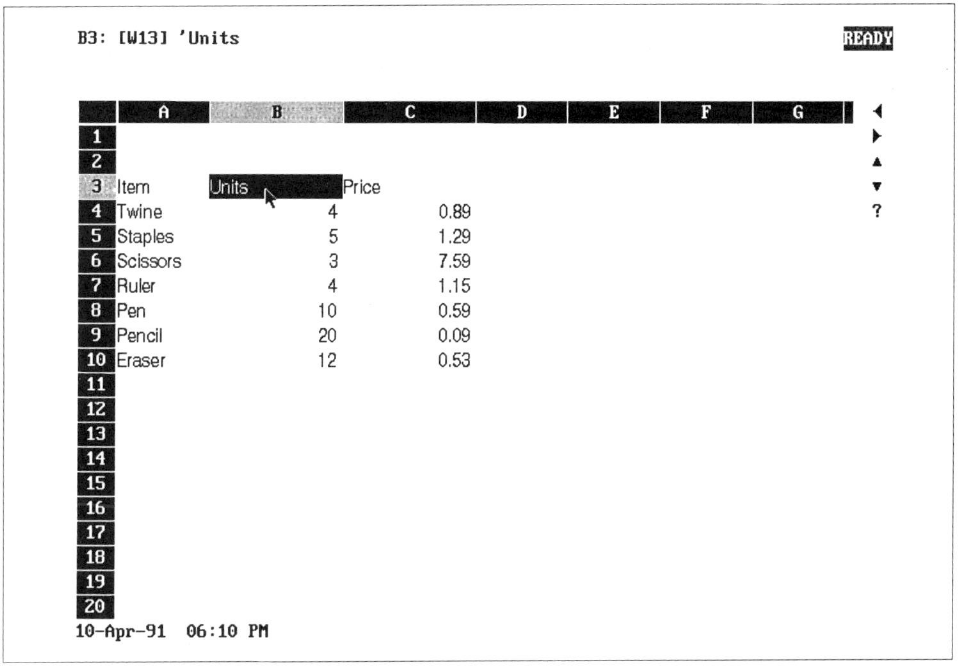

```
B3: [W13] 'Units                                          READY

        A         B           C        D      E     F     G
    1
    2
    3  Item      Units       Price
    4  Twine       4           0.89
    5  Staples     5           1.29
    6  Scissors    3           7.59
    7  Ruler       4           1.15
    8  Pen        10           0.59
    9  Pencil     20           0.09
   10  Eraser     12           0.53
   11
   12
   13
   14
   15
   16
   17
   18
   19
   20
   10-Apr-91  06:10 PM
```

Figure 4-3: Compare the alignment of these labels with the newly aligned labels in Figure 4-4 on the following page.

When you change the default label prefix character, none of the existing worksheet entries is affected. Likewise, you can still continue to use any label alignment when you enter the label prefix that you want before entering your data.

Changing the Appearance of Data

1-2-3 offers a number of options for affecting the way that your data appears on the screen or in a printed report. You will want to explore these options to ensure that the data you are working with is as understandable and as easy to work with as possible.

Using Range Format

1-2-3 offers a number of formats that can be applied to any value entry on the worksheet. If you do not select a special format option, 1-2-3 uses the General format

PUBLISHING 1-2-3

```
C3: {Bold} [W13] "Price                                          READY

      A         B           C        D       E       F       G
 1
 2
 3  Item       Units        Price
 4  Twine        4           0.89
 5  Staples      5           1.29
 6  Scissors     3           7.59
 7  Ruler        4           1.15
 8  Pen         10           0.59
 9  Pencil      20           0.09
10  Eraser      12           0.53
11
12
13
14
15
16
17
18
19
20
10-Apr-91  06:08 PM
```

Figure 4-4 shows the results of changing the alignment of label entries.

for every value entry. This can result in a worksheet that lacks a professional appearance and presents an image that is somewhat disorganized since the numbers do not line up. Figure 4-5 provides an example of this type of display. General format precedes decimal entries with a zero and varies the number of decimal digits displayed depending on the cell width and the number of digits in the number.

Extremely large numbers are displayed in scientific notation which presents the number and a power of 10 that it is raised to. For example, an entry of 3456789123 would display as 3.5E+09. Decimal fractions are truncated to fit within the display width of a cell. An entry of .0123456789 would display as 0.012345 in the default column width.

You can control the appearance of numbers with format selections. For most format options shown in Table 4-1 you can also select the desired number of decimal

BASIC 1-2-3 OPTIONS

Table 4-1
Formatting Options

All of the following options, except for Reset can be used when formatting a range or making a global format change. Reset is restricted to use with a range since it sets the range back to whatever has been selected for the global format setting.

Selection	Effect
Fixed	Establishes a fixed number of decimal places for every entry. If you select Fixed with 2 decimal places an entry of 5 will display as 5.00 and an entry of 5.127 will display as 5.13.
Sci	Uses scientific notation to represent a number. Selecting Sci with 1 decimal place displays an entry of 598.567 as 6.0E+02.
Currency	Places the currency symbol which is initially set as $ at the beginning of each value entry and uses commas as thousand separator. Negative numbers are shown in parentheses. The currency symbol, its location, and the character used as a thousand separator can be changed with Worksheet Global Default Other International. A format selection of Currency with 0 decimal places displays an entry of 5.45 as $5.
,	Uses the same display as currency with the currency symbol. An entry of -1234.679 will display as (1,234.68) with a format selection of , with 2 decimal places.

Table 4-1, continued

General	Uses several different formats depending on the entry. Extremely large numbers are displayed in scientific notation. Decimal entries are preceded by a zero. Extremely small entries are truncated to fit within the display width. An entry of .567 will display as 0.567.
+/-	Uses + or - symbols to represent the magnitude of a value. An entry of 5 displays as +++++\ and an entry of -3 displays as ---.
Percent	Multiplies the value entry by 100 and adds a percent symbol at the end. An entry of .0567 with displays as 5.67% with a format selection of Percent with 2 decimal places.
Date	Provides access to a variety of date and time formats.
Text	Displays the formula entered in a cell rather than the result computed by the formula.
Hidden	Eliminates the display of the entry from the worksheet although you can still see the contents of the cell in the control panel when the cell with the hidden format is the current cell.
Reset	Resets the format of a range of cells to use the global format setting.

BASIC 1-2-3 OPTIONS

places. A summary of the steps needed to format a range of numbers is shown in "A Closer Look: Formatting a Range of Values." A format selection of currency with zero decimal places would probably be the most effective format selection for the data in Figure 4-5. Follow these steps to make the format change:

1. Move the cell pointer to B3.
2. Select Range Format.
3. Select Currency.
4. Type 2 to indicate 2 decimal places and press ENTER.
5. Specify B3..B7 as the range and press ENTER.

Figure 4-6 shows the reformatted data.

Using Global Format

The Global Format command allows you to change the format of all worksheet cells that are not formatted with a range command. Worksheet Global Format affects existing entries without a format. And it affects cells that are currently blank. When an entry is made in these blank cells, the global format will be used unless the cell is formatted with a range command. The "Closer Look" box summarizes the steps needed to format the worksheet cells globally.

You have the same set of options for the Worksheet Global Format command as with Range Format with one exception. Range Format supports Reset which eliminates the current format setting for the range and causes the range to display with the global format.

A CLOSER LOOK

Changing the Global Format

1. Select Worksheet Global Format.

2. Select the desired format and supply a number of decimal places if prompted before pressing ENTER.

PUBLISHING 1-2-3

A CLOSER LOOK

Setting the Global Label Alignment

1. Select Worksheet Global Label-Prefix.

2. Select the desired alignment option. All empty cells will be affected although the result will not be evident until you make a change or check the global settings.

Formatting a Range of Values

1. Select Range Format.

2. Select one of the format options presented.

3. If prompted for the number of decimal places, press ENTER to accept 2 or type a new number and press ENTER.

4. Select a range and press ENTER unless you pre-selected a range before invoking the command.

Since this is not applicable to changing the format on a global basis, the Reset option will not be found in the Worksheet Global Format menu.

Using the Group Command in Release 3.1

When you work with 1-2-3 Release 3, you have multiple worksheets on which to place your data. Sometimes the contents of these worksheets and their formats are quite different and at other times you will want identical formats for different data. The Release 3 family offers a Worksheet Global Group command that allows you to format all the sheets in a group as you make changes to any one of the sheets. Changes such as format, label alignment, column width, inserting rows and columns, and adding page breaks will be applied to all sheets in the group allowing you to make your changes more quickly. The Release 2 family does not offer these features since you are always working with a single worksheet.

Imbedding Setup Strings

You can enter setup strings to invoke printer features with the Print Printer Options Setup command but any change made in this fashion will affect the entire worksheet that you print. In fact, it will also affect the printing of subsequent worksheets since the printer remembers your selections. You must resume printing with a setup string that turns the feature off.

Release 2 of 1-2-3 and later releases all support the use of the special label indicator '|'. Placing two of these symbols as the first character in a row to be

BASIC 1-2-3 OPTIONS

printed causes 1-2-3 to convert the characters that follow to their ASCII equivalents and to transmit them to the printer as control codes. You would enter the same setup string that could be used in the print menu within the worksheet using this option. Although you do need to insert blank lines in the worksheet for the sole purpose of entering these codes, you can use this capability to turn different printer features on and off as you are printing your document. Figure 4-7 shows boldface turned on in A1 and off again in A3. These codes will work for a Hewlett-Packard LaserJet Series II printer. You will need to look in your own printer manual to see which codes your printer requires. It is especially important to note the case of each character since the ASCII equivalents are different for upper and lower case characters.

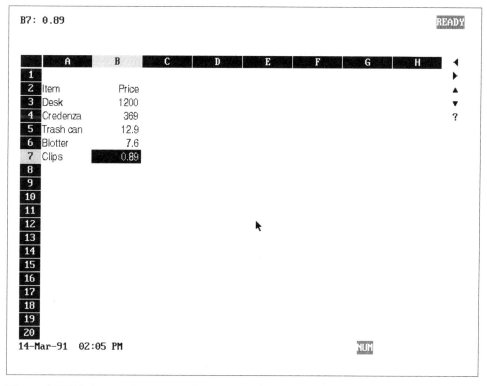

Figure 4-5: This format is not as effective as it could be. Compare this to Figure 4-6 on the following page where labels are right-aligned.

PUBLISHING 1-2-3

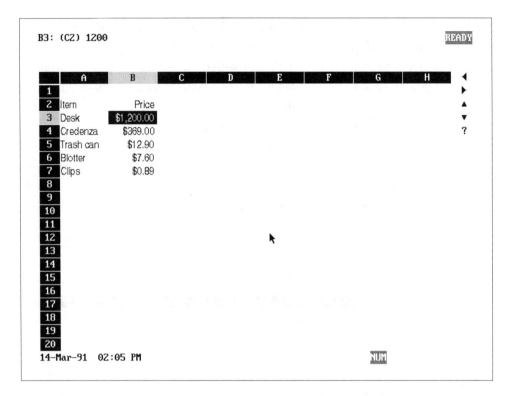

Figure 4-6: A format selection of currency with zeroes to hold decimal places is more effective than the formatting in Figure 4-5.

You will see the codes that you entered on the worksheet but the text that they affect will appear as normal. That is, you will not see the effect of these codes on your text until you print your document. It is also important to remember that the lines containing the codes are not printed. In Figure 4-7, a blank row was inserted as row 4 since without this addition there would have been no separation between the company name and the data. Later, you will see the advantage of using Wysiwyg since you will be able to make selections from menu choices and you will see the effect on your screen.

```
A1: |¦\027(s3B                                              READY

        A        B       C       D       E       F       G       H
  1  |\027(s3B
  2                   ABC COMPANY
  3  |\027(s0B
  4
  5             Q1      Q2      Q3      Q4
  6  Salaries 100,000 120,000 125,000 150,000
  7  Benefits  14,500  16,700  15,000  17,900
  8  Travel    25,500  32,000  23,000  21,000
  9  Rent       5,000   5,000   5,000   5,000
 10  Utilities  1,200   1,200   1,200   1,200
 11  Misc.        500     670     340     750
 12           ------------------------------------
 13  |\027(s3B
 14  TOTAL    146,700 175,570 169,540 195,850
 15  |\027(s0B
 16
 17
 18
 19
 20
 08-Feb-91  12:26 PM
```

Figure 4-7: Boldface is turned on in cell A1 and off in A3 through the use of imbedded setup strings.

Controlling Information at the Top, Bottom, and Sides

You can print consistent information at the top or sides of your screen or printout to create a more readable display. Depending on the technique used this information might be part of the worksheet, entered separately, or part of information maintained by your system.

Using Borders

Borders allow you to print the same information at the top or side of each page of a report. Without borders, pages following the first page of a report can appear as a sea of numbers without any identifying labels. The labels print on the first page because they are part of the print page but they do not automatically repeat on subsequent pages. When you define border rows or columns, this identifying information will print on every page of the report. It is important that you follow the procedure for using

A CLOSER LOOK

Adding Borders to Your Printout

1. Select Print Printer.

2. Select Range and the range containing your data. DO NOT include the border rows.

3. Select Options Borders.

4. Select either Rows or Columns depending on whether you want border columns or border rows.

5. Select the rows or columns you want to use.

6. Select Quit to return to the main print menu.

7. Select Go followed by Page and Align to print you data, advance to the next page, and reset the 1-2-3 counter.

border rows or columns summarized in "Adding Borders to Your Printout." If you inadvertently select border rows or columns as part of the print range you will think that you are seeing double since these rows or columns will print as borders then again as part of the print range on the first page of the report. You will need to re-specify the print range without the border rows and columns if this happens.

Figure 4-8 shows a small amount of employee data. If you assume that there are many additional rows of this data, a printout of later rows would not include the identifying information in rows 1 and 2. You can define rows 1 and 2 as border rows and print all the data by following these steps:

1. Select Print Printer Options Borders Rows.

2. Select A1..A2.

3. Select Quit to exit the Options menu.

4. Select Range then select A3..G100 as the range to print. Note that the border rows are not included in the print range.

5. Select Go Page Align. Figure 4-9 shows the top of two pages of the report assuming a header line was also entered to show the page number. You will learn how to add a header line later in this chapter.

BASIC 1-2-3 OPTIONS

```
A1: {Bold} [W10] 'First                                      READY

        A         B          C          D          E         F          G
   1  First     Last                             Job        Date of
   2  Name      Name       Dept.      Manager    Title      Hire      Salary
   3  Mary      Jones      Design     Green      Clerk      Jun-90    $23,500
   4  Jim       Harris     Production Smith      Engineer   Apr-89    $44,577
   5  Paul      Smith      Testing    Forest     Engineer   Sep-85    $54,288
   6  Harry     Javis      Production Forest     Clerk      May-82    $24,471
   7  Susan     Fordham    Testing    Ilian      Engineer   Jun-76    $43,047
   8  Bob       Kaylor     Design     Green      Clerk      Feb-78    $20,520
   9  John      Studnika   Production White      Accountant Jan-91    $58,688
  10  Jeff      Larson     Design     Steiff     Clerk      Oct-90    $20,159
  11  Liz       Greene     Production White      Accountant Nov-85    $69,581
  12  Linda     Statler    Testing    Ilian      Clerk      Jul-91    $22,416
  13  Cindy     Barton     Production White      Engineer   Apr-87    $64,358
  14  Wendy     Coyne      Testing    Parker     Engineer   Jun-78    $69,508
  15  Tova      Rogers     Design     Steiff     Mechanic   Apr-84    $57,075
  16  Paul      Link       Production Lark       Clerk      Sep-81    $31,930
  17  Steve     Umber      Design     Steiff     Supervisor May-88    $54,049
  18  Keith     Stark      Production Lark       Supervisor Jun-68    $64,454
  19  David     McFaul     Design     Steiff     Engineer   Feb-80    $69,719
  20  Dave      McCartin   Production White      Engineer   Jan-90    $64,409
  14-Mar-91  02:10 PM                                           NUM
```

Figure 4-8: Employee data fits here, however, if there were more than one page of data, subsequent pages of the printout would not include essential identifiers. See Figure 4-9, a printout where borders have been defined to reflect information consistently on the second page.

To eliminate borders you must select Print Printer Clear Borders. There is no way to remove borders from the Options Border menu although you would use this option to change them to other rows or columns without having to delete the existing ones first.

Using Titles to Work with Screen Data

Titles do not affect your printed output. Adding titles allows you to move your cell pointer to any area of the screen and have the titles visible as identifying information.

PUBLISHING 1-2-3

Figure 4-9: Adding borders makes identifying information on subsequent pages easier.

Just as borders prevent a sea of printed numbers, titles insure that your screen does not look like a sea of numbers, too.

You can add title rows at the top of your data or title columns on the side. You can also add titles in both directions at once. "A Closer Look: Adding Titles" summarizes the steps needed to make sure that all of the data that you work with has the titles you need on the screen at all times. When you no longer want these titles to appear you can use Worksheet Global Titles Clear to eliminate all titles.

Once you have selected titles, the cell pointer movement keys will not let you move to these rows or columns. You can make changes to entries in title rows or

BASIC 1-2-3 OPTIONS

columns by pressing F5 (GOTO) to temporarily duplicate these rows and columns. After typing your change, move your cell pointer until the duplicate copies scroll off your screen. The other option is to temporarily clear the titles with Worksheet Global Titles Clear and then define them again.

To create titles for the account categories in column A of the worksheet in Figure 4-10 follow these steps:

1. Press the HOME key to bring column A into view.

2. Press the RIGHT ARROW key to position the cell pointer to column B.

3. Select Worksheet Global Titles Vertical. After the titles are created you can move to the data for later months and still see the titles at the left as shown in Figure 4-11. You will notice in this figure that the titles remain in column A when you look at the data in columns I through M.

Adding a Header

A header is a line that appears at the top of every page of printed output. You can use a header to print the name of your department, the current date, or your name at the top of every page of your report. 1-2-3 allows you to divide a header into a left, center, and right section with the divider bar acting as the separator. You will use the split vertical bar (!) symbol to

A CLOSER LOOK

Adding Titles

1. Position the cell pointer immediately to the right of any columns you want to remain fixed on the screen. Also position the cell pointer below any rows that you want to remain on the screen.

2. Select Worksheet Titles.

3. Select Horizontal, Vertical, or Both.

PUBLISHING 1-2-3

A CLOSER LOOK

Creating a Header

1. Select Print Printer Options Header.

2. Type any entry that you want to place on the left side of the header then type a ¦ if you plan to make additional entries in other locations in the header.

3. Type the entry, if any, that you want to place in the center of the header and type a ¦ if you plan to make an entry on the right side of the header.

4. Type the entry, if any, that you want to place on the right side of the header and press ENTER.

5. Select Quit to return to the main print menu and make any other needed selections such as Range before choosing Go to print your data. Note: If you place a # in the header, 1-2-3 will substitute the page number at that location and if you use a @, 1-2-3 will substitute the current system date.

separate the various parts of the header— if you elect to use them. Header entries are entered after requesting the appropriate menu selections summarized in "A Closer Look: Creating a Header." Header entries support some special symbols. To create a header with your name at the left and your department name at the right you might enter the following as header text: Tim Smith¦¦Department of Accounting. The first split vertical bar ended the first section and the second split vertical bar ends the center section of the header without any text. Two special symbols can also be used in a header. These symbols are # and @. The # is replaced with the current page number when the header prints. The @ symbol is replaced by the current system date. The entry used for the header in Figure 4-9 was Stark Inc.¦Employee List¦Page #. Note that the split vertical bar (¦) is used to separate each section of the header. The pound symbol (#) is replaced with the page number when the header prints at the top of each page.

Adding a Footer

Footers are identical to headers except they appear at the bottom of every page of your output. To define a footer you will use the /Print Printer Options Footer command. You can use any of the special symbols discussed in the previous section on headers.

When the last page of your output finishes printing you will need to select Page to tell 1-2-3 that nothing else will be printed on the page. This allows 1-2-3 to print the footer information on the last page of your output.

BASIC 1-2-3 OPTIONS

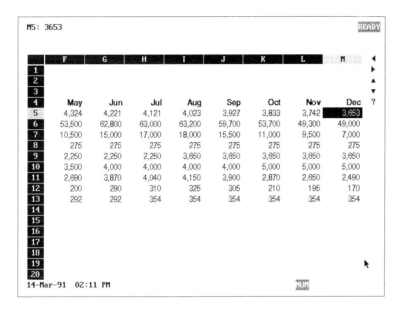

Figure 4-10 (l.) does not show the information in column since Titles were not set. Figure 4-11 (below) includes column A titles.

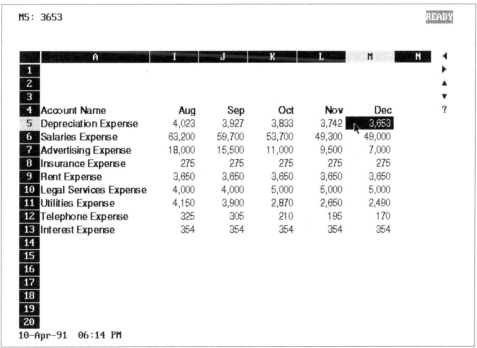

111

PUBLISHING 1-2-3

Separating Data

Separate elements of a worksheet are often easier to identify if you use design elements to separate them. You might set off totals from the detail or isolate assumptions from projections. Three popular ways of achieving this separation are adding lines, boxes, or white space to your data.

Adding Lines

Dividing lines can form a boundary between one section of the worksheet and another. You can create these lines in several different ways. Also you can use standard keyboard characters or special characters found in the Lotus International Character Set (LICS) or the Lotus Multibyte Character Set (LMBCS) character sets. The LICS codes offer 256 codes that will represent characters including characters accessible from the keyboard as well as those that are not. LICS codes are used with Release 2. In effect the LMBCS codes offer several sets of LICS codes but are only available with Release 3. They expand the potential options for entering special characters not accessible from the keyboard.

You can create many of the special characters with a compose key sequence of ALT-F1 (COMPOSE) followed by typing the two keyboard characters from Appendix A or B that create the character available with your release of 1-2-3. Another option is pressing the ALT key while you type the character number from the numeric keypad. The last option and perhaps the easiest is to ask 1-2-3 to produce the character for you with the @CHAR function and the code number of the character that you want. First, you will have a chance to look at the use of some repeated keyboard characters before attempting the complexities of composed characters.

Using the Repeating Label Indicator

The repeating label indicator allows you to create a label that will fill a cell regardless of its width. Unless you are creating a short line to separate a column of numbers from the total they represent, one repeating label entry will not be sufficient.

BASIC 1-2-3 OPTIONS

You can copy the label to other cells to create a much longer dividing line. To create a repeating label in a cell, type a backslash followed by the character or series of characters that you want to repeat. Figure 4-12 contains \- in B5 to create a line that separates the detail entries from the total in B6. A longer dividing line is created in A7..G7 by entering \/\ in A7 then copying this entry to B7..G7 as shown in Figure 4-13.

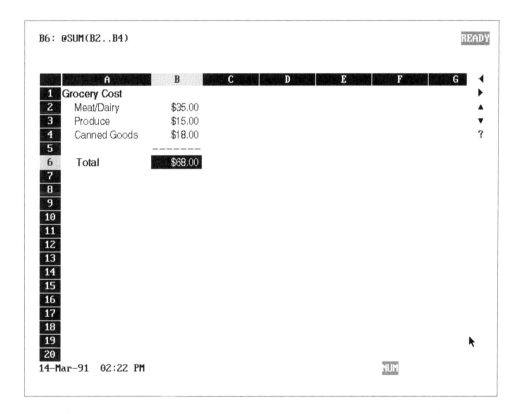

Figure 4-12: Using the Repeating Label Indicator separates out the total in B6.

113

PUBLISHING 1-2-3

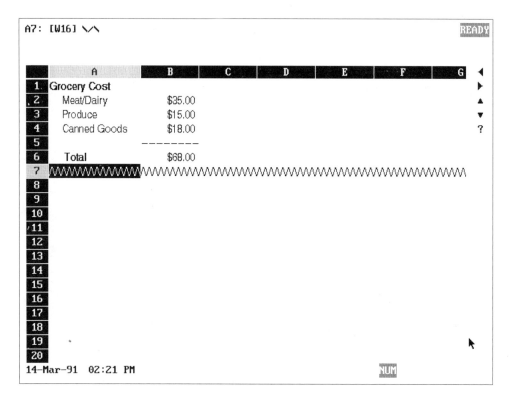

Figure 4-13: A long divider line is created using the Repeating Label Indicator.

Using @REPEAT

@REPEAT is a string function that allows you to repeat a character or series of characters a specific number of times. It has the same effect as using a repeating label but allows you to take advantage of 1-2-3's long label feature which will display a label that does not fit in the current cell placing that information into blank cells to the right. The syntax of the @REPEAT function is:

@REPEAT(string,number of times)

String is a character or series of characters enclosed in quotes. Number of times is the number of times the character string should be repeated.

BASIC 1-2-3 OPTIONS

Figure 4-14 uses @REPEAT("-",92) in both A14 and A16 to create the long lines that separate the total from the detail entries. The label generated with @REPEAT should not exceed the maximum label length in 1-2-3: 256 in Release 2 and 512 in Release 3.

Using a Compose Sequence

You can use the capabilities in Release 2 and higher to compose a character that does not display on your keyboard. This allows you to create a variety of special characters including foreign currency symbols and other specialized symbols.

```
A14: [W20] @REPEAT("-",92)                                              READY


                A           B        C        D        E        F        G
  1                              ABC Company
  2                            1991 Expense Budget
  3
  4  Account Name              Jan      Feb      Mar      Apr      May      Ju
  5  Depreciation Expense     4,762    4,649    4,538    4,430    4,324    4,2:
  6  Salaries Expense        49,500   49,850   49,900   51,100   53,500   62,8(
  7  Advertising Expense      7,000    7,000    7,000    9,500   10,500   15,0(
  8  Insurance Expense          275      275      275      275      275      2:
  9  Rent Expense             2,250    2,250    2,250    2,250    2,250    2,2!
 10  Legal Services Expense   3,500    3,500    3,500    3,500    3,500    4,0(
 11  Utilities Expense        1,090    2,100    2,160    2,320    2,690    3,8:
 12  Telephone Expense          160      175      180      195      200       2!
 13  Interest Expense           292      292      292      292      292       2!
 14  ---------------------------------------------------------------------------
 15  Total                   68,829   70,090   70,095   73,861   77,531   92,9!
 16  ---------------------------------------------------------------------------
 17
 18
 19
 20
10-Apr-91  06:20 PM
```

Figure 4-14 uses @REPEAT to create the long lines that separate the total.

PUBLISHING 1-2-3

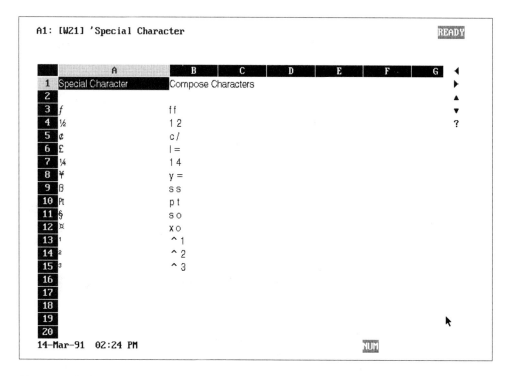

Figure 4-15 shows some of the characters that you can create using a compose sequence. The characters created appear in column A. The compose sequence used is shown in column B.

Different releases of 1-2-3 may support differing compose sequences. This is due to the fact the Release 3 uses LMBCS codes and Release 2 uses LICS codes.

The procedure for creating a composed character is to press ALT-F1 (COMPOSE) then type the two characters from the compose sequence. See the Compose Sequence column in Appendix A or B.

You need to check whether your printer can print the special character from a compose sequence. You can print the range in which you have stored this character to insure that your printer is not leaving the character blank or printing it in an unexpected fashion.

BASIC 1-2-3 OPTIONS

Using @CHAR

The @CHAR function is a string function that allows you to specify a character number in the LICS or LMBCS set. You can use this function as an argument for the @REPEAT function and draw a line consisting of special characters.

As mentioned earlier, the release of 1-2-3 that you are using will control which code set is in use and the number of options available to you.

In Figure 4-16, code numbers were entered in B3..B11. Since this example was created with Release 2.3, the LICS codes from Appendix A were used. A3 contains @CHAR(B3) to generate the special character. C3 contains @REPEAT(A3,60) to repeat this special character. The same result could have been achieved without the use of column A and B with the entry @REPEAT(@CHAR(170),60). The extra columns were used to clarify the process.

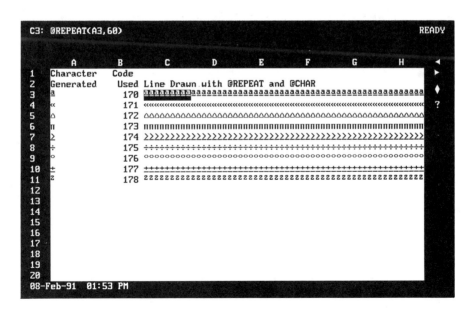

Figure 4-16: LICS codes were added to draw lines of special characters.

PUBLISHING 1-2-3

Adding Boxes

You can create boxes with a line at the top and bottom of your entries in a blank row using @REPEAT or the repeating label indicator (\). To create the side of the box you will need to use the same symbol as a left-aligned label for the left edge of the cell. Since a right-aligned label stops one character from the right edge of the cell you will only be able to use this approach if the line at the top and bottom of the box stop one character from the right edge of the cell.

The @REPEAT function in A1 of Figure 4-17 draws a line that extends one character into column H making it easy to complete the right edge of the box with an entry of '* in H2..H7. The same entry was used in A2..A7 for the left edge of the box. A1 was copied to H8 to complete the bottom edge of the box.

In situations where the box extends into middle of a cell on the right side, you will need to complete the right edge entries by preceding them with spaces.

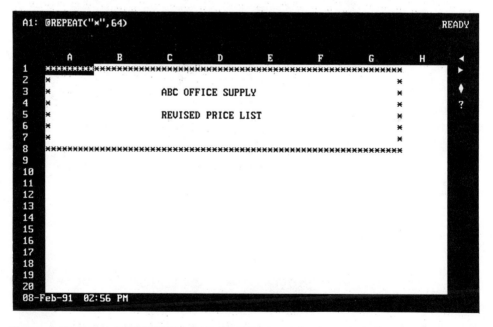

Figure 4-17: Using @REPEAT to draw boxes.

118

Using White Space

White space around your information can make it more attractive and easier to understand. 1-2-3 allows you to add white space to your printouts as well as to screen data. Usually, white space is evenly distributed on a page rather than concentrated at the right side and bottom of the page. Figure 4-18 shows the visual impression created by printing a tabular arrangement of 1-2-3 data using the default top and left margin setting. Figure 4-19 shows the improved appearance as the table of data is better distributed. This change was made by increasing the top and left margin.

Sometimes you have multiple ranges of 1-2-3 data that you want to print. If you print one range immediately followed by the second range, it will be hard to tell where one group of information stops and the second starts. Adding a few lines of white space or beginning the second range at the top of a new page can help prevent this problem.

Changing the Margins

You can use the Print Printer Options Margins command to change one of the margins. Your options after making this selection are Left, Right, Top, and Bottom. The default setting for the left is 4 and the right is 76. Both top and bottom margins are 2 lines. Sending setup strings to your printer that invoke compressed print or enlarged print can change the effect of margin settings since they are based on six lines of print to the inch.

Advancing to a New Page with Print Printer Page

If you wait until it is time to print and decide you want to separate two ranges by a few lines yet include them on the same page you can use the Print Printer Line command. Each time you invoke the command, 1-2-3 instructs your printer to generate a line feed. This means that you will need to invoke the command three times to add three blank lines to your document.

Adding a Page Break to the Worksheet

When you use the Print menu to add a page break between two ranges of data that you want to print, you will need to issue the Print Printer Page command every time

PUBLISHING 1-2-3

A CLOSER LOOK

Inserting Rows and Columns

1. Position the cell pointer beneath the row where you want to insert new rows or to the right of the column where you want to insert new columns. This step is essential since the inserted rows and columns are always positioned above or to the left of the cell pointer.

2. Select Worksheet Insert.

3. Select Row or Column.

4. Expand the range if you want to insert multiple rows or columns. Then press ENTER.

---

you finish printing the first range. If you forget to execute the Page request, the two ranges will print with no separation between them. Although, by using a macro, you could place the burden of remembering to execute the page request on 1-2-3, you may just want to include the page request within the worksheet. Every release of 1-2-3 as far back as 2.0 supports Worksheet Page.

Notice this request is not made from the print menu but from the Worksheet menu. 1-2-3 inserts a blank line at the location of the cell pointer when you request Worksheet Page and places !:: in the cell at the far left edge of the screen. As long as this cell is within the print range selected, a page break will always be generated at that location. Remember you may want to change the top and right margins to place the data from both ranges more in the center of the page.

Inserting Rows and Columns

If you want to separate different ranges of entries on the worksheet as well as printouts, the Worksheet Insert Row command will insert blank rows above the current location of the cell pointer. To add multiple rows you need to specify a range for those you wish to add. Worksheet Insert Column adds columns to the left of the cell pointer. If you accidentally add too many rows or columns, you can remove them with Worksheet Delete Row/Column. "A Closer Look: Inserting Rows and Columns" summarizes the steps you must follow to ensure the proper placement of blank rows and columns. With Release 3 you can even insert sheets with the same general procedure.

BASIC 1-2-3 OPTIONS

```
          Hillside Office Supply
            Quantity Discounts

                    1       10     100
Felt-tip pens     0.79    0.67    0.53
Erasers           0.59    0.53    0.29
Metal rulers      9.95    8.29    6.50
500 sheet bond    4.50    3.75    2.00
3-ring binders    5.50    4.20    3.59
Folders           0.79    0.59    0.35
Mailers 4"x6"     1.10    0.59    0.30
Mailers 8"x10"    1.29    0.75    0.45
```

Figure 4-18: Output created using the default margin settings.

Figure 4-19: Planning for a little more white space can make a difference.

```
              Hillside Office Supply
                Quantity Discounts

                        1       10     100
    Felt-tip pens     0.79    0.67    0.53
    Erasers           0.59    0.53    0.29
    Metal rulers      9.95    8.29    6.50
    500 sheet bond    4.50    3.75    2.00
    3-ring binders    5.50    4.20    3.59
    Folders           0.79    0.59    0.35
    Mailers 4"x6"     1.10    0.59    0.30
    Mailers 8"x10"    1.29    0.75    0.45
```

PUBLISHING 1-2-3

Labeling Data

Labels entered on the worksheet help make clear what the entries in the rows and columns of the worksheet represent. You can also add longer label entries to a worksheet. Rather than describing the contents of a row or column, these entries provide more lengthy descriptive information. Since the labels you type do not display on the worksheet until they are finalized, it can be difficult to decide on the correct length for achieving the most pleasing appearance on the page. 1-2-3 provides a command that allows you to enter the labels without regard to their length as long as they do not exceed maximum label length restrictions (256 characters, except for Release 3, which accepts 512 characters). Once the labels are entered you can have 1-2-3 rearrange them on the worksheet to achieve a desirable placement.

Labels can also be used to name ranges of data. Named ranges display the name of the range in any formula that references the range. This makes your formulas easier to understand. Since a range can be as small as one cell you can use this feature to name frequently used data. The labels that you use to name ranges can be stored in worksheet cells or entered when you apply the name.

Using Range Justify

The entries in rows and columns normally comprise most of the data printed from a worksheet. Figure 4-20 presents an example of typical worksheet entries. These entries show how unit prices are lowered when office supply items are purchased in quantity.

Adding descriptive text can strengthen the message that this data conveys. Unless you want to carefully count the number of letters that you enter in each row, it is easy to enter more text than can be displayed on the screen. Figure 4-21 provides an example of this situation. Although descriptive text was added to the right of the data, the length of the entries was not carefully monitored. The user would need to move the cell pointer to the right to continue reading the text. Also if the data on the worksheet was printed, the width of the page might not be sufficient to contain the recorded text.

BASIC 1-2-3 OPTIONS

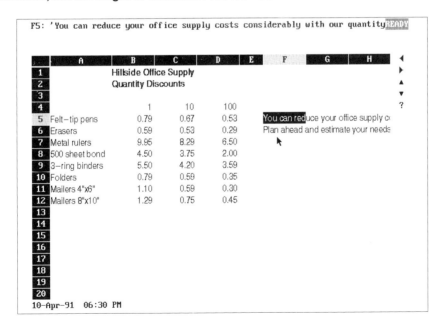

Figure 4-20 (above) shows typical worksheet entries. Figure 4-21: Descriptive text was added, but the length of worksheet entries was not monitored.

PUBLISHING 1-2-3

The Range Justify command offers a solution since it allows you to reformat long label entries and restrict them to any group of cells on the worksheet. Although more rows will be required to display the data it can be restricted to any columns that you want. The required steps for using this command are summarized in "A Closer Look: Steps for Using Range Justify."

To justify the text presented in Figure 4-21, you can use the Range Justify command. You will not need to be concerned with the depth of the range that you specify since the worksheet does not contain data beneath the labels that will be justified. Follow these steps:

1. Select Range Justify.

2. Select F5..H5.

3. Press ENTER to finalize the range selection.

The results are shown in Figure 4-22. The long labels are reformatted and display in F5..H11 although all the entries are actually long labels in column F.

Using Worksheet Entries to Name Cells

If you have labels entries on the worksheet that can be used as names for adjacent cells you can have 1-2-3 apply these names to their adjacent cell for you as described in "A Closer Look: Using Labels to Name Cells." If the labels exceed 1-2-3's maximum length of 15 characters for range names, they will be truncated. You can apply label entries to adjacent cells in any direction by choosing Right, Left, Above or Below after selecting Range Name Label. You can apply an entire row or column of label entries to cells with one execution of this command. Figure 4-24 shows a range of labels entries in A3..A10 that have been applied to the cells in column B. If you look at the control panel in the figure you can see that the formula that references some of these cells will display the range names rather than the cell addresses.

BASIC 1-2-3 OPTIONS

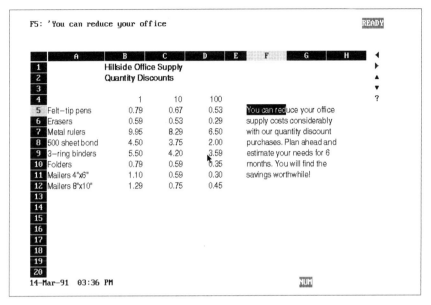

Figure 4-22: Using the Range Justify command to justify text.

A CLOSER LOOK

Steps for Using Range Justify

1. Enter the descriptive text in a column of worksheet cells. You can use long label entries that do not fit in the width of the cell. However, each cell cannot exceed the limit for a label entry. This limit is 256 characters for 1-2-3 releases through 2.3 and 512 characters for Releases 3 and 3.1.

2. Select Range Justify.

3. Specify the range for 1-2-3's use in reformatting your long label entries. The width should indicate the range of columns that can be used for the labels. If you only specify the top row in the range, 1-2-3 will overwrite data that follows the long labels if it needs the space. If you want to avoid this overwriting of data, you can specify a range that indicates the first and last row that can be used in this reformatting. But you must remember to select a range that has a sufficient number of rows to display the entries once the reformatting has been completed.

A CLOSER LOOK

Using Label to Name Cells

1. Select Range Name Label.

2. Select Right, Left, Above, or Below depending on the location of the data in relation to the labels.

3. Select the range of labels and press ENTER.

Creating a Table of Range Names

1. Select Range Name Table.

2. Specify the top leftmost cell in the table or a complete range where you want the table stored and press ENTER.

Entering Names from the Keyboard

You can use any label as a range name. To create a range name for a cell or range, select Range Name Create, type the name and press ENTER, then specify the range to apply the name to. If you are using Release 2.3 or Release 3, you can select the range before invoking the command if you prefer.

Keeping Track of the Names You Use

Just as the labels you use for rows and columns must be descriptive, your range names should be clear. Avoid cryptic range names (ZZZZ, FIDO), ones that look like cell addresses (A1, B3), and ones that use symbols representing arithmetic operations (Unit*Price).

You can create a list of the names that you have already used with the Range Name Table command available in Release 2 and above with the instructions in "A Closer Look: Creating a Table of Range Names." You will need an empty area of your spreadsheet that is two columns wide with as many rows as you have range names. Enter Range Name Table and provide either a range or the upper left cell in the area you want 1-2-3 to use. If you specify a range name, 1-2-3 will confine its list to the area you provide and stop listing range names when this area is full. When you provide the upper left cell, 1-2-3 uses as much space as it needs and so will overwrite entries in cells as necessary.

BASIC 1-2-3 OPTIONS

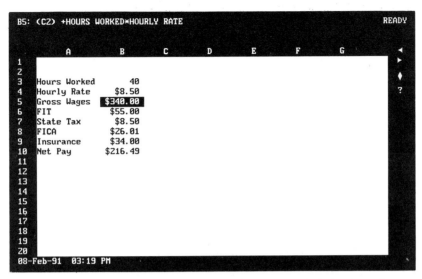

Figure 4-23 (above) shows a range of labels entries in A3..A10 that have been applied to the cells in column B. If you look at the control panel in the figure you can see that the formula that references some of these cells will display the range names rather than the cell addresses. In Figure 4-24 the table was placed in A12. All of the range names are listed in column A and the cells or ranges they are applied to are in column B.

127

Altering the Amount of Data Presented

There are many times when the data in your worksheet provides too much detail to convey a quick message. 1-2-3 provides numerous solutions to help you condense the detail in a form that is quicker to understand. You can use the Data Query command to locate a subset of records and even copy them to a separate area of your worksheet. You can print this range to create a quick exception report. You can use the database statistical functions to perform a computation on a selected group of records. To use either of these commands your data must be arranged with each field of information in its own column and each record of information in a different row in your spreadsheet. Later in the chapter you will learn how to represent data graphically in either a row or column format.

Extracting A Subset of Records

Although extracting records requires numerous steps, it provides a powerful capability to create any type of exception report that you want. You can look at a purchase database and select only records for purchases in December or only purchases for office supplies. You can choose to include all the fields in your original database or a subset of fields. The procedure is summarized in "A Closer Look: Extracting a Subset of Records."

Recording Criteria

You must place criteria for the records you wish to use on the worksheet before attempting an extract operation. The first step is the same for all types of criteria: You must always enter the field name in a cell. The field name is the label in the cell immediately above the data. It must be unique. If you look back at the data in Figure 4-8, you will find that you can use the field name in a database-like structure, but would need to change the entries in A1..B2. If left unchanged, both the first and last name fields would have a field name of Name because 1-2-3 only looks at the contents of row 2.

Options for recording criteria selections depend on whether you are using a field containing label or value entries. With label fields you can use exact match entries for

BASIC 1-2-3 OPTIONS

A CLOSER LOOK

Extracting a Subset of Records

1. Create criteria on the worksheet by entering a field name. Beneath it place the criteria for the desired field values.

2. Create an output area for the extracted records by placing the field names that you want to extract across a row of the sheet.

3. Select Data Query.

4. Select Input and specify the rows and columns containing the database. Be certain to include the field names in this range.

5. Select Criteria and specify the range containing your criteria specifications. This selection is Criterion in Release 2.01.

6. Select Output and specify the row containing the field names in the output area if there is no additional data under these names. If there is additional data specify the names and as many rows beneath them that you want to use for extracted records.

7. Select Quit to exit the Data Query menu.

a selection such as 'Jones'. You can also use wildcard entries such as J* to search for all entries that begin with J. And you can use logical string formulas. A logical string formula searches for all entries in the field that start with a letter greater than M might be +B3>"M" where B3 is the first data value in the field. Value fields support exact match entries and logical formulas such as +G3>25000, but they do not support the use of wildcards. You can check multiple fields at once using adjacent criteria areas. You can perform other Boolean logic operations, however such operations are more appropriately discussed in advanced 1-2-3 books.

Figure 4-25 uses the data in Figure 4-8 except the first two field names are changed to First Name and Last Name by erasing the entries in A1 and B1 and expanding the names in A2 and B2. The data in Figure 4-25 shows criteria entries in A37..B38. This set of criteria will only match with records where the Salary is greater than $50,000 and the Title is Engineer. The Output area was established in B41..E41 before invoking the command. After the extract was completed, a title was entered in row 40 which would allow the range from B40..E45 to be printed as a report.

Database Statistical Functions

Beginning with Release 2, all releases of 1-2-3 support the use of database statistical functions that can selectively compute basic statistics as described in Table 4-2. The basic difference between these functions and the statistical functions is that

```
A36: [W10]                                                              READY

            A           B          C          D          E         F         G
    26  Sam         Gilmore    Production Waters     Planner    Nov-85    $41,040
    27  Ruth        Johnson    Testing    Parker     Supervosor Jul-91    $50,735
    28  Neil        Young      Production Waters     Mechanic   Apr-87    $54,900
    29  Ray         York       Testing    Parker     Mechanic   May-77    $35,431
    30  Catherine   Walters    Design     Twiliger   Supervisor Sep-81    $66,990
    31  Tom         Peters     Production Waters     Supervisor May-88    $59,930
    32  Tim         Gregg      Design     Twiliger   Engineer   Jun-68    $24,433
    33  Tavis       Nance      Production Waters     Accountant Feb-80    $47,303
    34  Kim         Maurnee    Design     Twiliger   Engineer   Jan-90    $68,968
    35
    36
    37  Salary      Title
    38  +G3<50000   Engineer
    39
    40              Engineers Earing Less Than $30,000
    41              Last Name  First Name Dept.              Salary
    42              Harris     Jim        Production         $44,577
    43              Fordham    Susan      Testing            $43,047
    44              Boyd       Dorothy    Design             $40,597
    45              Gregg      Tim        Design             $24,433
    10-Apr-91   10:44 PM
```

Figure 4-25: Criteria entries in A7..B38.

you can selectively include data in the computations that they perform for you. Like the statistical functions, the database statistical functions can be used in place of arithmetic formulas in 1-2-3 cells. The database statistical functions perform comparable calculations to the statistical functions that operate on every value in a range such as @SUM, @AVG, and @MIN. The database statistical functions use similar keywords to the statistical functions except a D immediately follows the @ symbol and precedes the existing keywords. The resulting functions are: @DSUM, @DAVG, @DTOTAL, @DMIN, @DMAX, @DCOUNT, @DSTD, and @DVAR. Releases 3 and 3.1 support two additional functions @DSTDS and @DVARS which work with a population sample rather than the entire population like @DVAR and @DSTD. The procedure for using database statistical functions in your computations is described in "A Closer Look: Selectively Computing Statistics."

The database statistical functions each require three arguments rather than the single range specification required by the statistical functions. Each of the database statistical function follows this pattern:

@FUNCTION(database,column,criteria)

Database is the location of the 1-2-3 database of records. As you would expect, these records each require a single row of the database. Field names in the row preceding the first record are included in the range. *Column* is the column in the database that you want to

A CLOSER LOOK

Selectively Computing Statistics

1. Enter criteria for selecting the records you want to use in the computation.

2. Enter the keyword for the database statistical function you want to use in the cell where you will perform the computation.

3. Follow the keyword with an open parenthesis.

4. Enter the range containing the database and field names, and a comma.

5. Enter the column number on which you will perform the computation. 1-2-3 begins counting columns with the number zero and you will need to do the same for this computation.

6. Enter another comma as a separator and the range containing the criteria.

7. Close the parentheses and press ENTER.

PUBLISHING 1-2-3

use in your calculations. The first column in the database range is column 0, the second 1, and each subsequent column is numbered one higher than the last column. 1-2-3 expects this column to contain value entries for all database statistical functions except @DCOUNT which allows you to count the number of non-blank entries in any column. *Criteria* are worksheet entries that describe the records that should be included in the calculations. Criteria are created in the same fashion as criteria for use with the Data Query command described earlier.

You can select records for inclusion in the computation using any field in the record—not just the field used in the computation. A criteria entry consists of the name of the field from the database that will be used for selecting records with the matching entry which, in turn, will be used to select records.

Table 4-2
Database Statistical Functions

Function	Description
@DAVG	Computes an average selectively.
@DCOUNT	Computes a selective count.
@DMAX	Selectively looks for the maximum value.
@DMIN	Selectively looks for the minimum value.
@DSUM	Computes a total of the selected records for the a specified field.
@DSTD	Selectively computes the standard deviation when you have all the values in a population.
@DSTDS	Selectively computes the variance when you are working with a population sample. (Release 3 only.)
@DVAR	Selectively computes the variance when you have all the values in a population.
@DVARS	Selectively computes the variance when you are working with a population sample. (Release 3 only.)

BASIC 1-2-3 OPTIONS

Changing The Way Data Is Presented

You can change the way that your data is displayed on the worksheet by copying or moving the data to other locations. You can also use some commands that are not as commonly used to provide other options for displaying your data.

Using Copy and Move

Once you place data in a particular location you should not regard it as fixed. 1-2-3 offers flexibility in allowing you to copy or move data to any new location. Since it automatically adjusts formulas based on the new location, you do not need to worry about jeopardizing the validity of your model.

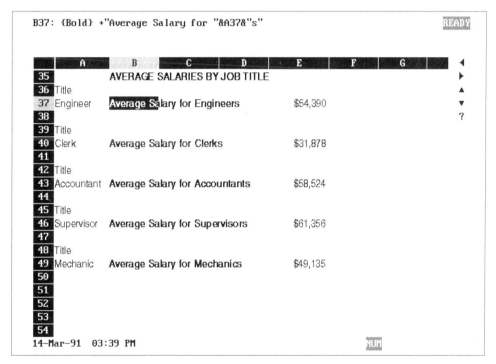

Figure 4-26 shows criteria in A36..A37, A39..A40, A42..A43, A45..A46, and A48..A49 to select records from the database in Figure 4-8 for each title. The criteria entries are also used to create the labels for each computation with string formulas such as +"Average Salary for "&A37&"s". The computation in E37 was created with @DAVG(A2..G34,6,A36..A37).

133

PUBLISHING 1-2-3

Data Tables

Once you create a model you can evaluate many different values for the variable used in the model by typing a new number for the variable and observing the effect. Although this approach allows you to reuse a model for many applications, it is not a good approach for exploring a wide variety of options since you will have forgotten the result from your first substitution by the time you complete your fifth substitution. Although you can print each iteration, often you will not take the time to do so. The Data Table command allows you to evaluate many values and display the result from substituting each of them in a model. You have a choice between changing one or two variables with releases of 1-2-3 through 2.3. If you vary one, you can look at the effect of change on many formulas, but if you change two variables you will have to restrict your observation of change to one formula. With Releases 3 and 3.1 you can create two additional types of tables. You can create a 3-way table that utilizes the multiple sheet options in these releases and allows a third variable to change. You can also create a Labeled table which eliminates the need for much of the table structure inherent in the other table options and allows you to change the values of more than three variables at one time. Labeled tables are more complex than the other types of tables and are beyond the scope of this book.

No matter what type of Data Table you create, you will need to complete some preliminary work before invoking the command. Each of the Data Table com-

A CLOSER LOOK

Creating a 1-Way Data Table

1. Place the values for the variable you want to alter down a column.

2. Move the cell pointer one cell above the top entry in this column and one cell to the right.

3. Enter the formulas you want to evaluate one per cell across the row. If the formulas are already on the worksheet, enter references to the cell that contains them.

4. Select Data Table 1-Way.

5. Specify a rectangular range for the table that includes all the values and all the formulas across the top row of the table.

6. Indicate the cell in the model that represents the variable values in the first column of the table and press ENTER.

BASIC 1-2-3 OPTIONS

mands can create a concise table of results that makes it easy to reference the effect of changing variable values.

Creating a 1-Way Command

A 1-Way table allows you to alter the value assigned to one variable in the spreadsheet. This variable can be referenced in one or more formulas and can have a direct or indirect effect on the results that you are observing. You can look at the effect on as many of the formulas as you wish. "A Closer Look: Creating a 1-Way Table" provides the exact steps needed to create one of these tables.

A 1-Way table was created in Figure 4-27. Criteria selection entries were entered as variable 1 in A41..A46. 1-2-3 will systematically insert these in A37 if you later specify that cell as variable 1. The formula results you want to examine are written in B40..D40 although they are formatted as hidden. The actual formulas entered are:

@DSUM(A2..G34,6,A36..A37)
@DAVG(A2..G34,6,A36..A37)
@DCOUNT(A2..G34,6,A36..A37)

With all the preliminary work finished you can use Data Table 1-Way to quickly compute a variety of summary statistics so that your readers may gain more information from than the detailed records presented earlier.

Creating a 2-Way Table

A 2-way table allows you to vary the value of two variables in a model. Since variable values are placed along both the left side and top of the table, only one formula can be evaluated. A reference to this formula is placed at the intersection of the row and column of variable values. You can follow the steps in "A Closer Look: Creating a 2-Way Table" to create your own 2-Way table to evaluate many variable values quickly.

PUBLISHING 1-2-3

```
B40: (H) @DSUM($A$2..$G$34,6,$A$36..$A$37)                          READY

        A         B          C          D       E       F       G
36  Title
37
38            Total      Average    # Emp
39            Salaries   Salary     in Title
40
41  Accountant  $175,572   $58,524     3
42  Clerk       $286,900   $31,878     9
43  Engineer    $543,904   $54,390    10
44  Mechanic    $147,406   $49,135     3
45  Planner      $74,359   $37,180     2
46  Supervisor  $245,423   $61,356     4
47
...
55
14-Mar-91  03:40 PM                                          NUM
```

Figure 4-27: A 1-way data table.

Figure 4-28 shows a 2-way table in B15..G20. This table shows projected profits in 1995 based on a variety of growth or decline assumptions about the sales of products 1 and 2.

Creating a 3-Way Table

Since Release 3 supports up to 256 sheets in one worksheet file, you can create 3-way tables with this release. This allows you to review the result of a formula as three different variables are systematically altered. "A Closer Look: Creating a 3-Way Table" provides the steps you will need to create a 3-way table on your own worksheets.

BASIC 1-2-3 OPTIONS

```
E19: (C0) 214231.1875                                              READY

        A        B         C         D         E         F      G    H
 1  Sales        1991      1992      1993      1994      1995
 2    Product 1  100,000   110,000   121,000   133,100   146,410
 3    Product 2  200,000   210,000   220,500   231,525   243,101
 4
 5  COGS        135,000   144,000   153,675   164,081   175,280
 6
 7  Profit      165,000   176,000   187,825   200,544   214,231
 8
 9  Growth Rate
10    Product 1  10%
11    Product 2  5%
12
13                              1995 Profit Projections
14                       Product 2 Growth
15              +F7      -5%       -2%       5%        10%       15%
16  Product 1   -5%      $134,394  $146,258  $178,504  $205,849  $237,189
17    Growth    -2%      $140,326  $152,191  $184,436  $211,781  $243,121
18              5%       $156,449  $168,313  $200,559  $227,904  $259,244
19              10%      $170,121  $181,986  $214,231  $241,577  $272,916
20              15%      $185,791  $197,656  $229,901  $257,246  $288,586
14-Mar-91  03:41 PM                                                NUM
```

Figure 4-28: A 2-way data table.

A CLOSER LOOK

Creating a 2-Way Data Table

1. Place the values for the variable you want to alter down a column.

2. Move the cell pointer one cell above the top entry in this column and one cell to the right.

3. Enter variable values for the second variable across this row.

4. Place the formula you want to evaluate or a reference to it at the intersection of the row and column of values.

5. Select Data Table 2-Way.

6. Specify a rectangular range for the table that includes all the values and all the formulas across the top row of the table.

7. Indicate the cell in the model that represents the variable values in the first column of the table and press ENTER.

8. Indicate the cell in the model that represents the variable values in the top row of the table.

A CLOSER LOOK

Creating a 3-Way Data Table

1. Place the variable values for variable one down a column of the table a sheet.

2. Place the variable values for the second variable one row above the top entry for variable 1 and beginning one column to the right.

3. Copy these entries to other sheets. You can insert new sheets with Worksheet Insert Sheet.

4. Select /Data Table 3-Way and define the variables. Note that the values for the third variable are the one that span sheets.

Figure 4-29 shows a 3-Way table created with Release 3. This table is used to look at loan payment amounts with different interest rates (variable 1), different loan amounts (variable 2), and different terms (variable 3). The concise data representation on the three sheets lets a reader quickly see the range of payments under different conditions.

Worksheet Column Hide

Although you can delete data that you no longer need, sometimes you do not want to eliminate it on a permanent basis. The Worksheet Column Hide command allows you to temporarily remove one or more columns from view. If you print the range that includes the hidden columns, the columns that are hidden will not print. This allows you to create an instant report that only presents the data that you need. You can create a report that removes confidential information or that highlights only the most important elements of data. This command is only available in Release 2.2 and above.

Changing the Column Width

Altering the width of columns can improve the appearance and readability of the data on your worksheet. Columns that are too wide limit the amount of data that can fit on the screen or on a page of a report. On the other hand, columns that are too narrow either cause 1-2-3 to truncate long label entries or make the information difficult to read. Figure 4-30 shows a worksheet containing journal entries with the columns at their default width of 9. The asterisks in D3 and E4

BASIC 1-2-3 OPTIONS

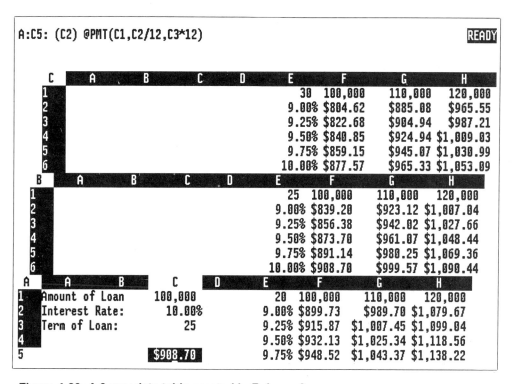

Figure 4-29: A 3-way data table created in Release 3.

indicate the column width is not wide enough to display the values entered. Numerous label entries are truncated since the cells to their right contain entries. Figure 4-31 shows the same data after the columns were widened. If you want other users to get the most from your spreadsheet you will need to check carefully to insure that each column is wide enough.

To widen all the columns on the worksheet with a single command, use Worksheet Global Column-Width. To widen a single column, use Worksheet Column Set-Width. With Release 2.3 and 3, you have an option that allows you to change the width of a range of columns with a single command. Using the Worksheet Column Col-Range command eliminates the need for individually changing the width of each column in the range.

PUBLISHING 1-2-3

```
B5: 'Owner made original investment of                              READY

         A         B         C        D         E       F    G    H
   1  1991                       Journal
   2  Date      Acct & ExLP      Debit    Credit
   3  Jan 1     Cash        101  *********
   4            Bob         401            *********
   5            Owner made original investment of
   6            $15,000 in business
   7
   8       1 Prepaid R   125  1,500.00
   9          Cash       101            1,500.00
  10       Paid rent for Jan-91
  11
  12       2 Supplies    121    500.00
  13          Cash       101             500.00
  14       Bought supplies for production of
  15       gidgets
  16
  17      15 Salaries    425  6,050.00
  18          Cash       101            4,000.00
  19          Sala       210            2,050.00
  20       Paid mid-month salaries
  09-Feb-91  03:30 PM                                      NUM
```

Figure 4-30 (above) shows a worksheet using the default column width. Figure 4-31 shows the same worksheet after the columns were widened.

```
D5: [W12]                                                          READY

         A              B                   C       D          E
   1  1991                                Journal
   2  Date     Acct & Explanation         LP   Debit      Credit
   3  Jan 1    Cash                       101  15,000.00
   4           Bob Babick, Capital        401              15,000.00
   5           Owner made original investment of
   6           $15,000 in business
   7
   8       1 Prepaid Rent                 125   1,500.00
   9          Cash                        101               1,500.00
  10       Paid rent for Jan-91
  11
  12       2 Supplies                     121     500.00
  13          Cash                        101                 500.00
  14       Bought supplies for production of
  15       gidgets
  16
  17      15 Salaries Expense             425   6,050.00
  18          Cash                        101               4,000.00
  19          Salaries Payable            210               2,050.00
  20       Paid mid-month salaries
  09-Feb-91  03:31 PM                                      NUM
```

BASIC 1-2-3 OPTIONS

Using Range Trans

The Range Trans command (Range Transpose in releases prior to 2.2) allows you to change the orientation of existing entries from rows to columns or vice versa. This allows you to transform a worksheet created for another application to one that suits your current needs or to adapt your existing entries in a new worksheet to a more attractive format.

Figure 4-32 contains data in B1..M1 representing the months of the year. You might decide after completing these entries that you want to run the month names down a column. This would eliminate the need for widening columns to achieve an appealing display. You can change the orientation of these entries without retyping them. To change the orientation of these entries Range Trans is selected and the range B1..M1 is selected. A2 is provided as the new location creating the display shown in Figure 4-33.

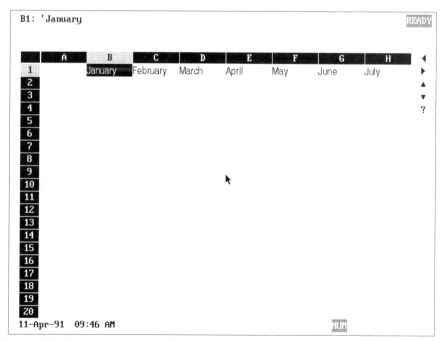

Figure 4-32: Data that you may decide to adapt to appear as in Figure 4-33.

PUBLISHING 1-2-3

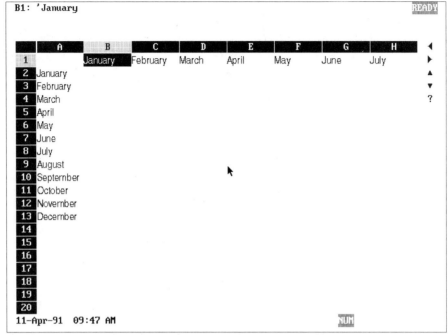

Figure 4-33: Range Trans allows you to re-orient data. Compare with Figure 4-32.

Data Sort

The Data Sort command allows you to alter the sequence in which records are displayed on your screen and printed. Data Sort physically rearranges the records in your 1-2-3 database according to the values in one or more columns. Release 2.0 through 2.3 let you select a primary or main sort key to control selection. Release 3.0 and 3.1 allow you to choose as many as 255 sort keys. The first or primary sort key controls the order of the records completely unless you select other sort keys. Even if selected, these other sort keys are only used as a tie breaker when higher level sort keys have duplicate entries. For example, you might sort a customer file by City only to learn that there are multiple City records that are identical. Specifying a secondary sort key of zip code would cause 1-2-3 to sequence records with the same entry in their city field by the zip code. "A Closer Look: Sorting Data" summarizes the steps that you will use to sort your records.

142

The data in the employee database originally shown in Figure 4-8 is sorted with Last Name as the primary key and First Name as the secondary key. A secondary key is selected in the event that there are duplicate entries in the Last Name field. As shown in Figure 4-34, the sorted results are much easier for readers who want to locate a specific employee's record.

Changing the Page Orientation

With the new laser printers, sideways output, known as landscape mode printing, is available. If you are using an early release of 1-2-3 you must request landscape printing with a setup string assuming your printer supports this option. Releases 2.2 through 3.1 support landscape printing with either Allways, Wysiwyg, or direct menu options. You will learn how to make the Allways and Wysiwyg selections in later chapters. In Release 3.1 you can print from 1-2-3 itself using landscape with the menu option Print Printer Options Advanced Layout Orientation Landscape. With releases where a setup string is required, your entry would be Print Printer Options Setup followed by the appropriate setup string obtained from your printer manual. The Hewlett-Packard LaserJet III would print in landscape mode if you entered \027&l1O as the setup string. Landscape mode would remain in effect until you sent the setup string for Portrait mode which is \027&l0O on the LaserJet III.

A CLOSER LOOK

Sorting Data

1. Select Data Sort.

2. Select Data-Range and specify the range containing all data records and fields but none of the field names across the top.

3. Select Primary-Key and choose any value in the column that you specified.

4. Enter A or D for ascending or descending sequence.

5. Specify a secondary key.

6. Select Go.

PUBLISHING 1-2-3

```
A1: {Bold} [W10]                                                    READY

        A          B         C         D         E         F         G
  1                                                    Job      Date of
  2  First Name  Last Name  Dept.     Manager   Title    Hire    Salary
  3  Cindy      Barton    Production  White    Engineer  Apr-87  $64,358
  4  Dorothy    Boyd      Design      Snow     Engineer  Feb-84  $40,597
  5  Wendy      Coyne     Testing     Parker   Engineer  Jun-78  $69,508
  6  Kenna      Donald    Production  Waters   Clerk     Jan-91  $34,316
  7  Susan      Fordham   Testing     Ilian    Engineer  Jun-76  $43,047
  8  Sam        Gilmore   Production  Waters   Planner   Nov-85  $41,040
  9  Liz        Greene    Production  White    Accountant Nov-85 $69,581
 10  Tim        Greene    Design      Twiliger Engineer  Jun-68  $24,433
 11  Jim        Harris    Production  Smith    Engineer  Apr-89  $44,577
 12  Harry      Javis     Production  Forest   Clerk     May-82  $24,471
 13  Ruth       Johnson   Testing     Parker   Supervosor Jul-91 $50,735
 14  Mary       Jones     Design      Green    Clerk     Jun-90  $23,500
 15  Bob        Kaylor    Design      Green    Clerk     Feb-78  $20,520
 16  Jeff       Larson    Design      Steiff   Clerk     Oct-90  $20,159
 17  Ilene      Link      Design      Snow     Clerk     Oct-90  $69,600
 18  Paul       Link      Production  Lark     Clerk     Sep-81  $31,930
 19  Eileen     Mathers   Production  Waters   Planner   Jun-76  $33,319
 20  Larry      Matthews  Design      Snow     Clerk     Feb-78  $39,988
 14-Mar-91   03:45 PM                                              NUM
```

Figure 4-34: Sorted records make it much easier to locate information.

Using Graphs to Convey Your Message

Graphs can convey a large quantity of information quickly. They are especially useful when you want to convey trends or comparisons between several sets of data. 1-2-3 offers a variety of graph types that allow you to tailor each graph to the data being displayed. The variety of options helps you maintain the audience's interest.

Options within the graph menu help you to increase the information presented with the graph by adding legends and titles or changing the scaling of the graph.

Choosing a Type

All releases of 1-2-3 support the five basic graph types of bar, stacked bar, line, pie, and XY. Release 2.3 adds HLCO, or high-low-close open, graphs and mixed graphs combining both lines and bars in one graph. In addition, a Features option in

BASIC 1-2-3 OPTIONS

the Release 2.3 Graph Type menu allows you to create either horizontal or vertical graphs and to add three dimensionality to a graph. Release 3 supports graphs with two Y axes and allows you to print graphs directly from the Print menu.

Figure 4-35 provides a look at a stacked bar graph that you can create from all versions of 1-2-3. You can show data for as many as six ranges on one graph. This type of graph provides a good way to look at the whole as well as the components although it is not very useful for comparing variables from the various ranges. Figure 4-36 shows an XY graph that is also available in early 1-2-3 releases. It can be a good way to show market or survey data since points are plotted using both axes then joined with a line. The line graph in Figure 4-37 can also be created with all releases of 1-2-3. There are options for showing only symbols, only lines, or both.

These new options are available only in Release 2.3 and 3. Figure 4-38 shows a bar graph with the bars shown in a horizontal position. The pie graph in Figure 4-39 is a popular way to show components of a whole. The 3-dimensional bars in Figure 4-40 were created with Release 2.3. This is one technique for adding interest and variety to graphs.

The HLCO graph created in Figure 4-41 is available in Releases 2.3 and 3 for graphing stock data. Figure 4-42 was created with Release 3 to show two Y axes. This allows you to create a graph with data that requires two very different Y axis scales.

In most releases of 1-2-3, you cannot print graphs directly from 1-2-3's main menu. You can use the Print Graph features to print graphs in Release 2.3 and below. You can also print graphs if you have Allways or Wysiwyg. Release 3 allows you to print graphs directly with Print Image.

PUBLISHING 1-2-3

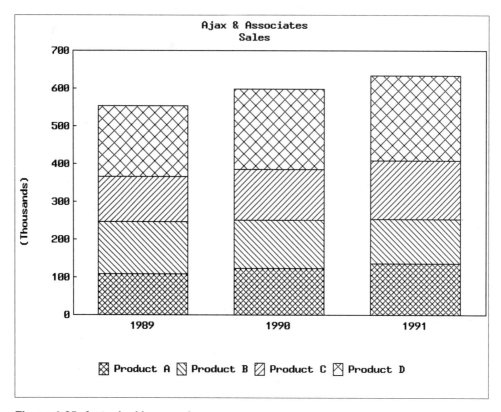

Figure 4-35: A stacked bar graph.

35mm Slides

You can create 35 mm graphs without an expensive investment in a film recorder. Although a film recorder may be a good investment if you create many graphs as slides, one of the overnight slide services may prove more cost effective for occasional use. Many companies that support the creation of slides from 1-2-3 .PIC files (file created with Graph Save). For approximately $10 a slide this can be a cost effective way to obtain a professional quality presentation cheaply.

BASIC 1-2-3 OPTIONS

A CLOSER LOOK

Creating A Graph Manually

1. Select Graph Type and choose a graph type from the options presented.

2. Select A for the A graph range and select the data that you want to use for this graph range.

3. Continue selecting as many additional ranges as you need through F to select as many as six data ranges if the graph type you selected supports multiple ranges.

4. Select X if you want to assign X axis data labels or labels for the pieces of a pie graph.

5. Select Options Legends and define graph legends for each data range used.

6. Select Options Titles and add titles to the graph.

7. Select Quit to return to the main graph menu and View the graph.

8. Make any desired changes then choose Graph Save and supply a name for the .PIC file that will be created with the graph image. Never save a graph for later printing on a black-and-white print device with after choosing Options Color. B&W must be the selection for a black-and-white print device or you will not be able to distinguish between data ranges on the graph.

9. Select Graph Name Create and name the graph before creating a second graph.

10. Select Quit then File Save to insure your graph definitions are part of the worksheet file.

PUBLISHING 1-2-3

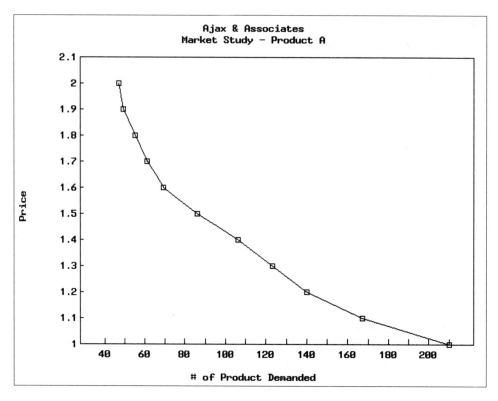

Figure 4-36: An XY graph.

Making Changes Easy with Macros

Macros make it easy to perform repetitive tasks. Rather than retyping the series of keystrokes each time you need to perform a task, you can store them in a macro and execute them as often as you want with one key combination. You will be more inclined to spruce up a spreadsheet if the task is quick and easy. You might decide to create a macro or two for repetitive formatting commands.

Macros are initially stored on a spreadsheet. Macros are named by using the Range Name Create command to assign a name to the top cell in the macro. The most common macro names consist of a backslash (\) and a single letter although Release 2.2 and above support the use of any valid range name using as many as 15 characters.

BASIC 1-2-3 OPTIONS

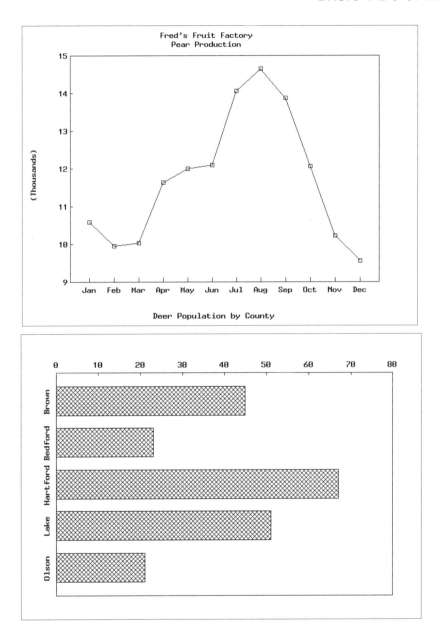

Figure 4-37 (top) shows a line graph. Figure 4-38 is a horizontal bar graph.

PUBLISHING 1-2-3

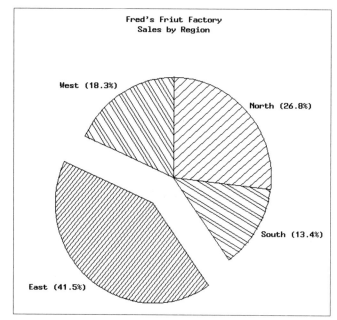

Figure 4-39 (r.): A pie graph with an exploded slice.
Figure 4-40: A 3-D bar graph.

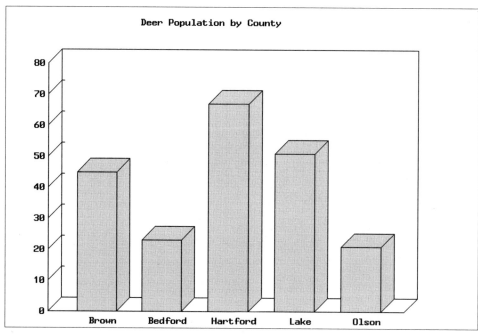

BASIC 1-2-3 OPTIONS

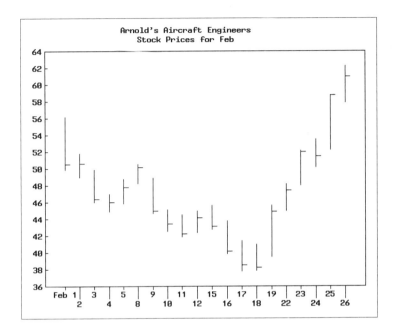

Figure 4-41 (l.): A high-low-close-open graph for stock bond prices.
Figure 4-42: A combination line/bar graph with two Y axes.

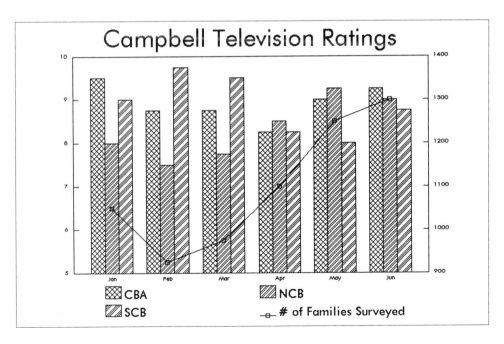

PUBLISHING 1-2-3

Figure 4-44 shows a simple macro to change the format of a cell to currency with 0 decimal places. You will find the steps for using the 1-2-3 Release 2.3 macro recorder in "A Closer Look: Using the Macro Recorder in Release 2.3."

With Release 2.2 and above you can use 1-2-3's Learn mode to record a macro as you try out the keystrokes. You can then name these keystrokes and make any desired changes before invoking the macro. To record a macro use ALT-F3.

A CLOSER LOOK

Using the Macro Recorder in Release 2.3

1. Select Worksheet Learn Range.

2. Specify a location out of the way of your data to record the macro keystrokes.

3. Press ALT-F5 to invoke LEARN mode.

4. Perform the procedure you want to record.

5. Press ALT-F5 to turn off LEARN mode.

6. Press F9 (CALC) to display the captured keystrokes in the LEARN range.

7. Select Range Name Create and name the top cell in the macro. When you are ready to run the macro you can use ALT-F3.

BASIC 1-2-3 OPTIONS

Figure 4-43: Macro keystrokes captured by the macro recorder.

CHAPTER 5

Using Wysiwyg with 1-2-3

Wysiwyg is an add-in product for 1-2-3 designed to provide a What-You-See-Is What-You-Get interface so that you see text enhancements and graphics on the screen. Because Wysiwyg can take advantage of all the features in new printers and allows you to create your own page layout, it is thought to add desktop publishing features to 1-2-3. Although Wysiwyg is a separate package, once you follow the special procedure for linking it to 1-2-3, the products operate together as one. If you are using another add-in, such as Allways, you will want to refer to Chapter 6.

Originally marketed as a separate add-in for users who already had a copy of 1-2-3, the Impress Wysiwyg add-in was included with Releases 3.1 and 2.3. You will find this chapter useful whether you purchased a copy of Wysiwyg separately or acquired it as part of your 1-2-3 purchase.

The coverage of the Wysiwyg features in this chapter is detailed enough to allow you to use them with your own worksheet. The organization of this chapter conforms closely to the design objectives discussed in Chapter 2, making it easy for you to cross-reference the types of changes you have decided to make to your information. You will find that there are sufficient features in this package to give you superior control over the layout of your information. This control includes the ability to use all the features of your printer most effectively and to combine text and graphics on the same page.

PUBLISHING 1-2-3

A CLOSER LOOK

Steps For Attaching the Wysiwyg Add-in

1) Select /Add-In or press ALT-F10.

2) Select Attach (Release 2.3 and below) or Load (Release 3) and select Wysiwyg.

3) Select No-Key or one of the hot keys that you can later use to display the Wysiwyg menu.

4) Select Quit to return to 1-2-3's READY mode or Invoke to display Wysiwyg's menu.

Installing and Attaching Wysiwyg

Although Wysiwyg now comes in the package with 1-2-3 Release 2.3 and 3.1, you must still install it on your hard disk. You can also set these two new 1-2-3 releases to automatically install Wysiwyg for you.

The Installation Process

If you are working with an older release of 1-2-3 and purchased the Impress Wysiwyg add-in separately, you will need to install the add-in after installing 1-2-3. You can follow the directions provided with the add-in. The process is straight-forward since all you do is copy Impress Wysiwyg files to your 1-2-3 directory.

Attaching the Add-in

Since Wysiwyg is a separate program, its code must be linked to the 1-2-3 code before you can use the Wysiwyg features. This linking process is referred to as *attaching* Wysiwyg. You only need to attach Wysiwyg once in each 1-2-3 session. You can even set up 1-2-3 to attach it for you automatically. The steps for attaching an add-in are shown in "A Closer Look: Steps for Attaching the Wysiwyg Add-in." It is not necessary to invoke Wysiwyg the way you do other add-ins to have it be operational.

To set 1-2-3 to attach Wysiwyg every time you launch the program, you would choose the Worksheet Global Default Other Add-In Set command (Release 2.3) or ALT-F10 Settings System Set (Release 3) and specify a number from 1 through 8, then select Wysiwyg as the add-in that you want to attach when 1-2-3 starts.

Once you update 1-2-3's configuration file with the Worksheet Global Update command, this selection will remain in effect unless you choose the Worksheet Global Default Other Add-In Cancel command (Release 2.3) or ALT-F10 Settings System Cancel (Release 3) and select the number for Wysiwyg.

Activating the Wysiwyg Menu

Activating the Wysiwyg menu is easy. All you need to do is press the hot key combination if you assigned one. The other option is to type a :. For most users the : is even more convenient than a hot key that requires the use of the ALT key with a function key. You can also activate the Wysiwyg menu with a mouse by pointing to the control panel. You will need to press the right mouse button if the 1-2-3 menu displays. The main Wysiwyg menu looks like Figure 5-1. Although some of the selections that you see look the same as the ones in 1-2-3's main menu, many of the options in lower level menus are different.

Many of the Wysiwyg commands add formatting to the worksheet. As you add formatting to the worksheet, Wysiwyg includes formatting indicators in the control panel to point out what formatting has been added to the current cell. These formatting instructions and the Wysiwyg commands that add them are listed in Table 5-1. We will describe these formatting features later in the chapter. The Wysiwyg features that you add to your worksheet are saved in a separate format file when you save the worksheet with 1-2-3's File Save command. The Wysiwyg formatting information is saved in a file with a .FMT (Release 2.3) or .FM3 (Release 3.1) extension.

Printing in Wysiwyg

Printing in Wysiwyg is similar to printing with 1-2-3. The steps are summarized in "A Closer Look: Summary of Steps For Printing." To see the results of your Wysiwyg enhancements on paper, you must print from within the add-in. If you print from within 1-2-3 your Wysiwyg enhancements will not appear. To print with Wysiwyg, set the range to print with the :Print Range Set command and then select a range just as you would for the 1-2-3 Print Printer Range command. When you select a range, Wysiwyg displays dotted lines to indicate where the output will be broken into

PUBLISHING 1-2-3

A CLOSER LOOK

Summary of Steps For Printing

1) Select :Print Range Set.

2) Select the worksheet range to print and press ENTER.

3) Check that the correct printer is listed under Configuration in the dialog box, otherwise, select Config Printer and the printer to use.

4) Check the print settings and layout options in the dialog box and make any changes as necessary.

5) Select Go to print to the printer, File and a filename to print to a file, or Background and a filename to print in the background with Release 2.3 (after running BPRINT).

pages and displays page information in the Wysiwyg format indicators in the control panel for the current cell. You can hide the lines or cause them to reappear with the :Display Options Page-Breaks and No to hide the lines or Yes to display them. Later you can remove the range setting with the :Print Range Clear command.

Once the range is selected, you can print the worksheet with the :Print Go, :Print Background (Release 2.3 only), or :Print File. The :Print Go and :Print Background commands print to the printer. In Releases 3 and above, 1-2-3 and Wysiwyg automatically print in the background while in Release 2.3, Wysiwyg only prints in the background with :Print Background after running the BPRINT program from DOS. If you use this command, you must provide a file name so that Wysiwyg can temporarily store the information it is sending to the printer. When you select :Print File, you must also supply a file name for storing the print information.

When you print with Wysiwyg, you do not need to advance or align the paper as you do in 1-2-3. Wysiwyg finishes each print job by advancing the paper to the top of the form. Wysiwyg also assumes that the paper in the printer starts at the top of the page.

While selecting the range and telling Wysiwyg to start printing are the two basic steps, you may also need to tell Wysiwyg which printer you are using by

USING WYSIWYG WITH 1-2-3

selecting :Print Config (or Configuration) Printer then selecting a printer. You may also need to change some of the other settings such as Interface to tell the program how the printer is connected to the computer; 1st and 2nd Cartridge to tell Wysiwyg which cartridges are installed on the printer; resolution to tell Wysiwyg the desired quality of your output; and bin to tell Wysiwyg which paper slot in the printer to use.

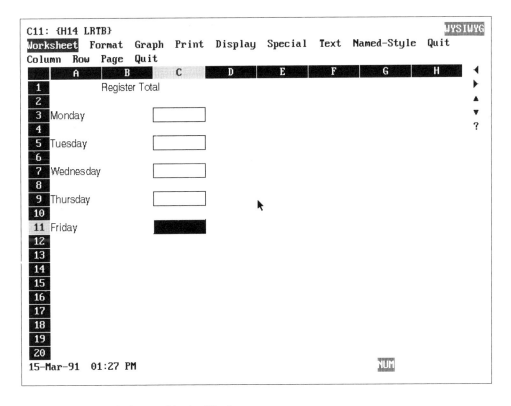

Figure 5-1: A worksheet with the Wysiwyg menu.

Table 5-1
Format Indicators and Wysiwyg Formatting Commands

Wysiwyg Formatting	Command Format Indicator
:Format Lines Bottom	B
:Format Bold Set	Bold
:Format Color Text	*color1*
:Format Color Background	/ *color2*
:Format Font 1 through 8	*font*
:Graph Add	Graph *name*
:Worksheet Row Set-Height	H*points*
:Format Italics Set	Italics
:Format Lines Left	L
:Worksheet Page	MPage
:Named Style 1 through 8	*named_style*
:Print Range Set	Page
:Format Lines Right	R
:Format Shade Light, Dark, or Solid	S1, S2, or S3
:Format Lines Shadow Set	Shadow
:Format Lines Top	T
:Text Set	Text
:Format Underline Single, Double, or Thick	U1, U2 or U3
:Format Color Negative	-

Changing Page Layout Options with Wysiwyg

The appearance of your printed pages depends as much on the amount of data that you put on the page as on the amount of room you leave for margins. In addition to page size and margins, layout is determined by whether you compress the data to fit within one page or several pages. As you create the page layouts, you can save them for future use or use them as the default for all worksheets. You can also see how the layout for any particular worksheet will appear and then select which pages you will print. Consult the "Checklist: Layout Options" to be certain that you have made all the desired adjustments before printing.

When working with Wysiwyg, you should also make most of your page layout changes from within the Print menu. Figure 5-2 shows the Print menu selections as well as the setting sheet/dialog box that appear when you select Print from the main menu. One of the main differences between selections in Wysiwyg and 1-2-3 is that Wysiwyg measurements are in inches whereas 1-2-3 shows them in characters. Once you start using proportional fonts—where the number of characters per inch varies—you will find that measuring in inches provides a much more meaningful look at the page layout. You can change the measurements from inches to millimeters in the event that you are using the metric system by entering a measurement followed by mm.

With Wysiwyg and Release 2.3 of 1-2-3, you can make changes to the layout and other Print menu

✔ CHECKLIST

Layout Options

Before you print, you may want to check to see if you've made all the adjustments you want.

✔ Adjusted the top and bottom margins.

✔ Added a header and/ or a footer.

✔ Added row or column borders at the top and left.

✔ Set the compression to expand or contract the output.

✔ Selected the correct page size.

✔ Checked the first and last page Wysiwyg will print.

✔ Previewed how Wysiwyg will print the worksheet.

PUBLISHING 1-2-3

commands through the dialog boxes. Dialog boxes are activated by clicking on them or by pressing F2 (EDIT). Once a dialog box is activated, you can select the option you want by typing the highlighted letter or clicking on it and entering an appropriate entry. While you can access most commands in this way, you cannot access print and preview commands through the dialog box.

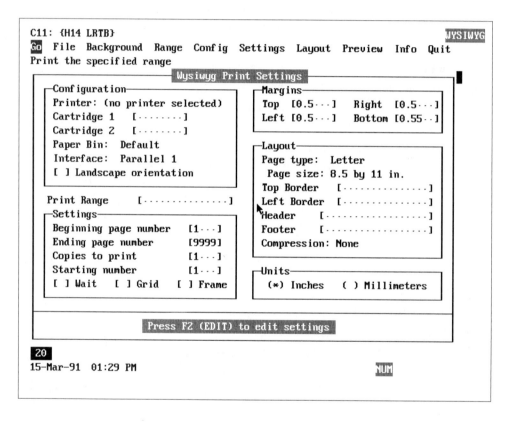

Figure 5-2: Wysiwyg :Print menu and its dialog box.

Setting the Page Size

Wysiwyg has a number of built-in options for the paper size. You can choose from 8 1/2" by 11", 8.268" by 11.693", 8 1/2"-by -11" fanfold, 14" by 11", 8 1/2" by 12", 8 1/2" by 14", and 6.929" by 9.843". You can also choose Custom and specify the size of the paper that you will put in your printer as long as your printer supports that size. Follow your custom width and length entries by typing in for inches or mm for millimeters. Most printers support both a minimum and a maximum size; you must stay within these guidelines even when using the custom option.

To change the paper size:

1. Type : to activate the Wysiwyg menu then select Print from the Wysiwyg menu.

2. Select Layout.

3. Select Page-Size.

4. Select one of the defined options or Custom. If you select Custom you will need to type a width and length.

Setting the Margins

The default left and right margin settings allow for 1/2 inch of white space on both sides. The top margin is also set at 1/2 inch initially. The bottom margin is a little larger at .55 inches. Any setting from 0 to 32 is acceptable although laser printers will require at least a small margin on all sides. The margins are set by selecting :Print Layout Margins and the side where you want to set the margin and typing the margin you want on that side.

Using the Preview Feature

Although, at this point, Wysiwyg displays your entries on the worksheet as they will print, it does not give you a feeling for how the information will appear on the

PUBLISHING 1-2-3

page. But the Print Preview screen shows the actual page and the placement of text on it. The Preview screen shows white space as well as text and allows you to make an assessment of the current margin settings. Figure 5-3 shows how the screen might look if you preview a worksheet in which you need to increase the top margin to better center the text on the page.

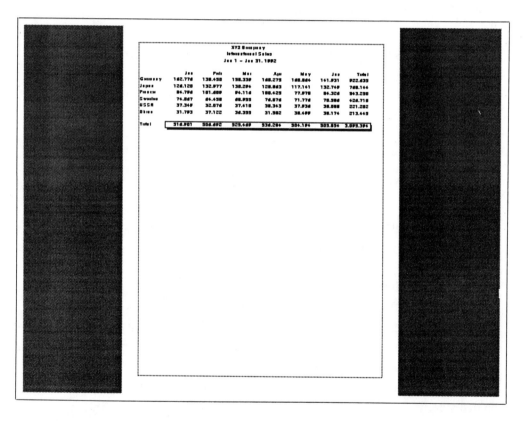

Figure 5-3: Previewing a worksheet to print.

USING WYSIWYG WITH 1-2-3

To preview the print follow these steps:

1. Press : and select Print.

2. Select Preview.

3. Press ESC to return to the Print menu or any key to continue displaying a preview of each page that will be printed.

The page that you previewed can be printed to a file—printed as a foreground task, requiring you to wait until the job is complete to continue other tasks, or pritned as a background activity that will allow you to work on other tasks. Wysiwyg does not actually start printing until you select an option like Go, File or Background.

Wysiwyg's display shows the worksheet as it will appear when printed. Once you select the range, dashed lines indicate page boundaries for each page. On a color monitor these lines will appear magenta, using the default settings. You may also want to hide the worksheet border that contains the column letters and row numbers by selecting :Display Options Frame None. You can recover the border with :Display Options Frame and one of the other options such as the default of Enhanced. If you are using a color monitor and want to display the worksheet as it will appear when printed, you might also select :Display Mode B&W, which changes the display to black and white. If you need to look at the worksheet up close or from farther away, select :Display Zoom and one of the options. The options to the left of Normal display the worksheet in smaller size and the options to the right display it larger. If you select Manual, you can enter a number less than 100 to shrink the worksheet or greater than 100 to enlarge it.

Using the Compression Feature

Although this feature is called Print Layout Compression, it will actually perform either compression or expansion on a range of data that you plan to print. Figures 5-4 through 5-9 show the different types of compression and expansion this command can perform. You would choose Print Layout Compression Automatic to have Wysiwyg try to fit the entire print range on a page. It will use a compression factor of up to 7 and will scale the fonts to a size where all of the data will fit on one page. You can use the Print Layout Compression Manual option to either expand or compress the print range. To expand the area occupied by the printed range, enter a number larger than 100. One hundred prints the data at its current size and 150 expands it by 50%. A number less than 100 causes the data to be compressed, thus, entering 75 causes the data to print at 75% of its original size.

Selective Printing

Although the range command lets you control the amount of data printed, it does not help when you want to replace several pages in the middle of a report. If you select the desired pages as a range, the first of these pages will print as page 1. If you retain the earlier selection of all the data you can use the Print Settings Begin and End options to specify the first and last pages that you want to print. This way, you can replace error-ridden pages.

USING WYSIWYG WITH 1-2-3

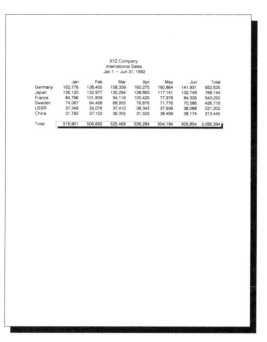

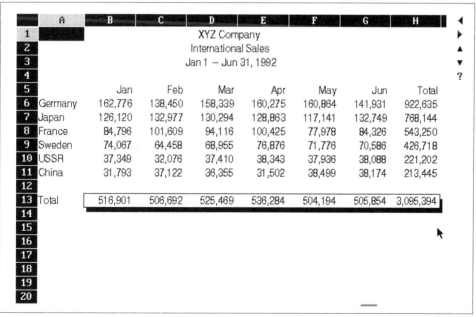

Figures 5-4 and 5-5: The Automatic setting compresses data just enough to fit on one page.

PUBLISHING 1-2-3

Figure 5-6 and 5-7: Manual can expand worksheet data and graphics.

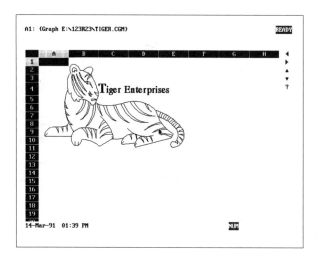

USING WYSIWYG WITH 1-2-3

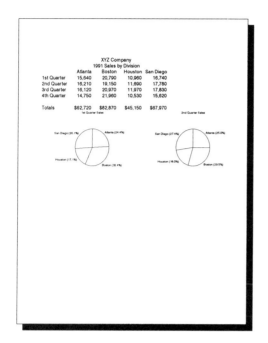

Figures 5-8 and 5-9: Manual can compress data to fit into a smaller area.

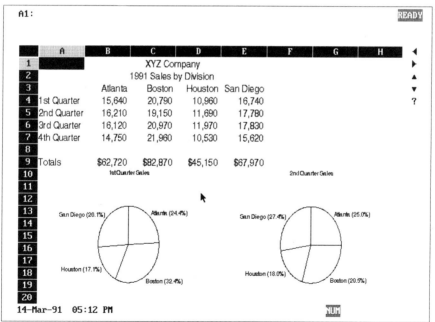

PUBLISHING 1-2-3

Creating a Library of Page Layouts

Once you perform the work of defining a page layout you may want to save it for other reports. You can even create libraries of these layouts and save a significant amount of time. This approach also ensures greater consistency among your reports without your having to go back to check the original.

To save the current print layout for later use:

1. Type : or point to the control panel to activate the Wysiwyg menu.

2. Select Print, Layout, Library, and Save.

3. Type the name of the file to store the layout settings and press ENTER. Wysiwyg will save all of the settings made with :Print Layout commands in the file with this name.

With a print layout saved, you can use it with any worksheet by selecting :Print Layout Library Retrieve and the file name of the layout you want to use. If you want to use the print layout as the default for all new worksheets, select :Print Layout Default Update. When you want to return a print layout to the default, select :Print Layout Default Restore.

Changing the Page Orientation

Wysiwyg supports portrait and landscape printing. Portrait uses an 8 1/2" -by- 11" sheet of paper by printing across the 8 1/2 inches. Landscape has the effect of turning the paper sideways and printing across the 11-inch side. Of course, your printer must support both print modes, too, and all popular laser printers do. You can make the change by pressing : and selecting Print Config (or Configuration) Orientation then choosing either Portrait or Landscape.

Adding Headers and Footers

Headers and footers provide a professional appearance to reports. Page numbers and dates at the top of a report make it easy to identify the latest copy and to return pages to their original sequence should they become separated. "A Closer Look: A Few Quick Steps For Adding Headers or Footers" covers the basics.

Although the process for entering headers and footers in Wysiwyg is the same as in 1-2-3, headers and footers from your worksheet will not automatically appear in Wysiwyg. Rather, you must re-enter them. In Release 2.3 you can enter up to 240 characters, and in 3.1, the header and footer can each contain up to 512 characters. In Wysiwyg you can access the header and footer option in the Print Layout Titles command. Don't confuse this command with 1-2-3's Worksheet Titles command since Print Layout Titles is equivalent to 1-2-3's Print Printer Options Header or Footer command. Headers and footers will use the default font 1 although you can use the formatting sequences discussed below to change fonts as well to add other font attributes to the header and footer text.

You can create three separate sections in Wysiwyg headers and footers just as you can with 1-2-3. The split vertical bar character (¦) divides information placed in the left, center, and right sections of the header. If you want to place NORTHEAST BRANCH on the left, ACCT. DEPT. in the center, and JOHN SMITH on the right, your entry would look like this: NORTHEAST BRANCH¦ACCT. DEPT.¦JOHN SMITH. If you enter

A CLOSER LOOK

A Few Quick Steps For Adding a Header or Footer

1) Select :Print Layout Titles Header or :Print Layout Footer.

2) Type the text you want on the top or bottom of each page. It can include these special characters: # for the page number; @ for the current date; | for dividing the text into left-aligned, centered and right-aligned sections; \ and a cell address for using a cell's contents as the header or footer. If this is used, do not include other information in the command prompt although the cell's entry can include them. Press CTRL-A and Format Sequences for adding formatting to the text

3) Press ENTER, then select Quit twice to return to the main :Print menu.

data in a header or footer without entering a split vertical bar, the entire contents of the header or footer will be placed at the left side of the header or footer. To center your entry, start with a split vertical bar. To place your entry at the far right side, place two split vertical bar characters at the beginning of the entry.

Just as in 1-2-3, you can use two special characters in the header or footer. The # represents the current page number and the @ represents the current system date.

With Wysiwyg you can set the number assigned to the first page printed with the :Print Settings Start-Number option. You might use a Start-Number of 9 making the entries on the first page show the page number as 9.

Another option, which is the same as headers and footers in 1- 2-3 is to enter the header or footer text in worksheet cells and reference them at the header or footer prompt. First select :Print Layout Titles and Header or Footer, then type \ and the cell address or range name containing the entry to use. Using the backslash in 1-2-3's headers or footers means you cannot include other information in the header or footer prompt, but you can include any special characters in the cell entry in the worksheet.

Just as when you use a header or footer in 1-2-3, it will print beneath the top margin or above the bottom margin. Two blank lines separate the header or footer from the body of the text. When you want to remove a header or footer that you have added in Wysiwyg, select :Print Layout Titles Clear and then select Header, Footer or Both to remove one or both.

Adding Borders

In 1-2-3, when you want to print the same columns or rows on each page, you use the Print Options Borders Columns or Rows command. In Wysiwyg, you use the :Print Layout Borders Top or Left command. Like adding a border row or column in 1-2-3, after selecting Top or Left, you only have to select one cell from each column or row that you want to use in the border. Make sure you do not include the range used by the

USING WYSIWYG WITH 1-2-3

borders within the range to print since Wysiwyg will print the range once as a border and then again as part of the print range. When you want to remove print borders, select :Print Layout Titles Borders Clear, and then Top, Left, or All to remove one border or both.

Adding Page Breaks

Page breaks can be inserted at any location. This allows you to place a chart, table, or other important information on a page by itself.

To add a page break from within Wysiwyg at the location of the cell pointer, you can use the Worksheet Page command. To add a page break at the current row you would type : then select Worksheet Page Row. To add a page break at the current column, use Worksheet Page Column. Figure 5-10 shows a worksheet where a page break has been added at both the rows and columns. Also note that the order of printing is shown on this page. Wysiwyg will use these page breaks alsong with :Print Layout Compression Automatic to decide how much to compress the data.

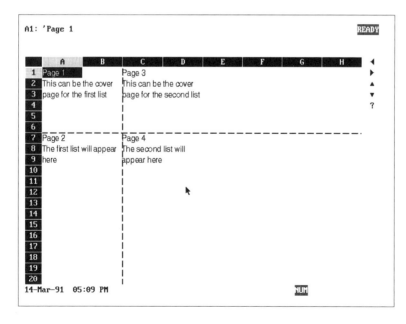

Figure 5-10: Wysiwyg displays page breaks it adds as well as those you've added.

PUBLISHING 1-2-3

Line Spacing

Although there is not a line spacing option per se, you can alter line spacing. To make such a change, use the Worksheet Row command and change the height of the row. Adding to the row height will make your entries look double-spaced or triple-spaced. Figure 5-11 shows an image that has several row heights increased.

You can also change row heights with a Wysiwyg text range to create double spacing. Figure 5-12 shows a text range that will print as double spaced because the :Worksheet Row Set-Height command is used to double each row's height in the range. Normally Wysiwyg sets the row height to be slightly taller than the tallest font in the row. When you select :Worksheet Row Auto, this is the row height Wysiwyg will use.

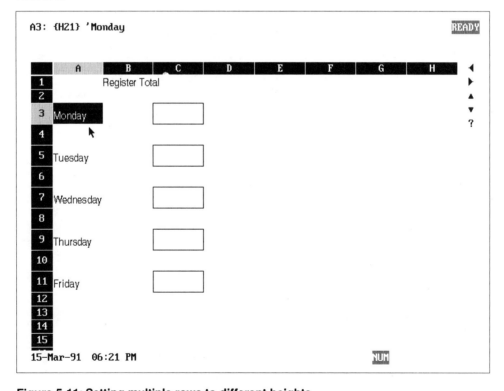

Figure 5-11: Setting multiple rows to different heights.

174

USING WYSIWYG WITH 1-2-3

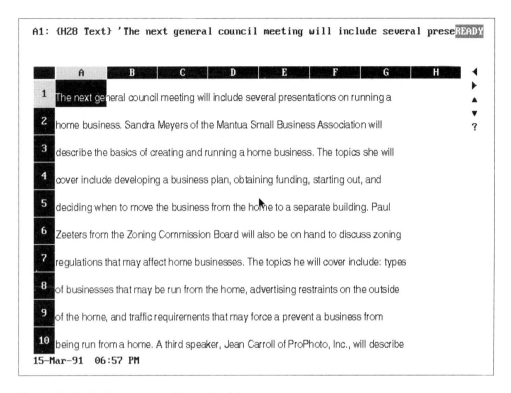

Figure 5-12: Making rows taller to double-space text.

Changing the Type

There are many different options for changing the type when printing from Wysiwyg. You can change the typeface or size. You can also choose formatting options that affect the font style. Wysiwyg puts all the capabilities of your printer at your fingertips making it easy to use both soft fonts and font cartridges without becoming an expert in the entry of setup strings.

Selecting a Different Typeface

Dot matrix and laser printers usually have a default font that 1-2-3 uses with the Print Printer command but these printers can actually print a wide range of fonts. Wysiwyg can take advantage of your printer's ability to print additional fonts. You can

PUBLISHING 1-2-3

A CLOSER LOOK

Changing the Font of a Worksheet Range

1) Select :Format Font.

2) Select a number 1 through 8 representing the font you want to add.

3) Select the worksheet range that should use this font.

use the different fonts to enhance the look of your printed worksheets and to emphasize portions of text. Wysiwyg lets you use up to eight fonts in a worksheet at once—more than enough in most cases. You can use the default fonts Wysiwyg has assigned, change them to your own, reset the default, or create libraries of font sets. With the eight fonts the worksheet has available, you can assign these fonts to any worksheet range or use them in command prompts and graphs. "A Closer Look" summarizes the steps for changing the font in a worksheet.

The eight fonts are listed when you select :Format Font. The numbers 1 through 8 appear next to the corresponding fonts. When you want to apply one font to a worksheet range, select the appropriate number and then the range. The worksheet display will show the font as it will appear when printed. Figure 5-13 shows a worksheet that uses several fonts for an improved appearance.

When you assign a font to a range, Wysiwyg remembers its font number rather than its name. Thus, when you assign font 2, which happens to be Swiss 14 point, for example, Wysiwyg assigns font 2 to the cell. If you change font 2 from Swiss 14 point to CG Times, 12 point, all worksheet data that uses font 2 will appear in CG Times.

To change the font assigned to the font number, select :Format Font Replace and the font number that

USING WYSIWYG WITH 1-2-3

you want to replace. Next select the typeface that you want to assign. The Swiss, Dutch, Courier and Xsymbol fonts are provided by Wysiwyg. These fonts appear in Figure 5-14. Additional fonts may be available under Other. They might include built-in fonts, cartridge fonts, downloaded soft fonts, and other installed Bitstream fonts that are not part of the original Wysiwyg package. After you select one of the initial Wysiwyg fonts or select Other and a font from the list Wysiwyg provides, type in the appropriate type size. Wysiwyg measures character sizes in points where each point is 1/72 of an inch. If you select a size that is not installed, Wysiwyg substitutes the closest installed size. "A Closer Look: Point Sizes" shows different point sizes. After you change the typeface and size, any worksheet data assigned to that font number will appear in the new selections.

	A	B	C	D	E	F
1			High Finance Incorporated			
2			Branch Performance Report			
3						
4	New Accounts by Branch				Money	
5			Savings	Checking	Market	Total
6	East		67	54	19	140
7	West		54	22	45	121
8	North		67	18	32	117
9	South		31	41	15	87
10	Total		219	135	111	465
11						
12	Total Deposits by Branch				Money	
13			Savings	Checking	Market	Total
14	East		$14,321,789	$3,214,321	$14,567,821	$32,103,931
15	West		$32,451,234	$54,321,234	$43,123,943	$129,896,411
16	North		$54,123,900	$34,123,783	$21,345,678	$109,593,361
17	South		$2,131,113	$14,321,599	$2,134,567	$18,587,279
18	Total		$103,028,036	$105,980,937	$81,172,009	$290,180,982

A4: {DUTCH14} [W13] 'New Accounts by Branch   READY

10-Apr-91 05:44 AM

Figure 5-13: Worksheet using multiple fonts and typefaces.

PUBLISHING 1-2-3

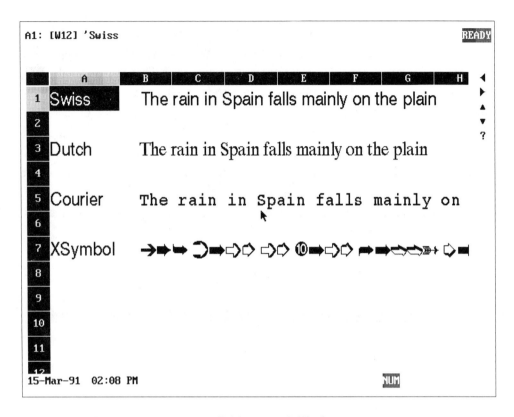

Figure 5-14: Different typefaces available through Wysiwyg.

If you use the same font selections for several worksheets, you may want to create a font library. Then, worksheets will use the same fonts and font numbers. To save a font library, select :Format Font Library Save and type a file name. To retrieve a font library select :Format Font Library Retrieve and select a file name. You can also erase libraries you no longer need with the :Format Font Library Erase command.

Finally, you can make a set of fonts the default fonts available for new worksheets by selecting :Format Font Default Update. When you want to return to the default font set, select :Format Font Default Restore.

Selecting a Different Type Style

Other formatting changes you can make with Wysiwyg include boldfacing, italicizing, and underlining text. As the name Wysiwyg implies, all of your changes will be visible on the screen display immediately. You can change formatting through either Wysiwyg commands or formatting sequences. Wysiwyg commands apply their formats to an entire cell entry while formatting sequences can be used to affect part of a cell entry. Some formatting options are not available as menu commands or as formatting sequences. If you are using Wysiwyg with a text range, you can use a special menu to add styles to your text.

Several of the :Format commands add styles to the text font. These include :Format Bold Set, :Format Italics Set, and :Format Underline. You would access all of these styles through the Wysiwyg format commands and then select the ranges they are to be applied to, although you can select the range before selecting the command. With underlining, you can choose Single, Double, Wide, or Clear. Figure 5-15 shows a worksheet that uses the :Format Bold Set and :Format Italics Set commands to add boldfacing and italics to a worksheet. If later you want to remove the formatting, select :Format followed by the style you want to eliminate, then select Clear as in :Format Bold Clear, :Format Italics Clear or :Format Underline Clear. If you want to remove all formatting, select :Format Reset. This selection removes all formats added with :Format commands but does not affect formats added with formatting sequences as described next.

A CLOSER LOOK

Point Sizes

This is Helvetica 10 point.

This is Helvetica 12 point.

This is Helvetica 16 point.

This is Helvetica 20 point.

This is Helvetica 24 point.

PUBLISHING 1-2-3

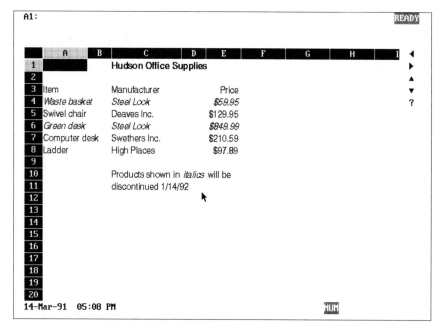

Figure 5-15: Using boldface and italics to enhance a worksheet.

Another option for adding styles is to apply them to text within a cell or to a header or graph title. For example, if you want to boldface only one word in a label entry, use formatting sequences. Wysiwyg formatting sequences can apply many of the standard formatting features to text within a cell. To add a formatting sequence that will apply a type style, press CTRL-A and type the letter of the formatting sequence for the format to add. This might be b, i, 1_, 2_, or 3_ for boldface, italics, single underlining, double underlining or wide underlining. Table 5-2 lists all of the formatting sequences and formats you may want to add (including ones for features covered later) with the Wysiwyg commands that apply the format to the entire cell. These formatting sequences are case sensitive. When you have entered the text to format or moved the cursor in the entry to where you want the formatting to end, press CTRL-E and type the same letter or formatting sequence combination. You can also press CTRL-N which returns all formatting to the default. CTRL-E must be used if you want to stop one type of formatting continue another. CTRL-N is also useful when you want to end several formatting sequences at once. You cannot apply formatting sequences to formula results. When you look at cell entries containing formatting sequences, you will see codes as well as your data. A Δ and a letter mark the beginning of the formatting. Another Δ and the letter mark the end. An example of an entry containing formatting sequences is creating this entry in a cell or in response to a command prompt:

Important: Read This Page First

This entry is created by pressing CTRL-A, typing b, pressing CTRL-A again, typing 1_, typing **Important:**, pressing CTRL-N and typing **Read This Page First.**

You can also add formatting sequences to text ranges. Text ranges, as described later in this chapter, let you treat a range of labels as if their contents were in a word processor. Once a range is selected as a text range, whenever you use the :Text Edit command, you can add formatting sequences by pressing F3 (NAME) and selecting the new formatting from the menu in the control panel. Wysiwyg will display the formatting currently in effect as you enter the text. When you want to finish a format, you press F3 (NAME) and select Normal. Adding formatting sequences this way produces the same result as pressing CTRL-A and CTRL-N to add formatting sequences.

Adding Arrows and Other Symbols

Most of the fonts you work with will provide a standard character set. This means that they will provide all the keyboard characters plus special symbols and even some other characters. All but one of the fonts provided with Wysiwyg are in this category. That font, called Xsymbol, provides unique symbols in place of the alphabetic characters.

PUBLISHING 1-2-3

You might use these symbols, such as arrows, to create dividing lines that draw attention to a caption, for example. Once you select the symbol set, typing in any character will generate an entirely different symbol than what appears on the keyboard. Appendixes A and B show which symbols are generated by the Xsymbol font. You can also add special effects by flipping these characters horizontally or vertically using formatting sequences.

Figure 5-16 shows a worksheet that uses these symbols. The numbers in A9 and A10 were added by pressing CTRL-A, typing 8F for the Xsymbol font, typing @ for the 1 and A for the 2, and pressing CTRL-N to return to the default font. The arrows in C9 and C10 were added by typing x in these cells and using the :Format Font command to apply the Xsymbol font. The arrow in D13 was added by typing r and using :Format Font to display the results using the Xsymbol font. The arrow in F13 was added by pressing CTRL-A and typing xr to reverse the symbol the r appears as in the Xsymbol font.

	A	B	C	D	E	F	G	H
1	Sales	1991	1992	1993	1994	1995		
2	Product 1	100,000	110,000	121,000	133,100	146,410		
3	Product 2	200,000	210,000	220,500	231,525	243,101		
4	Total	300,000	320,000	341,500	364,625	389,511		
5	COGS	135,000	144,000	153,675	164,081	175,280		
6	Profit	165,000	176,000	187,825	200,544	214,231		
7								
8	Growth Rate							
9	① Product 1	10% ←						
10	② Product 2	5% ←						
11								
12								
13	Total Sales Over Five Years				943,600			
14								
15								
16								

Figure 5-16: Creating circled numbers and arrows with the Xsymbol set.

Table 5-2
Wysiwyg Formatting Commands and Formatting Sequences

Style Feature	Wysiwyg Command	Formatting Sequence
Boldface	:Format Bold Set	b
Colors (Normal, Red, Green, Dark Blue, Cyan, Yellow, Magenta	:Format Color Text Color	1c to 7c
Colors Reversed	:Format Color Reverse	8c
Flashing	N/A	f
Flip text backwards	N/A	x
Flip text upside down	N/A	y
Fonts 1 through 8	:Format Font 1 through 8	1F to 8F
Italics	:Format Italics	Seti
Lines	:Format Lines	N/A
Outline of character	N/A	o or 1o to 255o
Reset	:Format Reset	CTRL-N
Shading	:Format Shade	N/A
Strike through	N/A	5_
Subscript	N/A	d
Superscript	N/A	u
Underline		
Single	:Format Underline Single	1_
Double	:Format Underline Double	2_
Wide	:Format Underline Wide	3_
Outline	:Format Lines Outline	4_

PUBLISHING 1-2-3

Using Color Effectively

For most business users color printouts are not a viable option. Even those early users who have acquired color printers, do not have office copiers capable of supporting color and using the printer for all copies simply is not practical.

However, color can add significant appeal to information. And even if the use of color has not yet arrived as a standard for business printing, most monitors purchased today support it. If your presentation will appear on a large screen monitor you will want to assess your color selections carefully. You may also choose to create an image that can later be placed on a 35-mm slide. Color is also a practical option when you consider creating transparencies with a pen plotter. You may have multiple pens with a different color in each or instruct the plotter to stop and allow you to change pens as you print each new section of a graph.

Color choice can be important to the dissemination of your message. Many studies have been done indicating the effect of certain colors on the audience. Whether you use cool or warm colors may have an effect. Some colors clash when placed together. Other colors blend so closely that you may not be able to differentiate between adjacent pieces of a pie graph.

Wysiwyg allows you to change the color of 1-2-3 information in several ways. You can change the colors that the worksheet uses to print and/or display. When you select colors with the :Format Color command, you change both how the selected range prints and displays. This command can change the text color, the background color (only of the cell, not of the area of the label uses to display), the color of negative numbers, and it can reverse the text and background colors. After selecting an option, you can select one of the colors from the menu. If you reverse colors, make sure to include the cells that long labels borrow for their display as well as the cells in which you typed the labels. You can use the color display features knowing that 1-2-3 will convert color to black and white when you print. If your printer can only print one color (presumably black), it will print variations in color as varying shades of black or gray—except for text.

You can also change the color of text within cells using the formatting sequences of CTRL-A followed by 1c to 7c. And you can reverse colors within an entry by pressing CTRL-A and typing 8c. These formatting sequences override the colors set by :Format Color.

You can also change the colors of your worksheet display without affecting your color output. You might do this when creating slides from screen captures. The display colors are changed by selecting :Display Colors and selecting the part of the display you want to change. You can change the background color of all cells, the text of all cells (unless changed from the default with the :Format Color command), the contents of unprotected cells, the cell pointer, the grid lines, the worksheet frame, negative numbers, lines added with :Format Lines, shadows added with :Format Lines Shadow). After selecting an option, select the color from the menu. Unlike the :Format Color command, the :Display Colors command affects the entire worksheet.

The :Display Colors Replace Command lets you substitute other colors for the seven default color selections available when you use the :Display Colors command. After selecting this command and the color you want to change, enter the number of the replacement color. These numbers represent the 64 colors that Wysiwyg can use for worksheets. They are not in any particular order.

The changes you make with :Display commands remain in effect for the period during which you use Wysiwyg and 1-2-3, the changes you make with :Format commands are saved to each worksheet. If you want the display changes to apply to all worksheets, select :Display Default Update. You can also return to the default display by selecting :Display Default Restore.

PUBLISHING 1-2-3

Adding Lines and Boxes

The use of lines and boxes in a report can add structure, help to create tables, and group related items together. You can add these lines and boxes to your worksheet with Wysiwyg's :Format Lines command. Boxes are created by adding lines on four sides. You can choose from several different line types. Note that lines differ from underlining because lines apply to cells whereas underlining applies to their contents. You can also add a shadow effect to create a three-dimensional box.

You can choose single, double, or single thick lines. Lines are added as an outline to the edge of the range—on its left, right, top, or bottom sides— or using All adds the lines in between all cells in the range. Single lines are created by selecting :Format Lines, where you want the lines drawn, and then selecting the range. Select :Format Lines Double for double line, :Format Lines Thick for thick lines. Figure 5-17 shows a printed schedule that uses the :Format Lines Single All command to create all of the lines in the table. To remove the lines, select :Format Lines Clear, where you want the lines removed, and then the range.

Portage Rapid Transit
Schedule Effective 6/1/91

Downtown	33rd & Lake	Euclid & 107th	Euclid & 200th
04:48 AM	04:55 AM	05:09 AM	05:22 AM
06:00 AM	06:07 AM	06:21 AM	06:34 AM
07:12 AM	07:19 AM	07:33 AM	07:46 AM
08:24 AM	08:31 AM	08:45 AM	08:58 AM
09:36 AM	09:43 AM	09:57 AM	10:10 AM
10:48 AM	10:55 AM	11:09 AM	11:22 AM
12:00 PM	12:07 PM	12:21 PM	12:34 PM
01:12 PM	01:19 PM	01:33 PM	01:46 PM
02:24 PM	02:31 PM	02:45 PM	02:58 PM
03:36 PM	03:43 PM	03:57 PM	04:10 PM
04:48 PM	04:55 PM	05:09 PM	05:22 PM
06:00 PM	06:07 PM	06:21 PM	06:34 PM
07:12 PM	07:19 PM	07:33 PM	07:46 PM
08:24 PM	08:31 PM	08:45 PM	08:58 PM
09:36 PM	09:43 PM	09:57 PM	10:10 PM
10:48 PM	10:55 PM	11:09 PM	11:22 PM

Figure 5-17 shows how :Format Lines adds lines so you can create tables.

USING WYSIWYG WITH 1-2-3

```
A1: [W8]                                                              READY

        A       B         C         D         E         F         G         H
  1                                 XYZ Company
  2                                 International Sales
  3                                 Jan 1 – Jun 31, 1992
  4
  5             Jan       Feb       Mar       Apr       May       Jun       Total
  6  Germany    162,776   138,450   158,339   160,275   160,864   141,931   922,635
  7  Japan      126,120   132,977   130,294   128,863   117,141   132,749   768,144
  8  France     84,796    101,609   94,116    100,425   77,978    84,326    543,250
  9  Sweden     74,067    64,458    68,955    76,876    71,776    70,586    426,718
 10  USSR       37,349    32,076    37,410    38,343    37,936    38,088    221,202
 11  China      31,793    37,122    36,355    31,502    38,499    38,174    213,445
 12
 13  Total      516,901   506,692   525,469   536,284   504,194   505,854   3,095,394
 14
 15
 16
 17
 18
 19
 20
15-Mar-91  03:04 PM                                              NUM
```

Figure 5-18: A drop shadow added to give a box a 3-D look.

You can also add a drop shadow like the one in Figure 5-18. These shadows are often combined with lines to create three-dimensional boxes. To add a drop shadow select :Format Lines Shadow Set and the range over which the shadow should appear on the right and bottom side—B13..H13 in Figure 5-18. If you need to remove a drop shadow, select :Format Lines Shadow Clear and the range. Set the color for the shadow's display and printing using the :Display Colors Shadow command.

Using Shading

Another option for emphasizing a cell or range is shading. Shading is also an alternative to changing colors. Figure 5-19 shows a worksheet that uses shading to draw attention to positive variances that need to checked. You can add shading by selecting :Format Shade and then Light, Dark, or Solid. Remove it by selecting

PUBLISHING 1-2-3

:Format Shade Clear and the range. Set the displayed color of shading using :Display Color Text.

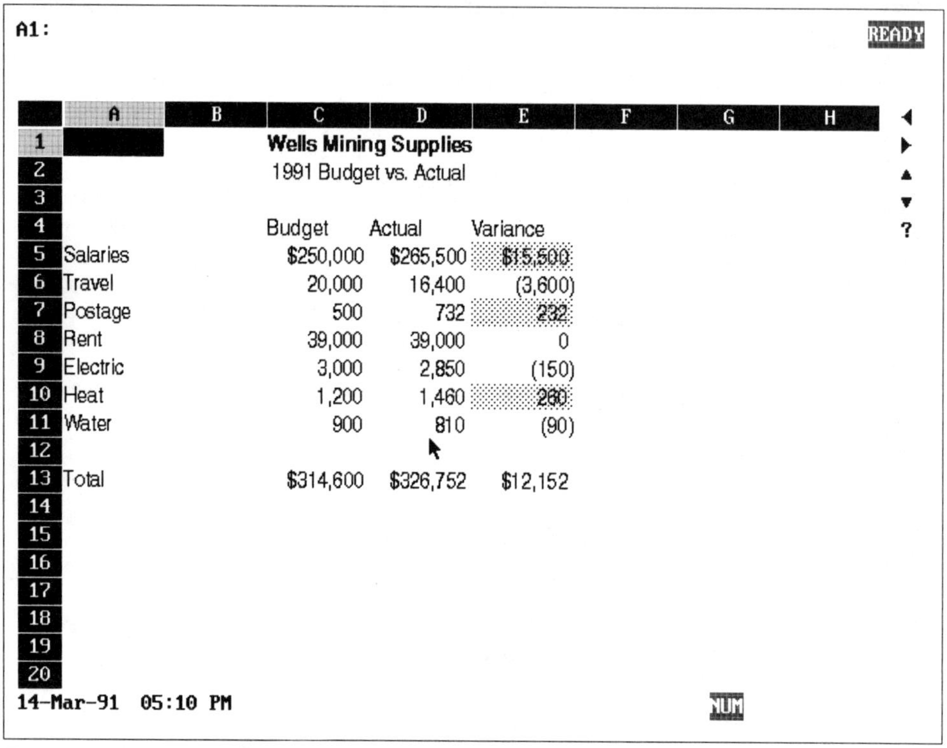

Figure 5-19: Shading emphasizes cell contents.

Using Captions, Labels and Other Explanatory Text

Labels in 1-2-3 are used for many purposes besides just labeling data that you calculate on the worksheet. They can be used for lengthy explanations, captions, and headings. Wysiwyg includes several features that simplify work with labels. One of these features is using a text range so you can treat text as if it were in a word processor.

Using Text Ranges

If you have text to include in a worksheet, you will find that the 1-2-3 Range Justify command does not do what you want for rearranging text over several rows since it doesn't adjust the cell entries for the font width. Also, when you enter a paragraph of text in 1-2-3, you may be annoyed that you continually have to move to the next cell. Using a Wysiwyg text range eliminates both problems since entering text in a text range is like entering text in a word processor. A text range is created by selecting :Text Set and the range. The number of columns determines how many columns will be used to display the text although the text is only stored in the first column. You can enter and edit a text range by selecting :Text Edit.

When you edit a text range by selecting :Text Edit and the range, you do not see your entry in the control panel since you are entering it directly into the worksheet. Additionally, several keys behave differently. Table 5-3 shows the keys you may use to edit a text range. These keys behave differently largely because Wysiwyg treats the entries as paragraphs within the range. When you are finished using a text range, press ESC.

Text ranges are readjusted for paragraph width using the :Text Reformat command. Unlike using Range Justify, when formatting a text range, Wysiwyg adjusts the text entries for the width of the characters in the selected font. Also, Wysiwyg will wrap text around graphics.

The other special command for working with text ranges is :Text Align which sets the alignment of paragraphs. Unlike the 1-2-3 Range Label command, paragraph alignment is done over a range rather than within cells. Also, the :Text Align command has another option, Even, which justifies both the left and right edges of text as is done in this book. The :Text Align command is used when you need to set the alignment of labels over several columns of entries. Figure 5-20 shows an example of when the :Text Align command is used to center labels over multiple columns so you do not have to manually add spaces to the beginning of the label entry. This worksheet also shows a text range that is evenly aligned, or justified.

Table 5-3
Keys to Use While Editing A Text Range

Key	Action While Editing A Text Range
Up arrow or down arrow	Moves cursor to the line of text above or below
Left arrow or right arrow	Moves cursor one character left or right
ESC	Ends editing text and returns to READY mode
Enter	Starts new line
Backspace	Removes character to the left of cursor
Ctrl-Left arrow	Moves cursor one word to the left
Ctrl-Right arrow	Moves cursor one word to the right
DEL	Deletes character at cursor's position
END	Moves cursor to end of line
HOME	Moves cursor to beginning of line
F3	Displays menu for adding text formatting
INS	Switches between Insert and Overstrike mode
Pg Up	Moves cursor up one screen
Pg Dn	Moves cursor down one screen

Working With Graphs

Using Wysiwyg you can add graphs to your worksheet and print with the standard Wysiwyg Print command. Earlier releases required a utility for printing the graph and refeeding paper through the printer in order to integrate text and graphics on the same page. Figure 5-21 shows an example worksheet display with both graphs and text.

All of the graphs that you work with in Wysiwyg must be created using 1-2-3's Graph menu. There are no menu options in Wysiwyg that allow you to create a graph

USING WYSIWYG WITH 1-2-3

```
A1: {SWISS14 Text} [W13] ^High Finance Incorporated                    READY
```

	A	B	C	D	E	F
1			High Finance Incorporated			
2			Branch Performance Report			
3						
4	New Accounts by Branch				Money	
5			Savings	Checking	Market	Total
6	East		67	54	19	140
7	West		54	22	45	121
8	North		67	18	32	117
9	South		31	41	15	87
10	Total		219	135	111	465

The 50 percent increase in new accounts is substantially caused by updating the premiums offered with the accounts. Premiums such as toasters and magazine racks have been replaced with microwavable dishes and digital electronics.

	A	B	C	D	E	F
17	Total Deposits by Branch				Money	
18			Savings	Checking	Market	Total

```
18-Apr-91  02:24 PM
```

Figure 5-20: Using center and even text alignment.

unless it has been previously defined; you can add images to existing graphs. And you can create graphics with Wysiwyg or other graphics packages and add them to your worksheet. These include files created in a standard Metafile format created by many packages, including Harvard Graphics, Freelance, DrawPerfect, CorelDRAW, 2D-Graphics, and 3D-Graphics.

Adding Graphics to A Worksheet

Wysiwyg allows you to add five different graph types to a worksheet. "A Closer Look" lists the steps for doing so. You can add the current graph, which displays when

PUBLISHING 1-2-3

```
A1:                                                              READY

        A        B         C         D         E       F     G     H
  1                        XYZ Company
  2                     1991 Sales by Division
  3              Atlanta    Boston    Houston  San Diego
  4  1st Quarter 15,640    20,790    10,960   16,740
  5  2nd Quarter 16,210    19,150    11,690   17,780
  6  3rd Quarter 16,120    20,970    11,970   17,830
  7  4th Quarter 14,750    21,960    10,530   15,620
  8
  9  Totals     $62,720   $82,870   $45,150  $67,970
 10              1st Quarter Sales            2nd Quarter Sales
 11
 12
 13    San Diego (26.1%)   Atlanta (24.4%)   San Diego (27.4%)   Atlanta (25.0%)
 14
 15
 16
 17
 18    Houston (17.1%)                        Houston (18.0%)
 19                        Boston (32.4%)                        Boston (29.5%)
 20
 14-Mar-91  05:12 PM                                         NUM
```

Figure 5-21: Adding two graphs to a worksheet.

you press F10, by selecting :Graph Add Current. Another 1-2-3 graph enhancement option in Wysiwyg is adding a named graph to a worksheet by selecting :Graph Add Named and selecting a named graph from the list. If you want to add a 1-2-3 graph stored in a .PIC file, you can do so by selecting :Graph Add PIC- File and selecting the graph name. 1-2-3 includes several Metafiles. You can add these graphic images to your worksheets as well as other graphic images stored in a Metafile format by selecting :Graph Add Metafile and the filename. The last type of graph is a blank graph which you can edit by adding objects to the graph. The last type of graph you can add to a worksheet is added by selecting :Graph Add Blank. Once you have selected the graph type to add, Wysiwyg asks for the worksheet range. You can select any range to display. The size of the range determines the size of the graphic and its height-to-width ratio.

If you want to remove a graphic, select :Graph Remove and then the graph or graphs you wish to eliminate. With all of the graph settings that you can make after you add the graphic, you must select the graphic to change. You can either select a cell in the range the graphic displays, select a range containing one or more graphics to affect, or press F3 (NAME) and select one of the listed graphics.

An advantage to using named and current graphs for the current worksheet is Wysiwyg will automatically update graphs. It will reflect changes to the worksheet data, changes to the settings of the graph, or updates to the graph made through the 1-2-3 Graph Name Create command. Figure 5-21 shows a worksheet with the current graph added to A11..H20. The graph changes to reflect new entries in A4..D9. You can also set Wysiwyg to update the graph at your instruction only by selecting :Graph Settings Sync No and the graph or graphs that you do not want instantly updated. When you want these graphs updated, select :Graph Compute. This command updates all graphic images in the worksheet and will even reread .PIC and Metafiles. When you want to restore the instant update feature, select :Graph Settings Sync Yes and the graph or graphs.

A CLOSER LOOK

Adding a Graphic to a Worksheet

1) Select :Graph Add.

2) Select one of these graphic types:

Current to add the current worksheet graph.

Named to add a named graph in the current worksheet.

PIC to add a graph saved in a .PIC file.

Metafile to add a graphic saved in a .CGM file.

Blank to add an empty graph.

3) Select the named graph to add, the .PIC file to add, or the .CGM file to add if you selected Named, PIC or Metafile.

4) Select the worksheet range to display the graph and press ENTER.

PUBLISHING 1-2-3

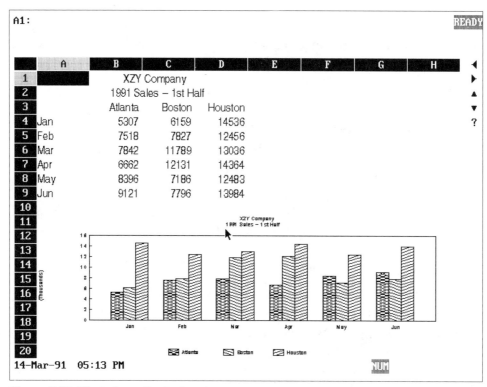

Figure 5-22: Worksheet displaying the current graph.

Although the graph size and position are intially determined by the range you select, you can change both size and position. Change the worksheet range used to display by selecting :Graph Settings Range, the graph, and the new range in which to display the graph. You may want to make the change when you add a graphic that does not have the proper height- to-width ratio. You can also change the graph's position by selecting :Graph Move, the appropriate graph, and the upper left cell where you want to place the graph.

While the graphics normally hide the underlying worksheet information in the range where the graphics display, you can change that. For example, you can combine graphics and worksheet data as in a company logo. Figure 5-23 shows the TIGER.CGM

USING WYSIWYG WITH 1-2-3

file added to the worksheet in A1..E11. Once the graphic file is added, the text is added in C4. The formatting sequences and the :Format Bold command are used to set the appearance of the text. To display both the graphic and the underlying worksheet data as in Figure 5-23, select :Graph Settings Opaque No and the appropriate graphs. You can later hide the worksheet data by selecting :Graph Settings Opaque Yes and the appropriate graphs.

You can change the type of name of a graphic or replace a .PIC file with a Metafile when the .PIC file was originally used as the basis for the Metafile. To change the graphic that displays in the worksheet, select :Graph Settings Graph, the graphic to

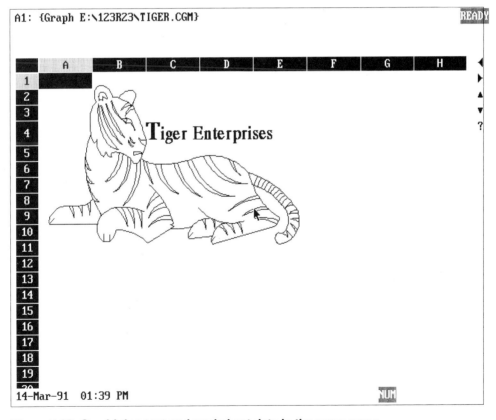

Figure 5-23: Combining text and worksheet data in the same range.

PUBLISHING 1-2-3

change, the type of graphic you want to display in its place, and, unless you select Blank or Current, the name of the graphic. Any enhancements you have made to the graph using Wysiwyg's graphics editing window and all of the graphics settings will remain.

If you want to speed your work with graphs, you may want to display graphics as a shaded region by selecting :Graph Settings Display No and the graph or graphs to hide. Figure 5-24 shows a hidden graph represented by a shaded area as well as showing how, when a graphic is included in a text range, Wysiwyg wraps text . When graphs are not displayed Wysiwyg behaves faster. Wysiwyg and 1-2-3 also perform faster when the display mode is set with :Display Mode Text. Graphics do not appear

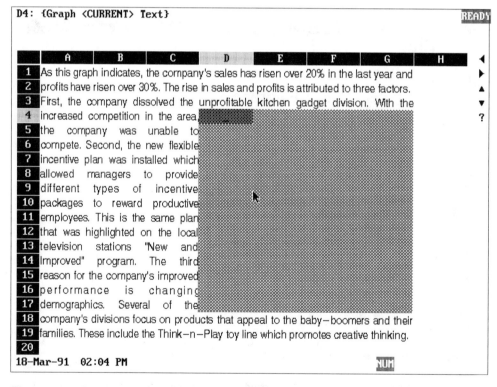

Figure 5-24: Shaded graph in the middle of a text range.

USING WYSIWYG WITH 1-2-3

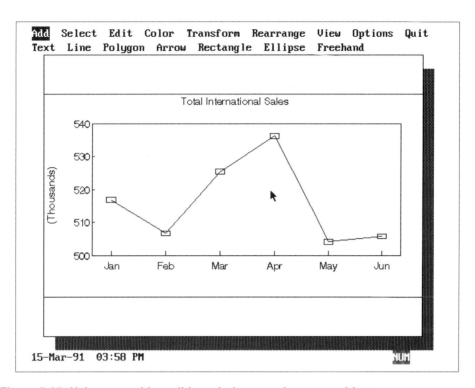

Figure 5-25: Using a graphics editing window to enhance graphics.

in this mode. You can return to the default graphics mode by selecting :Display Mode Graphics. You can also restore graphs to display on the worksheet in a graphics display mode by selecting :Graph Settings Display No and then the graph or graphs to display.

Creating a Graphic With Wysiwyg

You can also use Wysiwyg to create graphics. Graphics editing in Wysiwyg allows you to create new graphic images or to add enhancements to other graph types. New graphic images are created by adding a blank graphic to the worksheet and editing the graphic to add objects. Graph enhancements are made to any of the other types of graphics. You can enter the Wysiwyg graphics editing window by selecting :Graph Edit and the graphic to edit. This displays a graphics editing window like the one in Figure 5-24. Once you are in the graphics editing window, the only way you

PUBLISHING 1-2-3

can return to 1-2-3 and Wysiwyg is to select Quit. Pressing ESC multiple times will only return you to the initial graphics editing window. Figure 5-26 shows the purpose of each option in the graphics editing menu.

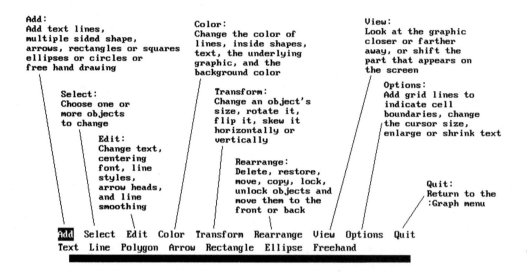

Figure 5-26: The graphics editing window menu and its functions.

In this graphics editing window, the lines in the drawing area represent the boundaries of the graphic. The menu lets you add and alter the graphic. Each part of the graph is called an object. To change an object, you must select it by clicking on it or by using the Select command. When an object is selected, small squares, or handles, appear on its sides. You can use other commands to change the selected object's appearance.

One of the objects you may want to modify is the underlying graphic. The underlying definition graphic is the original 1-2-3 graph or Metafile image that the graphic uses. For example, in Figure 5-23, the underlying graphic is the tiger stored in the file TIGER.CGM. With this file you can only make limited changes, such as changing colors or fonts. The underlying graphic's colors are set by selecting the Colors Map command. Then you can select one of the eight colors the graph uses and select a new color from the palette. The enhancements you can make to 1-2-3 graphs are more extensive. Although 1-2-3 graphs initially use font 1 for all the graph text, you can use formatting sequence to change the font. However, do not use formatting sequences in graphs you plan to save as .PIC file for use with Print Graph since these formatting sequences are not supported.

When you are creating or enhancing a graphic, you will want to add objects by selecting Add and the particular object. Table 5-4 shows the objects you can add and how you add them. You can also use the SHIFT key while adding objects. When you press SHIFT as you move the cursor, rectangles become squares, ellipses become circles and lines in lines, polylines, arrows and freehand objects are only drawn in 45-degree angles.

You may find that you frequently want to change the size of text with graphics. Since you are limited to using the same fonts that the worksheet uses, you may want to make the worksheet text smaller or larger. To do so, select Options Font-Magnification and then enter a number less than 100 to make all of the graphic's text smaller. A number more than 100 will enlarge the graphic's text.

Creating graphics with Wysiwyg has advantages and disadvantages. On the positive side, Wysiwyg may be more accessible than other graphics packages. Also, it enables you to see immediately how the graphic will appear in the worksheet. Wysiwyg includes many graphic editing features you expect from more expensive graphics packages.

One of the disadvantages of creating graphs in Wysiwyg is that transferring graphics created and enhanced in the add-in to other worksheets is difficult. Also, you cannot transfer the graphic images to other packages as you can .PIC files created by the 1-2-3 Graph Save command.

PUBLISHING 1-2-3

If you need to transfer a graphic that you have created or enhanced with Wysiwyg, or if you need multiple copies of a graphic you have created with Wysiwyg in the same worksheet, you can import the graphic in a format file using the :Special Import Graphs command. The steps for doing so are covered in "A Closer Look: Transferring and Copying Graphics." :Special Import Graphs only imports graphics without affecting the other Wysiwyg formats added to the current worksheet. The :Special commands are used for moving and duplicating Wysiwyg formats and graphics. You can also use this command to import formats from other worksheets, export formats to other worksheets, copy formatting information to another worksheet location, or move formatting information to another worksheet location. The use of :Special Import Graphs does not work for current or named graphs since importing the graphics from a format file imports the graph placeholders such as Current or the graph name as well as any graphics editing done in Wysiwyg.

A CLOSER LOOK

Transferring and Copying Graphics

To transfer or copy a graphic, follow these steps:

1. Save the file with the graphic to copy to a temporary file so you will not accidentally write over your original.

2. Remove the worksheet data and other graphics that you do not want to transfer from this temporary file.

3. Save this temporary file.

4. Retrieve the worksheet that you want to bring the graphic into.

5. Select :Special Import Graphs and the temporary filename containing the graphic.

6. Move the copy of the added graphic to wherever you want it.

Table 5-4
Objects You Can Add in a Text Graph

Graph Object	How to Add This Type of Object
Text	Enter the text (including any formatting sequences) and move the text and cursor to where you want it on the graphic and press ENTER. This font uses the same fonts the worksheet uses.
Line	Move to each point of the line and press the space bar. After selecting the last point of the line, press ENTER.
Polygon	Move to each point of the polygon and press the space bar. After selecting the last point of the polygon, press ENTER and Wysiwyg draws the line from the first point of the shape to the last.
Arrow	Move to each point of the arrow and press the space bar. After selecting the last point of the arrow, press ENTER.
Rectangle	Move to first corner of the rectangle, press the space bar, move to the rectangle's opposite corner, and press ENTER.

PUBLISHING 1-2-3

Table 5-4

 Ellipse — Move to first corner of the rectangle the ellipse will fill, press the space bar, move to the rectangle's opposite corner, and press ENTER. The ellipse uses the vertical height and horizontal width to determine the shape of the ellipse.

 Freehand — Move to where you want to start drawing, press the space bar and move the cursor to where you want the line drawn, pressing ENTER when finished.

CHAPTER 6

Using Allways with 1-2-3

If you read through the Wysiwyg features in Chapter 5, you will want to skip to Chapter 7 at this time. Allways is an alternative to the newer Wysiwyg add-in that will only be of interest if you are using an older version of 1-2-3. The Allways add-in was originally marketed as a separate add- in for 1-2-3. This add-in was included with the release of 2.2. Allways adds spreadsheet publishing capabilities to 1-2-3. With Allways you can utilize all the features of your printer including fonts and other typeface enhancements. You will find this chapter useful whether you purchased a copy of Allways separately or acquired it as part of your 1-2-3 purchase.

This discussion of the Allways features is detailed enough to help you enhance your worksheets. The organization of this chapter conforms closely to the design objectives discussed in Chapter 2, making it easy for you to cross reference to the types of changes you have decided to make to your information. The Allways features are sufficient to give you superior control over your layout. This control includes the ability to use all the features of your printer effectively and to combine text and graphs on the same page.

Installing and Attaching Allways

Whether you purchased Allways as an add-in or it came as part of your 1-2-3 package, it must be installed separately. Unlike 1-2-3, you cannot run Allways without a hard disk.

PUBLISHING 1-2-3

The Installation Process

After you install 1-2-3, you can install Allways by putting the first Allways disk in drive A, making drive A active, and typing AWSETUP. Once AWSETUP is loaded, it guides you through the selections. These steps are listed in "A Closer Look: Steps for Installing Allways."

A CLOSER LOOK

Steps For Installing Allways

1) Put the first Allways disk in drive A.

2) Type A: and press ENTER to make drive A the active drive.

3) Type AWSETUP and press ENTER to start the installation program.

4) Press ENTER after reading the initial screen.

5) Press ENTER to select First-Time Installation.

6) Enter the drive and directory information for the location of your 1-2-3 program files.

7) Select Yes if the display driver shown is correct, or select No and then the correct display driver from the list.

8) Select the printer you are using from the list.

9) Enter the disks in drive A as Allways prompts for them so Allways can copy the printer information from the correct floppy to your hard disk.

10) Select No to only select one printer or select Yes and repeat steps 8 and 9 to add another printer.

11) Enter the disks in drive A as Allways prompts for them so Allways can copy the fonts from the floppies to your hard disk.

12) Select Exit to DOS from the main Allways menu and select Yes to confirm that you want to leave the AWSETUP program.

USING ALLWAYS WITH 1-2-3

Attaching Allways

You only need to attach Allways once in each 1-2-3 session. You can even set 1-2-3 to attach Allways automatically. The steps for attaching Allways are shown in "A Closer Look: Steps for Attaching Allways."

To set 1-2-3 to attach Allways automatically, choose /Worksheet Global Default Other Add-In Set, select a number 1 through 8, specify ALLWAYS.ADN as the add-in that you want to attach when 1-2-3 starts, and select the hot key you want this add-in to use. Once you update 1-2-3's configuration file with the /Worksheet Global Update command, this selection remains in effect unless you choose /Worksheet Global Default Other Add-In Cancel and select the number associated with Allways.

Activating Allways

Activating Allways is easy. Simply press the hot-key combination if you assigned one. You can also activate the Add-in menu by typing /Add-In (Release 2.2 only) or pressing ALT-F10, selecting Invoke and Allways. Your Allways selections affect only the appearance of the worksheet—without affecting the data. Allways provides a WYSIWYG (what-you-see-is-what-you-get) display which shows the worksheet as it will appear when printed. The mode indicator changes to ALLWAYS to indicate that your selections will affect how Allways displays and prints your worksheet data.

A CLOSER LOOK

Steps For Attaching the Allways Add-in

1) Type /Add-In or press ALT-F10.

2) Select Attach and select Allways.

3) Select No-Key or one of the hot keys that you can later use to display the Allways menu.

4) Select Quit to return to 1-2-3's READY mode or Invoke to display Allways' menu.

PUBLISHING 1-2-3

The top line of the control panel displays the formatting added to the current cell. As in 1-2-3, the next two lines display the menu. Also as in 1-2-3, this menu is activated by typing /. The main Allways menu is shown in Figure 6-1. Although some of the selections that you see look the same as the ones in 1-2-3's main menu, many of the options in lower level menus are different. The Allways features that you add to your worksheet are saved in a separate format file when you save the worksheet with 1-2-3's /File Save command. The formatting file will have a .ALL extension.

When you want to exit Allways to edit your worksheet, use the /Quit or /1-2-3 command. You can also press ESC from the ALLWAYS mode. The Allways interface will disappear but it is available simply by pressing its hot-key. Just as you cannot change worksheet data while you are in Allways, you cannot change the Allways worksheet formatting while you are in 1-2-3.

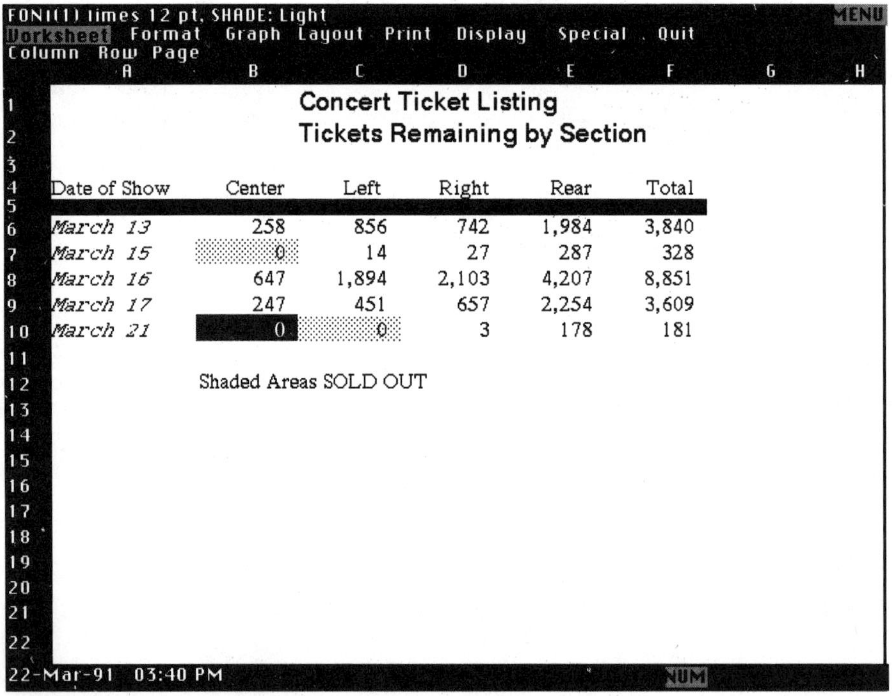

Figure 6-1: 1-2-3 worksheet with Allways menu.

206

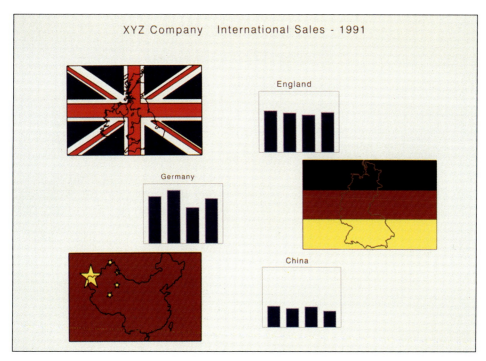

Figure 1: Three 1-2-3 bar graphs with clip art flags.

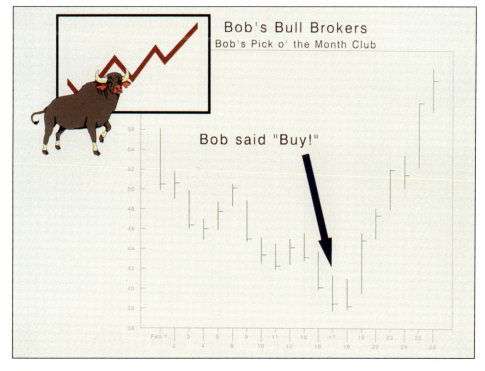

Figure 2: 1-2-3 High-Low-Open-Close graph with clip art.

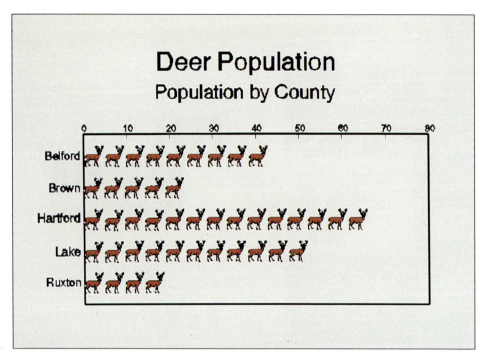

Figure 3: Vertical 1-2-3 bar graph with deer added.

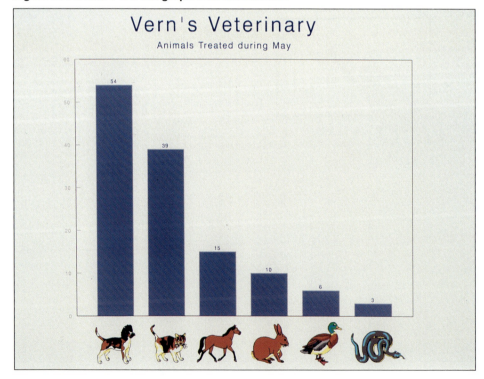

Figure 4: Bar graph created with 1-2-3 and enhanced with clip art.

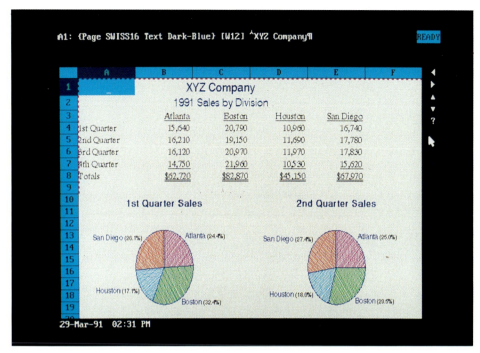

Figure 5: 1-2-3 Release 2.3 Wysiwyg screen with graphs added.

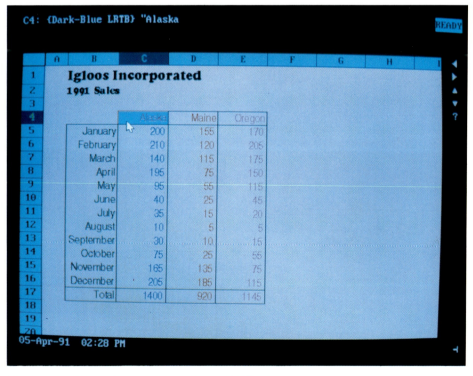

Figure 6: Color text on a 1-2-3 Release 2.3 Wysiwyg screen.

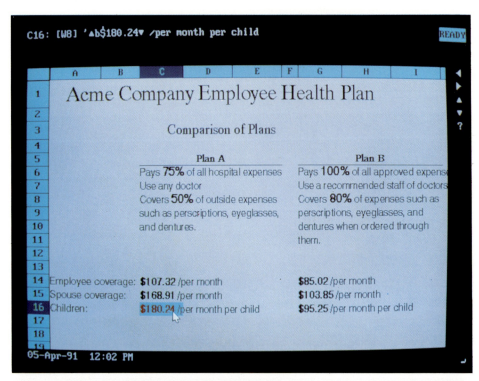

Figure 7: Different size fonts on a Wysiwyg screen.

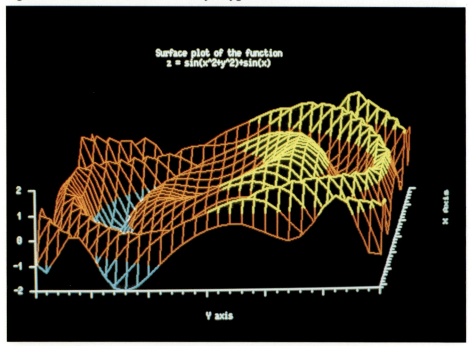

Figure 8: Surface chart created with the Intex 3D Graphics add-in.

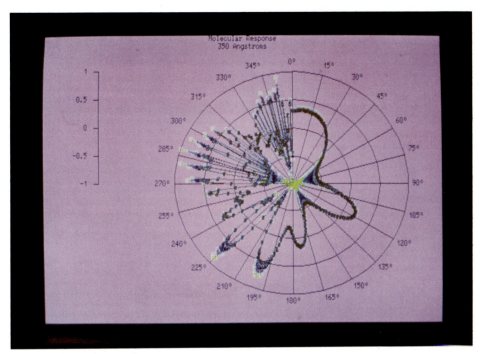

Figure 9: Polar chart using 2D Graphics add-in by Intex.

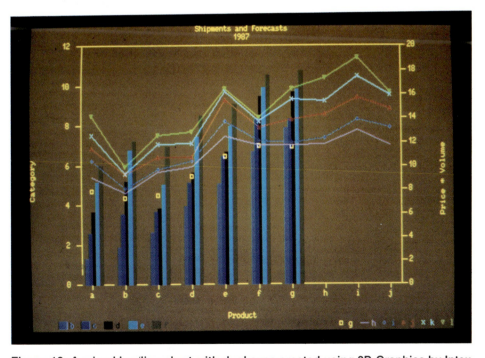

Figure 10: A mixed bar/line chart with dual axes created using 2D Graphics by Intex.

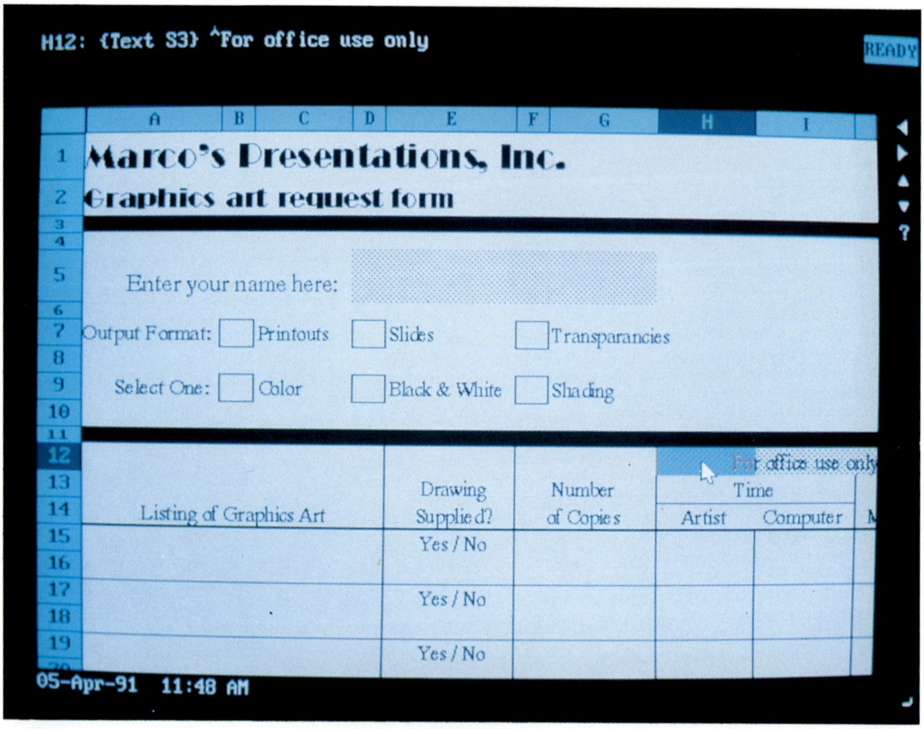

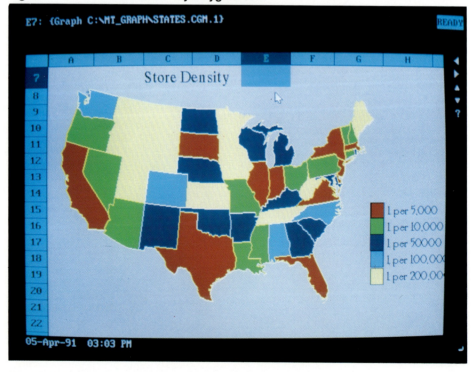

Figure 11: Lines added to the Wysiwyg screen.

Figure 12: Graphic images added to the Wysiwyg screen.

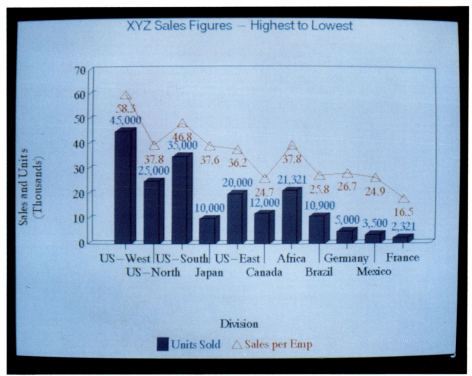

Figure 15: Mixed graph created with 1-2-3 Release 2.3.

Figure 16: Combining graphics and text with Allways.

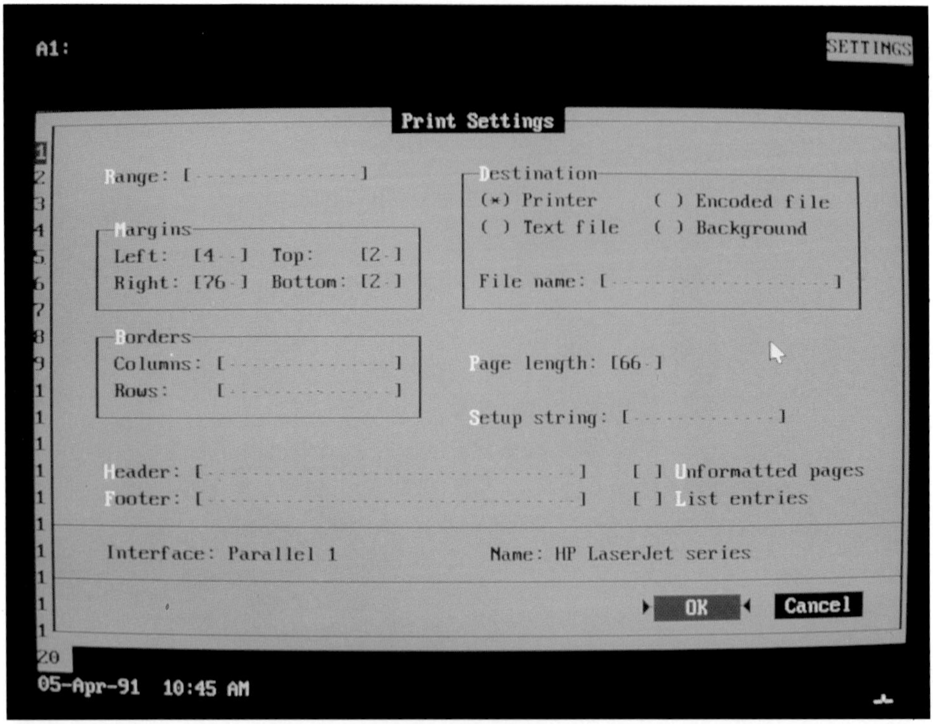

Figure 13: Dialog boxes from 1-2-3 Release 2.3.

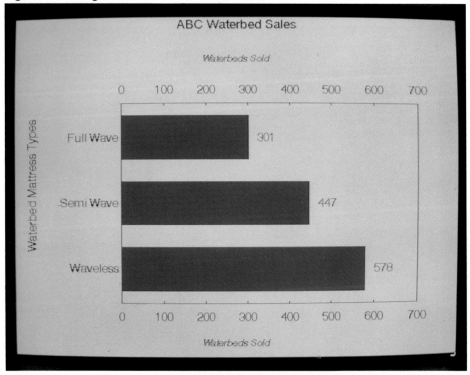

Figure 14: Horizontal bar graph created with 1-2-3 Release 2.3.

USING ALLWAYS WITH 1-2-3

Printing in Allways

Printing in Allways is similar to printing from 1-2-3. The steps are summarized in "A Closer Look: Summary of Steps For Printing." When you print from 1-2-3, your output will not include the newly-added formatting. To add the spreadsheet publishing enhancements you have made in Allways, you must print using Allways. To do so, set the range to print with the /Print Range Set command and then select a range just as you would for the /Print Printer Range command in 1-2-3. When you select a range, Allways displays dashed lines to indicate where the output will be broken into pages. You can remove this range setting with the /Print Range Clear command.

Once the range is selected, you can print the worksheet by selecting /Print Go or /Print File. The /Print Go command prints to the printer. When you select /Print File, you must also supply a file name to which Allways will add a .ENC extension. This file will store the printer information.

When you print with Allways, you do not need to advance or to align the paper as you do in 1-2-3. Allways finishes each print job by advancing the paper to the top of the form. Allways also assumes that the paper in the printer starts at the top of the page.

While selecting the range and telling Allways to start printing are the two basic steps, you may need to tell Allways about the printer you are using with the /Print Configuration command. To select one of the installed printers, select Printer and one of the listed printers. You may need to select Interface to tell the program how the printer is connected to the computer. To use an additional font cartridge in your worksheet, select Cartridge and the installed cartridge. You can also print at different quality levels by selecting Resolution and specifying one of the listed options. The Bin option tells Allways which paper slot in the printer to use. Some of these options will not appear if they do not apply to your printer.

PUBLISHING 1-2-3

Allways displays the worksheet as it will appear when printed. Once you select the range to print, the dashed lines indicate page boundaries for each page. If you need to look at the worksheet from different perspectives, choose /Display Zoom and one of the options: Tiny, Small, Large, or Huge. Figure 6-2 shows the worksheet magnified by selecting /Display Zoom Huge. Now the Allways screen looks like a magnified version of the printed worksheet. Selecting Normal returns the display magnification to the default. Allways also lets you expand and reduce the display using function keys. Each time you press F4, you reduce the size of the display and each time you press ALT-F4 (SHIFT-F4 in some releases of Allways), you enlarge it.

```
FONT (1) Times 12 pt, SHADE: Light                              ALLWAYS
B10: 0
              A           B          C          D          E
1                            Concert Ticket Listing
2                          Tickets Remaining by Section
3
4     Date of Show      Center      Left      Right       Rear
5
6     March 13           258        856        742       1,984
7     March 15             0         14         27         287
8     March 16           647      1,894      2,103       4,207
9     March 17           247        451        657       2,254
10    March 21             0          0          3         178
11
12                     Shaded Areas SOLD OUT
13
14
15
16
22-Mar-91  03:42 PM
```

Figure 6-2: Close-up view of a worksheet.

Changing Page Layout Options With Allways

The appearance of your pages depends as much on the amount of data on the page as on the amount of white space allotted. Layout is determined by the page size, margins and headers, footers, and borders. You can save page layouts to reuse them, or you can make them the default for all worksheets. You can also select which pages of the output you will print. Consult the "Checklist: Layout Options" to be certain that you have made all desired adjustments before printing.

Unlike 1-2-3, in Allways you make most of your page layout changes from the Layout menu. Figure 6-3 shows the Layout menu selections as well as the setting sheet that shows the current layout settings. One main difference between Allways and 1-2-3 is that 1-2-3 selections are measured in characters, whereas Allways selections are measured in inches. Once you start using proportional fonts—where the number of characters per inch varies—you will find that measuring in inches provides a much more meaningful look at page layout.

Setting the Page Size

Allways will use any page size that your printer accommodates. Allways will list your printer's page sizes as well as Custom so you can print non-standard pages. For example, if a Hewlett-Packard LaserJet printer is selected, you can select from Standard (8 1/2" by 11"), Legal (8 1/2" by 14"), Executive (7 1/4" by

A CLOSER LOOK

Summary of Steps For Printing

1) Select /Layout and check the settings sheet to see if there are any layout settings you want to change.

2) Select Quit to return to ALLWAYS mode.

3) Select /Print Range Set.

4) Select the worksheet range to print and press ENTER.

5) Select Configuration and check that the correct printer and printer settings are listed under in the settings sheet, otherwise, change the appropriate settings.

6) Select Quit to return to the /Print menu.

7) Select Go to print to the printer or File and a filename to print to a file.

✔ CHECKLIST

Layout Options

✔ Adjusted the top, bottom, left and right margins.

✔ Added a header and/or a footer.

✔ Added row or column borders at the top, left and bottom.

✔ Selected the correct page size.

✔ Checked the first and last page Wysiwyg will print.

---

10 1/2"), Fanfold A4 (8 1/2" by 12"), International A4 (8.27" by 11.69"), International B5 (7.1" by 10.2"), and Wide (14" by 11").

To change the paper size:

1. Type / to activate the Allways menu.

2. Select Layout.

3. Select Page-Size.

4. Select one of the defined options or Custom. Like all list boxes in Allways, select an option by typing the corresponding number or by using the arrow keys to highlight the option and then pressing ENTER. If you select Custom you will need to type your page's width and length in inches.

Setting the Margins

The default left and right margin settings allow for one inch of white space on all sides. Any setting from 0 to 99.99" is acceptable although laser printers require at least a small margin on all sides. Set margins by selecting /Layout Margins, the side where you want to set the margin and typing the appropriate number of inches.

Selective Printing

Although you can control the amount of data printed with the range command, this is not a good method for replacing several pages in the middle of a report. If you select the desired pages as a range, the first of these pages will print as page 1. If you retain the earlier selection of all the data you can use the Print Settings Begin and End commands to specify the first

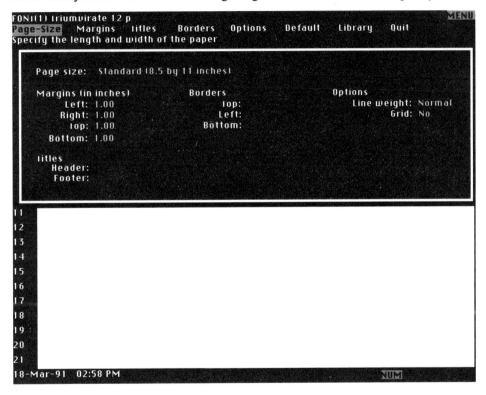

Figure 6-3: The Allways /Layout menu.

and last pages that you want to print. This way you can replace the error-ridden pages. After selecting Begin or End, enter the number of the first or last page you want to print. You can also print multiple copies of the pages by selecting Copies and specifying the appropriate number. /Print Settings are not saved with the worksheet so Allways will return to printing one copy of all subsequent pages.

PUBLISHING 1-2-3

Creating a Library of Page Layouts

Once you've defined a page layout you may want to save it for future reports. Creating libraries of layouts will save a significant amount of time for most users. This approach ensures greater consistency among reports without your having to check the appearance of the original.

To save the current print layout for later use:

1. Type / to activate the Allways menu.

2. Select Layout, Library, and Save.

3. Type the name of the file where you will store the layout settings and press ENTER. Allways will save all of the settings made with /Layout commands in this file.

You can use a saved layout with any worksheet by selecting /Layout Library Retrieve and the layout's file name. If you want to use the print layout as the default for all new worksheets, select /Layout Default Update. When you want to return a print layout to the default, select /Layout Default Restore.

Changing the Page Orientation

Allways supports the use of both portrait and landscape printing. Portrait uses an 8 1/2"-by-11" sheet of paper by printing across the 8 1/2 inches. When printed in landscape, your output will print sideways and across the 11-inch side. Of course, your printer must support both print modes and all popular laser printers do. To switch print modes, press / and select Print Configuration Orientation then choose either Portrait or Landscape. Figure 6-4 shows worksheets printed with the two different options.

USING ALLWAYS WITH 1-2-3

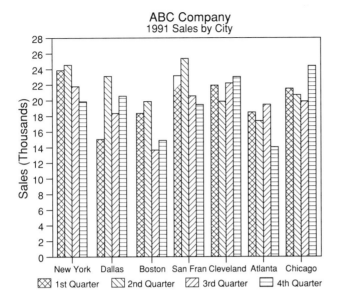

Figure 6-4: Printing in Portrait and Landscape mode with Allways.

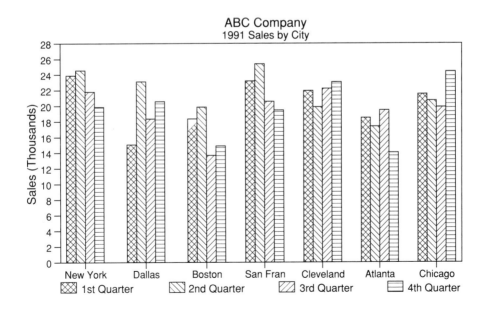

Adding Headers and Footers

Headers and footers add a professional appearance to reports. Placing page numbers and dates in headers easily identifies the latest copy of a report and can be helpful if pages should fall out of sequence. "A Closer Look: A Few Quick Steps For Adding a Header or Footer" covers the basics of adding a header or footer.

Headers and footers are entered in Allways in much the same way that they are entered in 1-2-3, but Allways will not automatically read your 1-2-3 headers and they must be re-entered. You can enter headers with up to 240 characters. In Allways you can access the header and footer option with the /Layout Titles command. This command is equivalent to 1-2-3's /Print Printer Options Header or Footer. Unlike Release 2.2 of 1-2-3, you cannot use the backslash and a cell address to use the contents of the cell as the header or footer. But as in 1-2-3, you can use "#" to include the current page number and "@" to include the current system date. Allways starts printing with the page number set in the /Print Settings First option. If you use this command and enter 9, the first page uses 9 in place of #, the second page uses 10, and so on.

As with 1-2-3, you can enter three separate sections in Allways' headers and footers. The split vertical bar character (!) is used as the dividing character between information placed in the left, center, and right sections of the header. If you enter data in a header or footer without entering a split vertical bar, the entire contents of the header or footer is placed at the left side

---

A CLOSER LOOK

A Few Quick Steps For Adding a Header or Footer

To add a header or footer:

1) Select /Layout Titles Header or /Layout Titles Footer.

2) Type the text you want on the top or bottom of each page. It can include these special characters:

\# for the page number.

@ for the current date.

¦ for dividing the text into left-aligned, centered and right aligned sections.

3) Press ENTER then select Quit twice to return to READY mode.

of the header or footer. To center your entry, start with a split vertical bar. To place your entry at the far right side, place two split vertical bar characters at the beginning of the entry. Here is an example of how vertical bars align header and footer text:

NORTHEAST BRANCH|Page -#-|Date: @

When you print a report with this header, it will look like the one in Figure 6-5.

As in 1-2-3 when you use a header or footer, it will print beneath the top margin or above the bottom margin. Two blank lines separate the header or footer from the body text. When you want to remove a header or footer that you have added in Allways, select /Layout Titles Clear and then select Header, Footer or Both to remove one or both.

NORTHEAST BRANCH   Page -1-   Date: 25-Mar-91

ABC Company
1991 Sales by City

	New York	Dallas	Boston	San Fran	Cleveland
1st Quarter	23,910	15,070	18,425	23,160	21,940
2nd Quarter	24,625	23,145	19,780	25,410	19,845
3rd Quarter	21,845	18,430	13,565	20,605	22,310
4th Quarter	19,860	20,625	14,950	19,535	23,100

Figure 6-5: Using #, @ and | special characters produce these results in headers.

Adding Borders

In 1-2-3, when you want to print the same columns or rows on each page, you use the /Print Options Borders Columns or Rows command. In Allways, you use the /Layout Borders Top or Left command. Allways has another option, Bottom, which lets you select rows appearing at the bottom of each page. As in 1-2-3, after selecting Top, Left, or Bottom in Allways, you only have to select one cell from each column or row that you want to include in the border. Also, note that you should not include the range used by the borders in the range to print since Allways will print the range once as a border and then again as part of the print range. When you want to remove print borders, select /Layout Titles Borders Clear, and then Top, Left, Bottom, or All to remove one border or both.

Adding Page Breaks

Page breaks can be inserted at any location regardless of how much space is left on the current page. This feature allows you to place charts, tables, and other important information on separate pages.

To add a page break from within Allways at the location of the cell pointer you can use the /Worksheet command. To add a page break at the current row, type / then select Worksheet Page Row. To add a page break at the current column, use /Worksheet Page Column. Figure 6-6 shows a worksheet where a page break has been added at both the rows and columns. You will also note the order of printing shown in that figure. The page breaks that you add with this command are used in addition to the page breaks Allways adds.

Line Spacing

Although Allways does not have an option for line spacing, you can create that effect by setting row heights. To set a row's height, select /Worksheet Row Set-Height and change the height of the row. By doubling the current row height, you can make a range of text look double- or triple-spaced. Figure 6-7 shows an image that has

USING ALLWAYS WITH 1-2-3

several row heights increased. Normally Allways sets the row height to be slightly taller than the tallest font in the row. When you select /Worksheet Row Auto, this is the row height Allways will set the row height depending on the font selected.

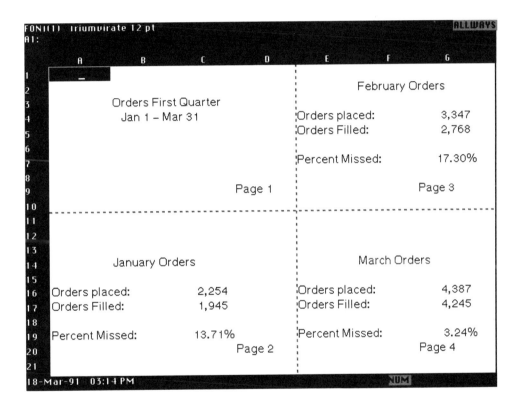

Figure 6-6: Allways displays both page breaks it adds and you add.

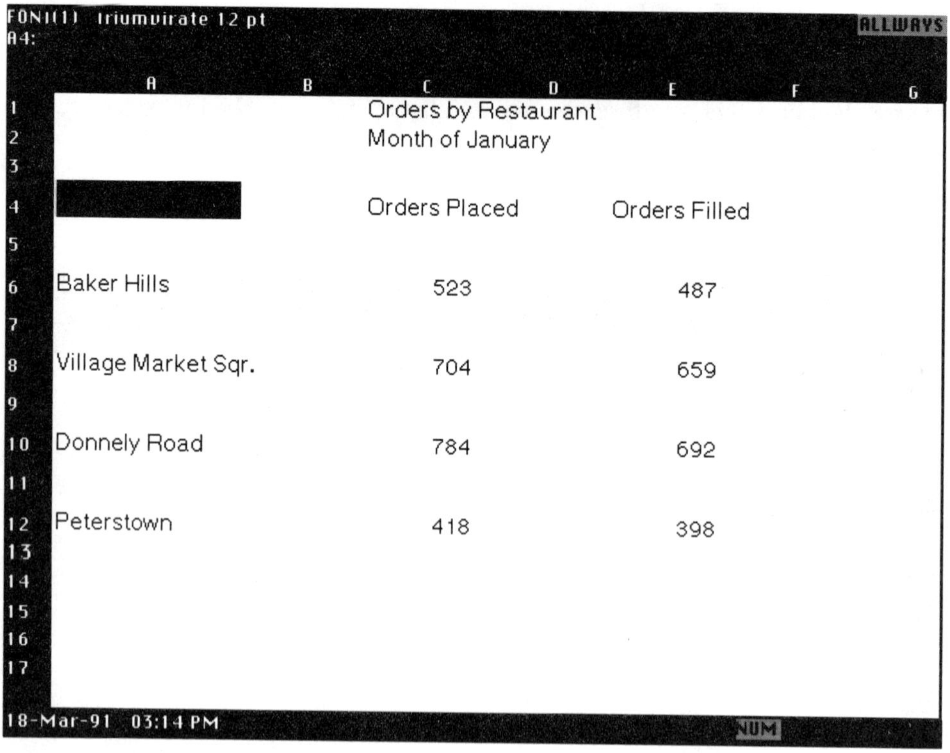

PUBLISHING 1-2-3

```
FONT(1) Triumvirate 12 pt                              ALLWAYS
A4:
         A        B       C        D       E       F       G
 1                       Orders by Restaurant
 2                       Month of January
 3
 4                       Orders Placed      Orders Filled
 5
 6      Baker Hills          523                 487
 7
 8      Village Market Sqr.  704                 659
 9
10      Donnely Road         784                 692
11
12      Peterstown           418                 398
13
14
15
16
17
18-Mar-91  03:14 PM                              NUM
```

Figure 6-7: Setting multiple rows to different heights.

Changing the Type

There are many different options for changing type when printing a 1-2-3 document from Allways. You can choose another font to change the typeface or size. You can also choose formatting options that affect font style. Allways puts all the capabilities of your printer at your fingertips making it easy to use both soft fonts and printer fonts without becoming an expert in the entry of setup strings. Allways also includes shortcuts, called accelerator keys, that make formatting such as changing fonts easier. We will discuss the use of accelerator keys later in this chapter.

Selecting a Different Typeface

When you print with 1-2-3, your printer uses its default font. But most printers can print a wide range of fonts using either built-in font information or font-specific software. Allways can print any of the fonts your printer provides as well as with the three font styles that come with Allways. Varying the fonts in a worksheet will improve the overall look and help emphasize key points. You can use up to eight specially select fonts in any one worksheet. You can use the fonts Allways initially assigns, change them, make a new of fonts the default, or create libraries of font sets. You can assign the eight fonts available to any worksheet range. "A Closer Look: Changing the Font of a Worksheet Range" summarizes the steps for changing fonts in a worksheet.

The current eight fonts the worksheet uses in Allways are listed when you select /Format Font. The numbers 1 through 8 are assigned to each font and appear beside them. When you want to apply one of the fonts to a worksheet range, you can select that font's number, Use and the appropriate range. The worksheet display will show the font as it will appear when printed. Figure 6-8 shows a worksheet enhanced by the variation in fonts.

When you assign fonts in a worksheet, Allways remembers the font number—rather than font name—assigned to cells. This means that when you assign font 5 which is initially Times 10 point to a cell, Allways

A CLOSER LOOK

Changing the Font of a Worksheet Range

1) Select /Format Font.

2) Select a number 1 through 8 representing the font you want to add.

3) Select Use.

4) Select the worksheet range to use this font.

PUBLISHING 1-2-3

remembers font 5 is assigned to the cell, rather than "Times 10 point." Later, if you change the typeface, point size or other attributes of font 5, all worksheet data that uses that font changes to the new selection. The top line in the control panel displays the font number assigned to the cell followed by the description of the corresponding font.

```
FONT(1) Times 12 pt                                                  ALLWAYS
A4: 'Date of Show

              A         B         C         D         E         F         G    H
                             Concert Ticket Listing
                          Tickets Remaining by Section

    Date of Show      Center     Left      Right     Rear      Total

    March 13           258        856       742      1,984     3,840
    March 15             0         14        27        287       328
    March 16           647      1,894     2,103      4,207     8,851
    March 17           247        451       657      2,254     3,609
    March 21             0          0         3        178       181

18-Mar-91  03:14 PM                                               NUM
```

Figure 6-8: Worksheet using multiple typefaces and sizes.

Initially, the entire worksheet uses Font 1. And, while you can reassign fonts to worksheet ranges, as we've described, you cannot reassign fonts to headers and footers. You can only change the header or footer font by assigning different attributes to Font 1. To change the typeface assigned to a font number, select /Format Font, the font number to change, and Replace. Next select a typeface from the display. Allways provides Times, Triumvirate, and Courier typefaces as soft fonts. These fonts appear

USING ALLWAYS WITH 1-2-3

in Figure 6-9. The printer fonts are fonts built into your printer, or installed through a cartridge (after selecting /Print Configurations Cartridge). After you select a typeface, select a character size from the display. Character size is measured in points or pitch. A point is 1/72 of an inch. Characters measured in pitch are the same height but have a different number of characters across the line width. Figure 6-10 shows different point and pitch sizes. After you select a character size, the size is applied to the font that matches a specific font number. All worksheet data assigned to that number will appear in the newly selected font, at the new type size. When you change a font in the current font set, it only affects the current worksheet since each worksheet has its own independent font set.

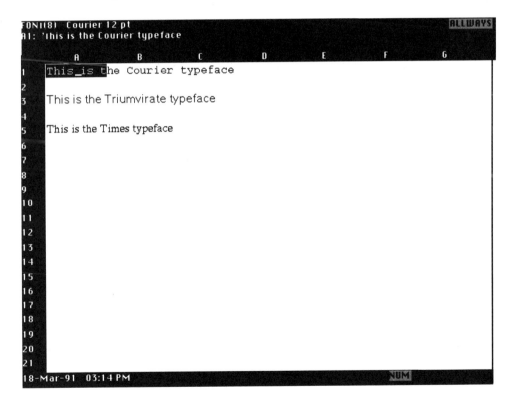

Figure 6-9: Different typefaces available through Allways.

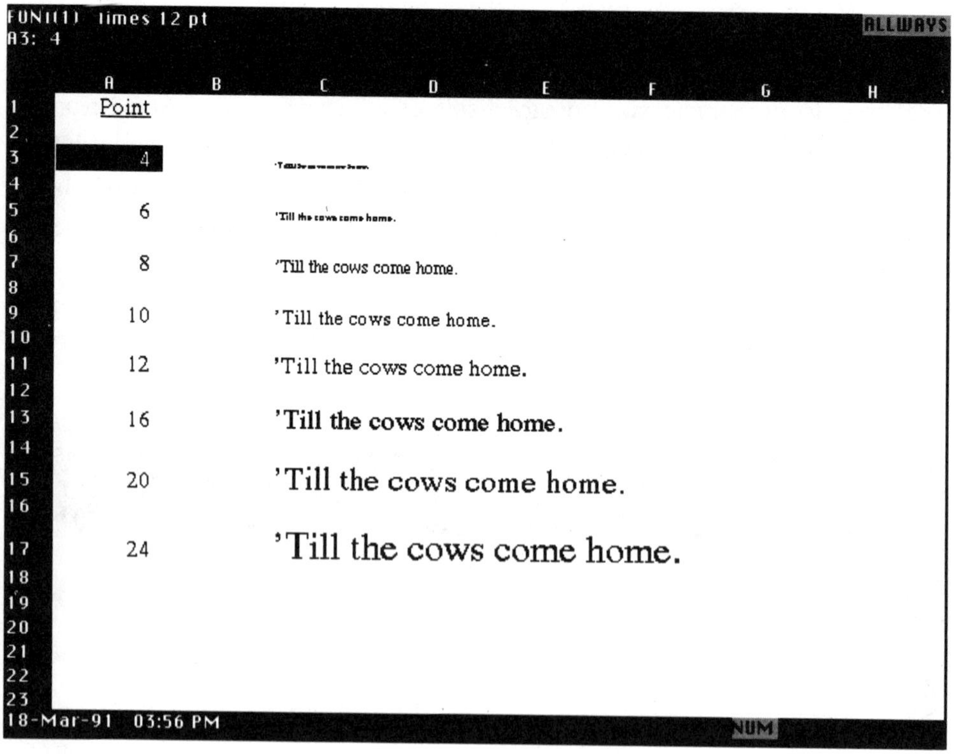

PUBLISHING 1-2-3

```
FONT(1)  times 12 pt                                    ALLWAYS
A3: 4

         A      B      C      D      E      F      G      H
  1    Point
  2
  3      4      ·T...
  4
  5      6      'Till the cows come home.
  6
  7      8      'Till the cows come home.
  8
  9     10      'Till the cows come home.
 10
 11     12      'Till the cows come home.
 12
 13     16      'Till the cows come home.
 14
 15     20      'Till the cows come home.
 16
 17     24      'Till the cows come home.
 18
 19
 20
 21
 22
 23
18-Mar-91  03:56 PM                                      NUM
```

Figure 6-10: Different point sizes.

If you use the same font selections for several worksheets, you may want to create a font library. These libraries can be retrieved into a worksheet and used to replace the worksheet's selected fonts. To save a font library, select /Format Font Library Save and type a file name. To retrieve a font library select /Format Font Library Retrieve and select a file name. You can erase libraries you no longer need with /Format Font Library Erase.

You can create a set of default fonts for new worksheets by selecting /Format Font Default Update. You can return to this default font set at any time by selecting /Format Font Default Restore.

Selecting a Different Type Style

Besides changing the typeface to improve a worksheet's appearance, you can add other types of formatting, such as boldface and underline. The /Format Bold Set, /Format Underline Single, and /Format Underline Double commands add styles to the text font. After selecting one of these commands, select the range of text for formatting changes. The control panel will show "Bold" when boldfaced cells display are highlighted, "Underline" when underlined cells are highlighted, and so on. Figure 6-11 shows a worksheet that uses boldface and underline commands. You can see from this worksheet that single underlining underscores only the characters within the entry, whereas double underlining covers the width of the cell. /Format Bold Clear or /Format Underline Clear remove formatting. You can also select /Format Reset but this removes all formatting added with /Format commands.

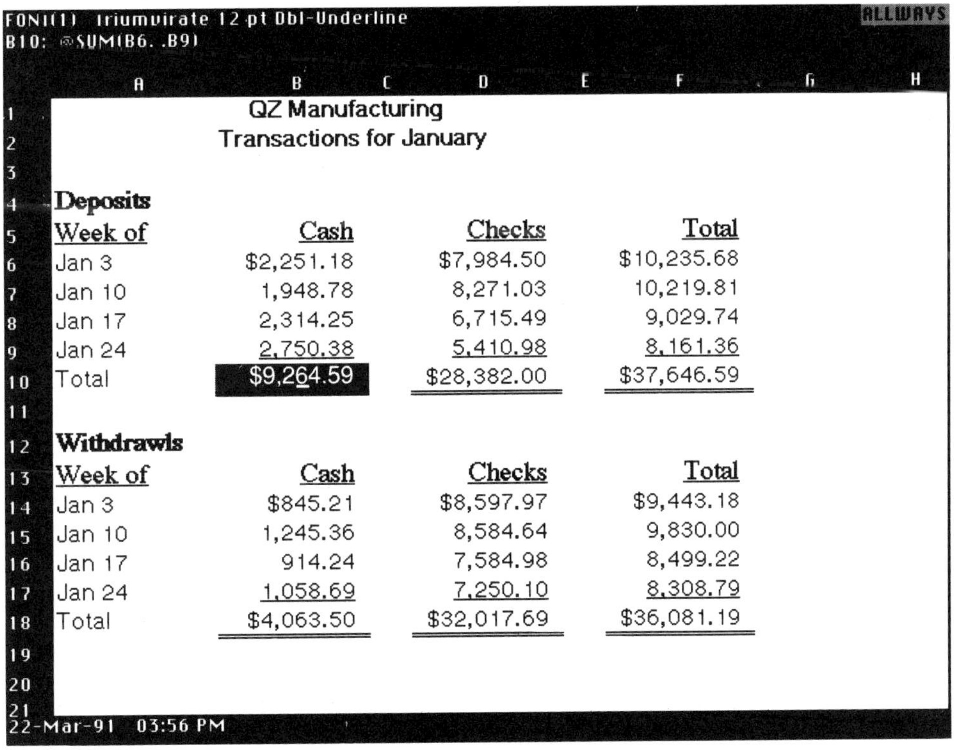

FONT(1) Triumvirate 12 pt Dbl-Underline ALLWAYS
B10: @SUM(B6..B9)

	A	B	C	D	E	F	G	H
1		QZ Manufacturing						
2		Transactions for January						
3								
4	**Deposits**							
5	Week of	Cash		Checks		Total		
6	Jan 3	$2,251.18		$7,984.50		$10,235.68		
7	Jan 10	1,948.78		8,271.03		10,219.81		
8	Jan 17	2,314.25		6,715.49		9,029.74		
9	Jan 24	2,750.38		5,410.98		8,161.36		
10	Total	$9,264.59		$28,382.00		$37,646.59		
11								
12	**Withdrawls**							
13	Week of	Cash		Checks		Total		
14	Jan 3	$845.21		$8,597.97		$9,443.18		
15	Jan 10	1,245.36		8,584.64		9,830.00		
16	Jan 17	914.24		7,584.98		8,499.22		
17	Jan 24	1,058.69		7,250.10		8,308.79		
18	Total	$4,063.50		$32,017.69		$36,081.19		
19								
20								
21								

22-Mar-91 03:56 PM

Figure 6-11: Using boldface and underlining to enhance a worksheet.

PUBLISHING 1-2-3

Using Accelerator Keys to Apply Formats

Besides using /Format Bold and /Format Font to apply formats to worksheet cells, Allways has accelerator keys that let you add formats by selecting a range and pressing a key combination. The accelerator keys and the Allways commands they represent are shown in Table 6-1. Some of these accelerator keys perform a cycle of features. For example, if you press ALT-U for cells without any underlining, Allways adds single underlining to the selected range. If the cells currently have single underlining, pressing ALT-U will change that to double underlining. If you press ALT-U on cells with double underlining, Allways removes underlining.

To apply an accelerator key or use an Allways menu command on a range of text, move the cell pointer to the first cell of the range and type a period. This displays ANC in the status line to indicate that you have anchored a corner of a range. With one corner anchored, move the cell pointer to the opposite corner to select the entire range. Press an accelerator key or enter an Allways menu command. The range remains selected after a menu command or accelerator key is applied but the range is no longer anchored. Thus, as soon as you move the cell pointer, the selected range becomes deselected.

Using Color Effectively

For most business users color printouts are not a viable option. Even users who have color printers, probably do not have copiers that support color, and printing all originals is usually not practical.

Color can add significant appeal to information. Although it has not yet "arrived" as a standard in business printing, today most monitors support color. If you are planning a presentation with a large-screen monitor, you will want to assess you color selections carefully. You may also choose to create an image that can later be transformed into a 35-mm slide. Color is also practical for creating transparencies with a pen plotter. You may have multiple pens of different colors or you may instruct the plotter to stop to allow you to change pens as you print each new section of a graph.

Table 6-1
Allways Accelerator Keys

Style Feature	Allways Command	Accelerator Key
Boldface	/Format Bold Set	ALT-B
Fonts 1 through 8	/Format Font 1 through 8 Use	ALT-1 through ALT-8
Grid Lines (On/Off)	/Layout Options Grid	ALT-G
Lines (Outline/All/None)	/Format Lines	ALT-L
Shading (Light/Dark/Solid/None)	/Format Shade	ALT-S
Underline (Single/Double/None)	/Format Underline	ALT-U

Color choice can be important to the dissemination of your message. Many studies have been done to indicate the effect of certain colors on the audience. Cool colors have a different effect than warm colors. Some colors are thought of as more masculine whereas others could be categorized as feminine. Some colors clash when placed together. Other colors blend so that there may not be sufficient differentiation between adjacent pieces of a pie graph.

Allways allows you to change the color of 1-2-3 information in several ways. You can change the colors that the worksheet uses to print and display with the /Format

PUBLISHING 1-2-3

Color command. This command changes the text color or displays negative numbers in red. After selecting this command, select one of the colors from the menu. If your printer cannot print in color, this command will not affect your output. When you change the color of a range, the newly selected color will appear in the control panel.

You can also change the Allways display colors. You would want to do so when you are creating slides from screen captures. The display colors are changed by selecting /Display Colors. After selecting this command, you can select the part of the display you want to change. You can change the background color of the worksheet, the color of the worksheet foreground, and the color of the cell pointer. After selecting an option, select a color from the menu. Unlike the /Format Color command, the /Display Colors command affects the entire worksheet. The changes you make with /Display commands remain in effect while you are using Allways and 1-2-3 , the changes you make with /Format commands are saved to the worksheet.

Adding Lines and Boxes

Lines and boxes in a report can add structure, help to create tables, and group related items together. You can add these lines in Allways to your worksheets using the /Format Lines command. Boxes are created by adding lines on four sides. You can change the thickness of the lines this command adds. You can also add dashed lines to mark the boundaries of cells.

Lines are added as an outline to the edge of the range, on the left, right, top, or bottom sides of the range, or in between all cells in the range, using All. These lines are created by selecting /Format Lines, where you want the lines drawn, and the range over which the lines should be drawn. Figure 6-12 shows a printed schedule that uses the /Format Lines All command to create all of the lines in the table. If you later want to remove the lines, select /Format Lines Clear and the range over which to remove lines. As you add lines, Allways displays where lines are drawn in a cell in the control panel.

USING ALLWAYS WITH 1-2-3

```
FONT(1) Triumvirate 12 pt, LINES:LRIB                          ALLWAYS
C6: 2.15

        A    B      C       D       E       F       G       H       I
   1                        Ohio State Turnpike
   2                        Entrance at Exit 8
   3
   4                                CLASS
   5                1        2       3       4       5       6       7
   6          1   $2.15   $2.47   $3.46   $4.85   $7.75   $10.08  $15.12
   7          2    1.85    2.13    2.98    4.17    6.67    8.67   13.01
   8          3    1.35    1.55    2.17    3.04    4.87    6.33    9.49
   9    E     4    1.15    1.32    1.85    2.59    4.15    5.39    8.09
  10    X     5    0.95    1.09    1.53    2.14    3.43    4.45    6.68
  11    I     6    0.80    0.92    1.29    1.80    2.89    3.75    5.63
  12    T     7    0.50    0.58    0.81    1.13    1.80    2.34    3.52
  13          9    0.60    0.69    0.97    1.35    2.16    2.81    4.22
  14         10    1.10    1.27    1.77    2.48    3.97    5.16    7.74
  15         11    1.35    1.55    2.17    3.04    4.87    6.33    9.49
  16         12    1.55    1.78    2.50    3.49    5.59    7.27   10.90
  17         13    1.85    2.13    2.98    4.17    6.67    8.67   13.00
  18
  19
  20
  21
18-Mar-91  04:25 PM                                            NUM
```

Figure 6-12: /Format Lines adds lines so you can create tables.

The lines and boxes you create can use different line thicknesses. The thickness of the lines is determined by the /Layout Options Line-Weight command. After selecting this command, select either Normal, Light, or Heavy to set the thickness. This command will apply to all lines in the current worksheet. The different line thicknesses may not have any effect on how the printed worksheet looks since some printers cannot print varying line thicknesses. If you need to create very thick lines, you can do it by solidly shading cells and setting the row height to the line thickness you want.

Another type of line you can add to your worksheet is grid lines that define the boundaries of each cell. Figure 6-13 shows part of a worksheet with the grid displayed.

The grid appears when you select /Layout Options Grid Yes and disappear when you You can also add grid lines by pressing ALT-G.

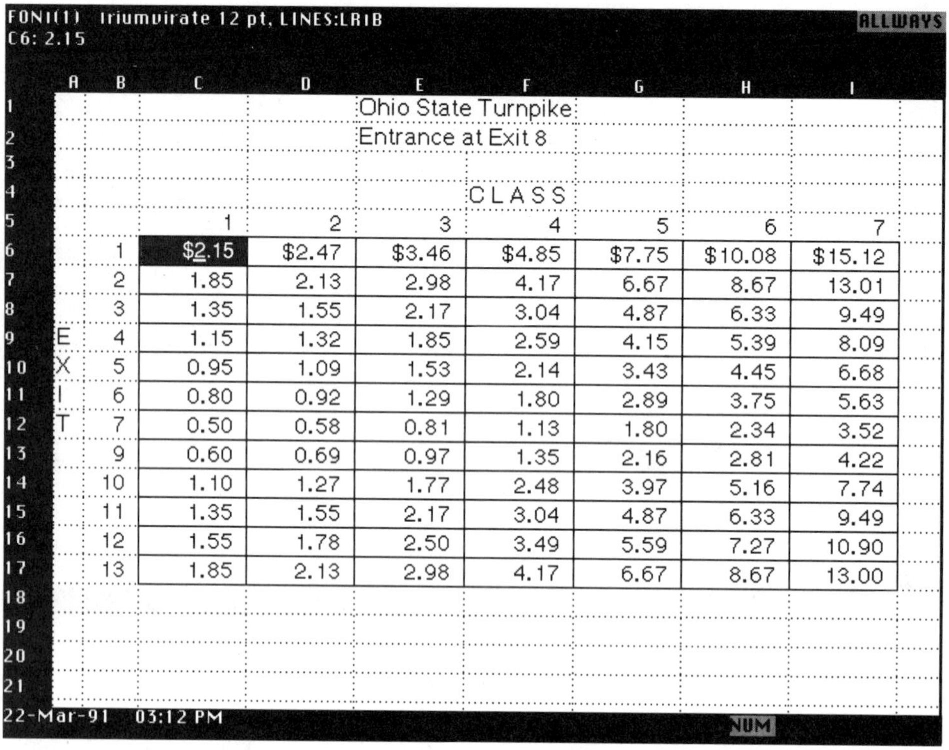

		1	2	3	4	5	6	7
	1	$2.15	$2.47	$3.46	$4.85	$7.75	$10.08	$15.12
	2	1.85	2.13	2.98	4.17	6.67	8.67	13.01
	3	1.35	1.55	2.17	3.04	4.87	6.33	9.49
E	4	1.15	1.32	1.85	2.59	4.15	5.39	8.09
X	5	0.95	1.09	1.53	2.14	3.43	4.45	6.68
I	6	0.80	0.92	1.29	1.80	2.89	3.75	5.63
T	7	0.50	0.58	0.81	1.13	1.80	2.34	3.52
	9	0.60	0.69	0.97	1.35	2.16	2.81	4.22
	10	1.10	1.27	1.77	2.48	3.97	5.16	7.74
	11	1.35	1.55	2.17	3.04	4.87	6.33	9.49
	12	1.55	1.78	2.50	3.49	5.59	7.27	10.90
	13	1.85	2.13	2.98	4.17	6.67	8.67	13.00

Figure 6-13: Worksheet with grid displaying.

Using Shading

Another option for emphasizing a cell or range is shading. Shading can be an alternative to color for drawing attention to a range or cell. It can also hide data Figure 6-14 shows a worksheet that uses shading to draw attention to sold-out concerts. You can add shading to cells by selecting /Format Shade and then Light, Dark, or Solid. After shading is added to a cell, Allways displays Light, Dark or Solid in the control panel. Shading can be removed by selecting /Format Shade Clear and the range. The

USING ALLWAYS WITH 1-2-3

thick line that is drawn in Figure 6-14 is created by using solid shading and setting the row height to the width of the line.

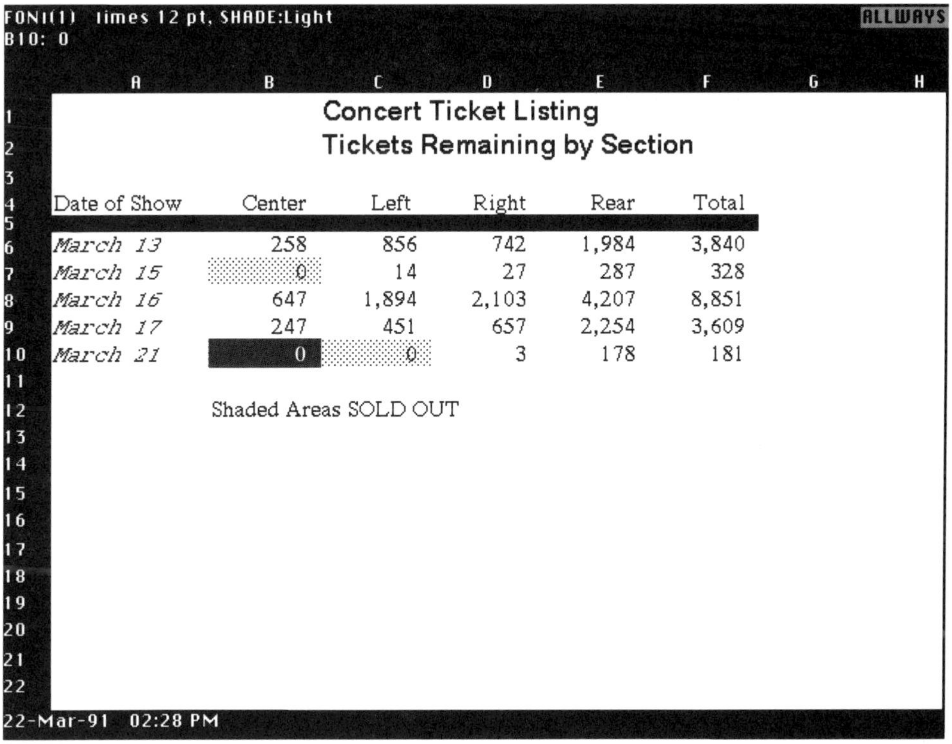

```
FONT(1) Times 12 pt, SHADE:Light                                    ALLWAYS
B10: 0
           A          B          C         D         E         F       G    H
                              Concert Ticket Listing
                            Tickets Remaining by Section

      Date of Show     Center      Left      Right     Rear      Total

      March 13          258        856        742      1,984     3,840
      March 15            0         14         27        287       328
      March 16          647      1,894      2,103      4,207     8,851
      March 17          247        451        657      2,254     3,609
      March 21            0          0          3        178       181

                    Shaded Areas SOLD OUT




22-Mar-91  02:28 PM
```

Figure 6-14: Adding shading to emphasize cell contents.

Using Captions, Labels and Other Explanatory Text

Labels in 1-2-3 are used for many purposes besides labeling data that you calculate on the worksheet. Labels can be used for lengthy explanations, captions to graphs, and headings to a report. Allways includes several features that make working with labels easier. These features include adjusting text entries to fit within a range and using different alignments.

PUBLISHING 1-2-3

Using Text Ranges

If you have text that you need to include in a worksheet, you will find that the /Range Justify command does not help to rearrange text over several rows since it doesn't adjust the cell entries for the font width. The Allways /Special Justify command removes this problem by moving text from one cell to another to fit within a range's width, taking into account the font the text uses. This command is the only Allways command that affects worksheet data since it actually moves text from one cell to another. Using this command is similar to using the /Range Justify command in 1-2-3 except you must include the entire range you want the labels to use. If the cells use different fonts, the cells change to using the font of the first cell in each paragraph where paragraphs are defined as labels being broken by an empty row. Figure 6-15 shows the same text in its original format, then redefined using the /Range Justify command and the /Special Justify command rearrange text to fit between columns A through F.

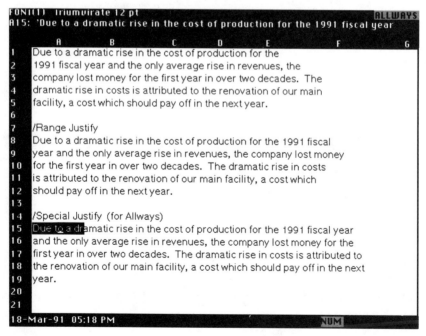

Figure 6-15: Rearranging text with /Range Justify and /Special Justify.

USING ALLWAYS WITH 1-2-3

Label Justification in Allways

You are probably accustomed to aligning labels within 1-2-3 cells. But in Allways, you can align labels within a range. Allways uses the label indicator to decide the starting point and direction the label should take. This means that a left-aligned label starts from the left edge of the cell and continues to the right until they cannot borrow more display space. Unlike 1-2-3, this also means that centered labels start from the middle of the cell and continue in both directions. Right-aligned labels start at the right side of the cell and continue to the left until they cannot borrow more display space. Figure 6-16 shows a worksheet using these label justifications. The label in E4 is right aligned so it starts from E4 and uses C4..E4 for display space. The label in D2 is centered so it is stored in D2 but borrows display space from columns B through F. Allways also uses the | label indicator differently as Figure 6-16 shows. In G4..G5, the cell entry of |Percent and |Change means that the last letter of the two labels is aligned with the percentage signs below it.

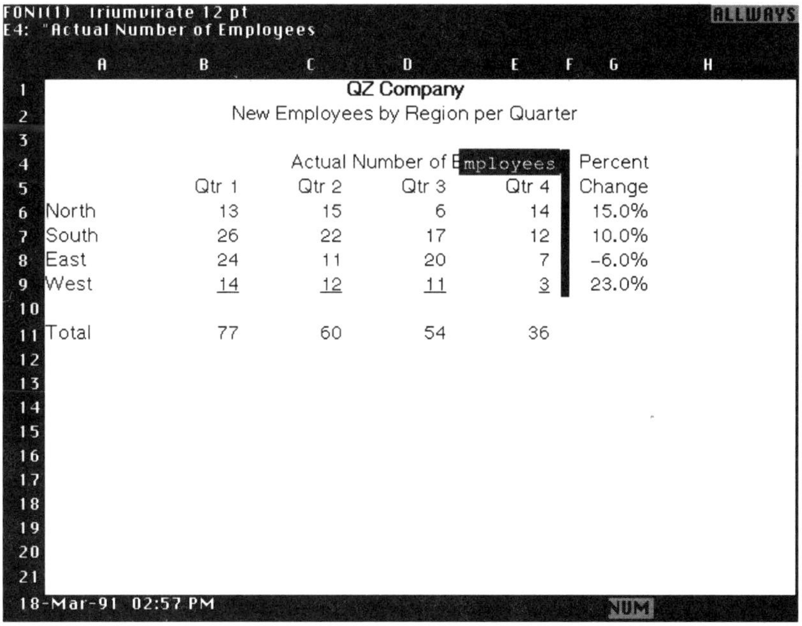

Figure 6-16: Different alignment options.

PUBLISHING 1-2-3

Column Widths in Allways

When you use Allways to enhance text, you will find that column widths in Allways work a little differently than they do in 1-2-3. Since Allways uses proportional fonts, the number of characters that fit into a cell is not always the same as the cell's width. Allways measures character width according to the width of numbers that use font 1.

In both 1-2-3 and Allways, you can also use different column widths. This means you can set the column width in Allways to exactly match the width of your text without worrying about how the change will appear in 1-2-3. In Allways column widths are set with the /Worksheet Column Set-Width command. This command draws a dotted line on the right side of the column indicating where the column width is set. You can use the arrow keys to move one character at a time and use CTRL with the arrow keys to move the column width by tenths of a character in either direction. Another option is to type the column width using up to two digits after the decimal point. When you set the width in Allways, you are only setting the width of the column in Allways. When you return to 1-2-3, the column is still at the width set by the 1-2-3 /Worksheet Column Set-Width command. You can return a column width in Allways to the column width set by 1-2-3 using the Allways command /Worksheet Column Set-Width.

Working With Graphs

The biggest news in the latest 1-2-3 release is that you can add graphs to your worksheet and print the graph and any worksheet text with the standard Allways Print command. This means you do not have to use PrintGraph to print the graph nor do you need to refeed paper through the printer to integrate text and graphs on the same page. Figure 6-17 shows an example of putting graphs into the worksheet so you can display graphs and worksheet data simultaneously.

All of the graphs that you work with in Allways must be saved to a .PIC file just as in 1-2-3, when you use the /Graph Save Command. There are no menu options in

Allways that allow you to create a graph or edit one. You can create .PIC files with 1-2-3 or other packages and add them to your worksheet. For example, you can create a graph file with 1-2-3, enhance it with another package such as 3D-Graphics, and then display it in an Allways worksheet.

Adding Graphs to A Worksheet

The /Graph Add command adds graphs to your worksheet. "A Closer Look: Adding a Graphic to a Worksheet" lists the steps for adding a graph to a worksheet. To add a 1-2-3 graph, select /Graph Add and the name of the .PIC file. Once you select the file, Allways prompts you for the worksheet range to display the graph. You can select any range and the size of the range determines the size of the graph and its height-to-width ratio. Every time you switch from 1-2-3 to Allways, Allways will re-read the .PIC file to make sure that it is using the most up-to-date version of the file.

If you want to remove a graph from the worksheet display, select /Graph Remove and the graph to remove. With this command, Allways displays a box listing the .PIC files that will be removed from the worksheet display. With the /Graph Settings commands that let you enhance how the graph appears on your worksheet, you can select the graph to modify before or after selecting /Graph Settings. You can select the graph by moving the cell pointer to a cell in the range where the graph displays and then the /Graph Settings command, or select /Graph Settings and then the .PIC file displayed

A CLOSER LOOK

Adding a Graphic to a Worksheet

1) Select /Graph Add.

2) Select the .PIC file to add.

3) Select the worksheet range to display the graph and press ENTER.

PUBLISHING 1-2-3

in the worksheet to change. For example, one setting you may want to change is the .PIC file that appears in a range. To change the graph file, either move to a cell in the range where the graph you want to replace appears and select /Graph Settings PIC-File and the graph to display in its place or select /Graph Settings PIC-File, the graph to replace from the list, and the graph file to display in its place.

The graph originally has size specified when you select the range to display the graph but you can change its size and position. The graph's size is set by the column widths and row heights of the range it displays in. You can change the worksheet range the graph displays in by selecting /Graph Settings Range, the graph to change, and the new range to display the graph. You may want to do this when a graph needs its height-to-width ratio changed.

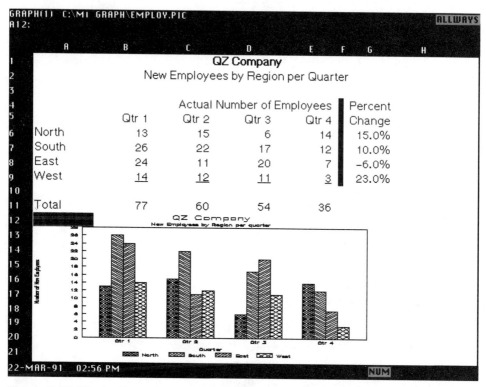

Figure 6-17: Displaying a graph an worksheet data.

Besides setting the graph size and position on the worksheet by selecting its worksheet range or changing the column widths or row heights in the range the graph displays, you can also shift the graph's position within the worksheet range. This is done by adding margins. A graph normally uses the full worksheet range to display but you can add margins to leave a small space on any of the four sides of the range. Margins lets you make finer adjustments than you can make with the graph range. To set a margin for a graph, select /Graph Settings, the graph to change, Margins, the side to set the margins for and the amount of margins in inches that you want.

If you want Allways to work faster, you can display graphs as a shaded region as in Figure 6-18 by selecting /Display Graphs No. Displaying the graphs as a hatched box applies to every graph in the worksheet. You can eliminate the display of graphs on the worksheet by selecting /Display Graphs No. You can switch between displaying graphs and displaying hatched boxes by pressing F10 (GRAPH). Allways and 1-2-3 also perform faster when the display mode is set to text with /Display Mode Text. This displays the worksheet with the same appearance as when Allways is not loaded except the Allways formatting information appears in the control panel. In this mode graphs appear as ranges filled with G's. You can return to the default graphics mode by selecting /Display Mode Graphics. You can also switch between the two display modes by pressing F6.

Changing A Graph's Appearance

When you print your graphs with PrintGraph, you can make menu selections that let you enhance how the graph prints. Allways includes the same selections so you can customize the fonts, colors, text size, and position of each graph in a worksheet range.

The graphs you add to your worksheet use the same font files that the PrintGraph program uses. You can select which fonts the graph uses from any of the ones PrintGraph provides. You may want to change the fonts so they closely match the fonts the worksheet data uses. These fonts appear in Figure 6-19. You can select which one a graph uses by selecting /Graph Settings, the graph to change, Fonts, 1 or 2, and one

PUBLISHING 1-2-3

of the fonts shown in Figure 6-19. The graph's first title uses font 1 and the remaining graph text uses font 2. For Allways to use these fonts, it must know where they are before you can add graphs to your worksheet. To tell Allways where it will find font files, select /Graph Fonts-Directory and supply the drive and directory information for where these graph font files are located.

You can also improve the legibility of the added graphs by increasing or decreasing the size of the graph. Since a graph usually is smaller than when you print it with PrintGraph, you may need to enlarge the graph text to make it legible. To change the size of the graph text without affecting other parts of the graph, select /Graph

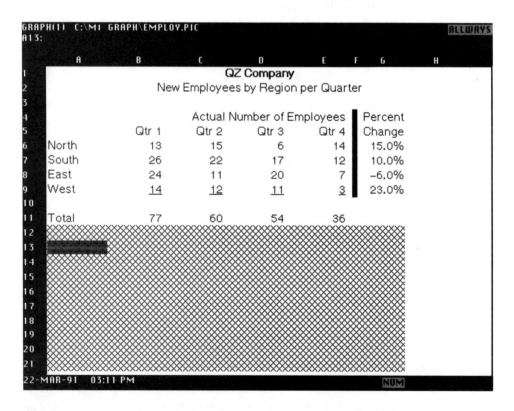

Figure 6-18: Displaying graphs as shaded regions to increase speed in Allways.

USING ALLWAYS WITH 1-2-3

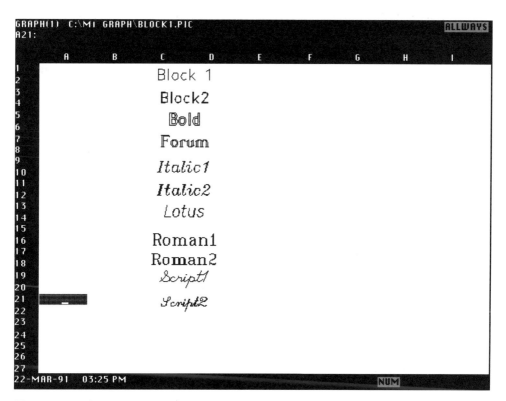

Figure 6-19: Fonts available through PrintGraph.

Settings, the graph to change, Scale and type a number between .5 and 3 where .5 represents text that is fifty percent of its original size and where 3 represents text that is three times its original size. Figure 6-20 shows two graphs with the second one using the larger text to make it easier to read.

Another enhancement you may want to make to your graph is selecting the colors of the graph. Initially, Allways is set to display all of the graph in black (unless you change the default as described later). Graph colors are set by selecting /Graph Settings, Colors, X or A through F for the data range to set the color, and then a color. After selecting the colors the graph uses, select Quit to return to the worksheet. Changing the color changes both how the graph displays and prints although if your

PUBLISHING 1-2-3

printer cannot print colors, changing the colors the graph displays does not effect the printout. If your printer can only print one color, you and you are including a bar, stacked bar, or pie graph, you will want to make sure to save the graph after using 1-2-3's /Graph Options B&W command so the saved graph file uses patterns to distinguish the series instead of solid colors.

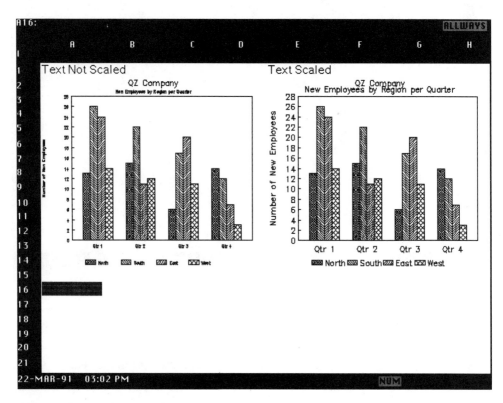

Figure 6-20: Two graphs showing different text scaling.

While Allways lets you set the graph settings for each graph separately, you may want to apply them to all new graphs that you add to a worksheet. This makes adding more graphs easier since they will use the same scaling, fonts, colors, and margins. To make a set of graph settings the default, select /Graph Settings, the graph using the graph settings you want to be the default, and Default Update. When you want a graph to use the default graph settings, select /Graph Settings, the graph to change, and Default Restore.

CHAPTER 7

Moving Beyond the Print Features in 1-2-3

1-2-3 Release 2.3 and 3.1 offer most of the features discussed in the print utilities covered in this chapter. The discussion of Bitstream soft fonts will be of special interest to 1-2-3 Release 2.3 and 3.1 users since these versions make it especially easy to install Bitstream fonts.

Primarily this chapter will provide information for the many users of earlier 1-2-3 releases. It is possible that 1-2-3 Releases 2.01 or 2.2 users may have a copy of one of these utilities around the office and not realize the extra power that they can squeeze from 1-2-3 by combining it with an add-in utility.

In upcoming months, more add-ins to extend the functionality of Release 2.3 will certainly be introduced. Since these are not available at this time, it is not possible to comment on features which might extend print capabilities in Release 2.3 even further.

This chapter covers Sideways, P.D. Queue, and JetSet utilities. In addition, it explains the use of Bitstream soft fonts and a cartridge containing 25 fonts.

A CLOSER LOOK

Bitstream Fonts

Here is a sampling of bitstream fonts you might want to use.

This is Futura Bold.

This is Futura Light.

This is Garamond.

This is Garamond bold.

This is Goudy.

This is Goudy bold.

This is Bodoni.

This is Bodoni bold.

Using Bitstream Fonts

Bitstream is the leading producer of fontware. Many fonts that are available from Bitstream are available for both the Macintosh and PC, making it possible to produce compatible type in the two different computing environments.

Bitstream offers 52 different typeface packages for the PC at a price of $195 each. Each typeface package contains a regular, italic, bold, and bold italic style. The fonts are scalable to any size from headlines to footnotes. "A Closer Look: Bitstream" shows some of the options available.

Bitstream offers six font collections for the PC. There are three different typefaces in each collection with each typeface available in all four type styles. At $295 each, these collections provide a savings over individual packages since each collection includes the equivalent of three packages. Collections are named for the types of documents that you might want to create from them. Table 7-1 shows each of the collections as well as the names of their typefaces.

Using 25 Cartridges in One

The 25 Cartridges in One product is marketed by Pacific Data Products. As the name implies, the package offers many different cartridges packed into one. It occupies one cartridge slot yet provides 172 fonts and 20 different symbol sets. You can select special driver files as a printer when you install 1-2-3. When

Table 7-1
Bitstream Font Collections

Collection	Fonts Included
Newsletter	Charter Headlines 1 Swiss Light
Books and Manuals	Baskerville Goudy Old Style Zapf Calligraphic
Flyers	Futura Light Headlines 2 Headlines 4
Reports and Proposals	Activa Zapf Humanist Bitstream Amerigo
Presentation	Slate Swiss Condensed Headlines 5
Spreadsheet	Zurich Monospace Zapf Elliptical

you use the Wysiwyg and Allways add-ins, you can select the various cartridge fonts from the menu. At less than $400, 25 Cartridges in One can provide a low-cost solution for someone wanting a variety of high-quality fonts at a low price.

Since the fonts are provided in a cartridge rather than on a disk, you do not have to download them into the printer's memory. This cartridge includes a special spreadsheet font that creates an attractive worksheet display.

P.D.Queue

If you are using 1-2-3 Release 2.01 through 2.2 you can use the P.D.Queue add-in to provide background printing capabilities. Although users of later releases take background printing for granted, earlier releases do not have a print spooler. Print Spoolers allow all of your print jobs to be written to disk until, one by one, they are printed. Without a print spooler you must sit idly until 1-2-3 finishes printing. P.D.Queue automatically intercepts print requests made directly from 1-2-3 or other add-ins such as Sideways.

P.D.Queue provides print queue management tools that allow you to make changes to print requests. You can access the add-in anytime you need to make changes.

Using P.D.Queue to Print

To use P.D.Queue for printing just install the add-in, configure, and invoke it. Installation is simple. All you need to do is run PDQINST to copy the files onto your hard disk, run PDQSETUP to communicate with your hardware, and select the parallel or serial port with which you will use P.D.Queue. If you select a hot-key during installation, you will be able to pop up the program by pressing ALT-7, ALT-F8, ALT-F9, or ALT-F10.

Subsequently, as you choose the Print Go command your information will not be sent directly to the printer, rather it will be written to your hard disk. Since writing to a hard disk is much faster than writing to a printing device, you can return to other 1-2-3 tasks while P.D.Queue slowly sends your output to the printer without disrupting your work. As many as 99 print requests can be stored in the print queue.

Working With the Print Spooler

P.D.Queue's pop-up menus offer many other options for managing print jobs. Figure 7-1 shows this menu and "A Closer look: P.D.Queue" provides a summary of

A CLOSER LOOK

P.D.Queue

Task	P.D.Queue Command
Cancel the current job	Kill Yes
Cancel all jobs	Job Flush
Change the job name	Job Name
Change the number of copies	Job Copies
Change the priority of a job	Job Move
Create a disk file for the next print job	Options Spooling File
Keep a job after printing	Job Action Keep
Release a held job	Job Release
Remove a job from the queue	Job Remove
Restart a printout at the beginning	Restart
Resume a job after pause	Continue
Temporarily stop printing	Pause

PUBLISHING 1-2-3

some frequently used P.D.Queue commands. Directly below this menu is a status area that provides information current print jobs. The queue lists as many of your print jobs as possible.

Each time you print, the job is queued behind preceding jobs. Using P.D.Queue's File command, you can print output stored on a disk created with 1-2-3's Print File command. Print jobs are automatically removed from the queue as they finish printing. You can delete jobs before they are printed, change the print order, hold a job, and even cancel a job that is currently printing.

P.D.Queue also allows you to change a job's name, request a different number of copies, and send print output to a disk file—rather than to the spooler.

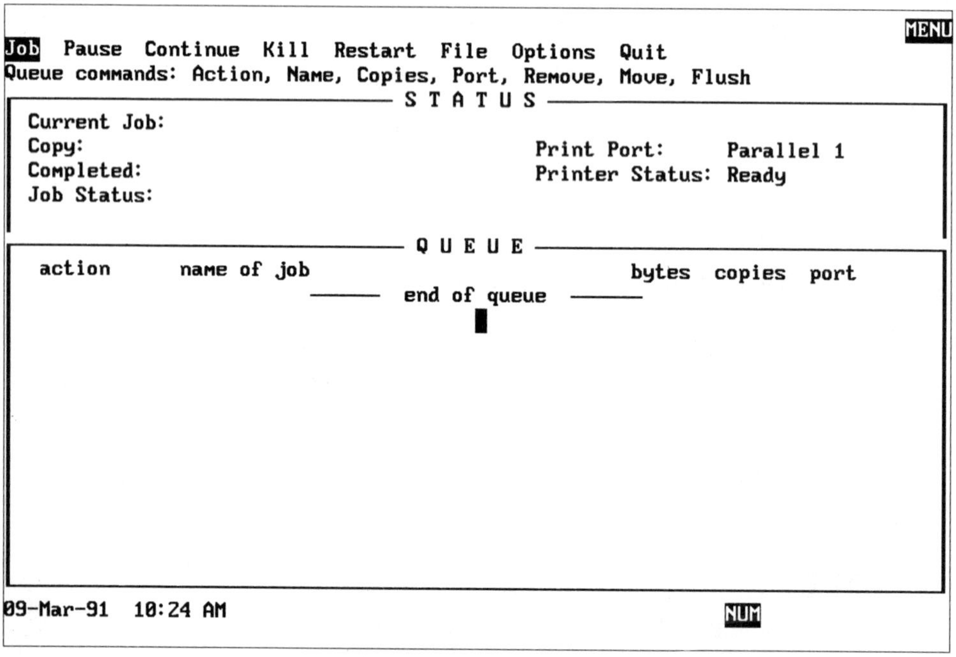

```
                                                                      MENU
 Job  Pause  Continue  Kill  Restart  File  Options  Quit
 Queue commands: Action, Name, Copies, Port, Remove, Move, Flush
 ─────────────────────────── S T A T U S ───────────────────────────
  Current Job:
  Copy:                            Print Port:      Parallel 1
  Completed:                       Printer Status:  Ready
  Job Status:

 ─────────────────────────── Q U E U E ─────────────────────────────
     action       name of job                   bytes   copies   port
                     ───────── end of queue ─────────
                                  ■





 09-Mar-91  10:24 AM                                         NUM
```

Figure 7-1: The PD Que popup menu.

MOVING BEYOND THE PRINT FEATURES IN 1-2-3

JetSet

If you're not using Wysiwyg and Allways to select fonts and landscape mode on your printer, you must resort to lengthy setup strings for such instructions. Setup strings are tedious to enter since they do not use acronyms for features but instead rely on unique combinations of upper- and lowercase characters and special symbols. There is no help menu to locate setup strings; instead, you must have your printer manual handy for the correct sequences.

With 1-2-3 Release 2.01, the JetSet add-in provides an easy-to-use menu interface to your printer. JetSet also supplements later 1-2-3 releases that do not work with Wysiwyg—adding such features as printing multiple ranges with one print request.

The next sections provide an overview of some JetSet features. "A Closer Look: JetSet" provides the actual key sequences for some tasks. You can see that these options are very similar to 1-2-3 features.

Selecting a Range to Print

First you must install and attach JetSet just as you would any add-in. When you invoke the JetSet print menu shown in Figure 7-2, JetSet assumes you want to print the entire worksheet unless you specify a range.

Just as in 1-2-3, you can use the Range command to specify a print range. When you want to print multiple ranges, use the Range Several command. You can also edit your list of print ranges or insert print range into an existing list.

Using JetSet's Print Options

Many of the Option menu commands have 1-2-3 Print menu equivalents — for example, Margins, Borders, Header, and Footer. Conveniences included in the JetSet interface are margins measured in inches, and a graphic display of the page layout is adjusted for font size 5. Changing the left or right margin settings automatically adjusts the graphic page layout display as shown in Figure 7-3.

PUBLISHING 1-2-3

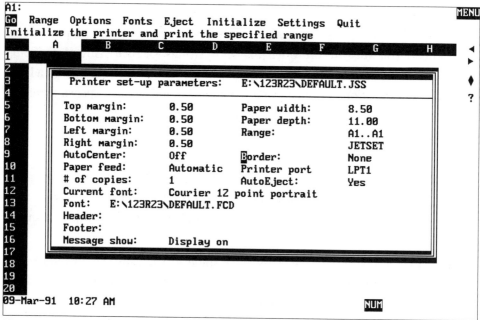

Figure 7-2: The JetSet Print menu.

Among its other options, JetSet will specify the number of copies to print. It also frees you from adjusting the margin to center the selected range; instead, you can tell JetSet to center the range on the page. The AutoEject option ejects the page after the last page of your document has printed.

Changing Fonts

JetSet supports Courier 12-point portrait and landscape as well as 8-point (16.66 cpi) line printer portrait font on some HP models. The add-in provides two compressed fonts that will print 12 rather than 10 characters to the inch like the 10-point fonts in the laser printer.

JetSet comes with a set of font cartridge description files for the Hewlett-Packard soft fonts and cartridges. If you use other fonts you will need to create your own

MOVING BEYOND THE PRINT FEATURES IN 1-2-3

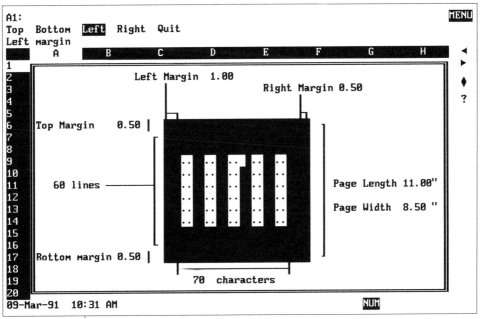

Figure 7-3: JetSet's graphical representation of the page layout.

A CLOSER LOOK

JetSet

Task	JetSet Command
Change fonts	Font Select
Change the margin settings	Options Margin
Print the worksheet	Go
Select multiple print ranges	Range Several
Set the margins	Options Margins
Set the paper size	Options Paper
Set the print margins	Options Margin

PUBLISHING 1-2-3

description files containing such information as orientation, typeface, style, character set, height, pitch, weight, lines per inch, and the width of a space in 1/120th-inch increments.

Fonts are either proportional or fixed. Although many proportional fonts have attractive characters that could improve the spreadsheet's appearance, you can ruin your column settings if you try to use these fonts with Setup strings. But in JetSet, these proportional fonts will not disturb your columns of labels or values.

JetSet's Special Printer Control Codes

With JetSet you can also use printer control codes to change fonts and print attributes in the middle of a page. These codes are similar to embedded setup strings but are much easier to remember and use. Each printer control code begins with an ampersand and is followed by a mnemonic, such as ul for underline, or by some font identification code.

Sideways

Sideways is an add-in that works with 1-2-3 Release 2.01, 2.2 and 3. As the name suggests, Sideways allows you to print in landscape mode either printing across the perforations in paper or printing over them if you have a dot matrix printer. You might have a worksheet that prints across four, five, or even ten sheets of paper in landscape mode using a technique where the selected range covers two sheets of paper. You can also select a character size, specify row and column borders, vary spacing between characters and lines, and use different styles such as underline, bold, and expanded in different worksheet ranges.

Installing Sideways

How you install Sideways depends on which Release of 1-2-3 you are working with. The manual provides detailed instructions for each release and the package includes all the files needed for any release. As you look at some of the tasks that Sideways will perform, you might also look at "A Closer Look: Sideways" to see how similar the menu selections are to the 1-2-3's already-familiar menus.

MOVING BEYOND THE PRINT FEATURES IN 1-2-3

Selecting a Print Range

Like JetSet, Sideways assumes that you want to print the entire worksheet unless you specify a range. To change the range you can choose Range from the main Sideways menu shown in Figure 7-4. Sideways calculates the number of pages to be printed based on your print settings. Sideways assumes that the entire width of your worksheet will comprise a page regardless of how many pieces of paper it is printed across.

Using Other Sideways Options

You can use the Sideways Options menu to change margins, page size, perforation skipping, or character options. The margin and page size options are straight forward and correspond to similar options in 1-2-3. The Options Character command allows

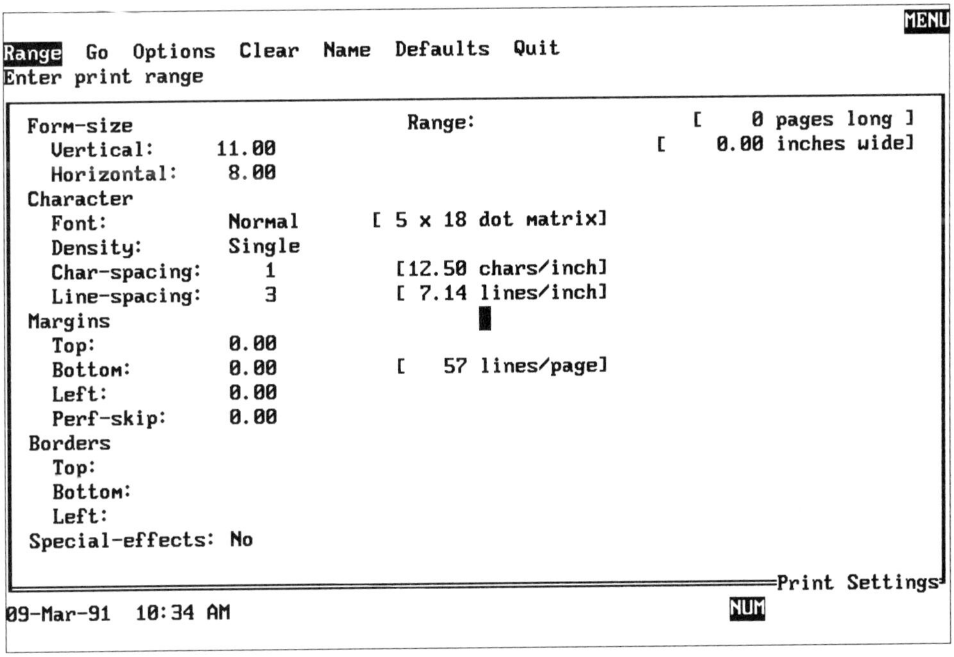

```
                                                                    MENU
Range  Go  Options  Clear  Name  Defaults  Quit
Enter print range
┌─────────────────────────────────────────────────────────────────────────┐
│  Form-size                   Range:              [    0 pages long ]    │
│    Vertical:    11.00                            [ 0.00 inches wide]    │
│    Horizontal:   8.00                                                   │
│  Character                                                              │
│    Font:        Normal       [ 5 x 18 dot matrix]                       │
│    Density:     Single                                                  │
│    Char-spacing:    1        [12.50 chars/inch]                         │
│    Line-spacing:    3        [ 7.14 lines/inch]                         │
│  Margins                                                                │
│    Top:          0.00                                                   │
│    Bottom:       0.00        [   57 lines/page]                         │
│    Left:         0.00                                                   │
│    Perf-skip:    0.00                                                   │
│  Borders                                                                │
│    Top:                                                                 │
│    Bottom:                                                              │
│    Left:                                                                │
│  Special-effects: No                                                    │
│                                                       =Print Settings=  │
│ 09-Mar-91  10:34 AM                              NUM                    │
└─────────────────────────────────────────────────────────────────────────┘
```

Figure 7-4: The SideWays main menu.

PUBLISHING 1-2-3

you to choose from any of nine different size fonts. The default setting is normal but you can select increase or decrease or a descriptive name such as Extra Large or Tiny. You can also choose single or double density if your printer supports these. Character spacing allows you to either crowd characters or separate them. Line spacing allows you to determine the space between lines.

Options Special-Effects lets you select bold, underlined, and expanded. All are options for changing the appearance of ranges of worksheet entries. Once you begin making selections you will be able to see the list of the ranges and the effects that you have selected as shown in Figure 7-5.

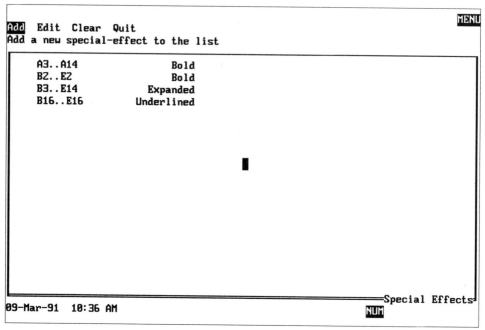

Figure 7-5: A list of the ranges and effects selected with Sideways.

MOVING BEYOND THE PRINT FEATURES IN 1-2-3

Sideways adds a few more options to 1-2-3 Release 3. It can support a range over multiple worksheets although it will not span worksheet files to include sheets from multiple files in one range. Sideways also supports Release 3's Group mode when setting special effects. This allows you to make special effects changes to an entire group of sheets as you change the current sheet.

You can also use Sideways in a stand-alone mode that allows you to print worksheets stored in files with a .WK1 or .WKS format without having 1-2-3 in memory. You also have the option of using Sideways with text files (.PRN) files.

Using Sideways with a Laser Printer

Since laser printers do not print across the edge of the paper it is possible that a page break could fall in the middle of a column. You will want to set Perf-Skip to at least .5". This will provide a clean break between columns. To use the manual feed option with the laserjet you will need to use a special manual feed printer driver.

A CLOSER LOOK

Sideways

Task	Sideways Command
Change the font	Options Character Font
Change the line spacing	Options Character Line-spacing
Define the page size	Options Form-size
Select a print range	Range
Set border rows or columns	Options Borders
Set margins	Options Margins

CHAPTER 8

Bringing 1-2-3 Data Into Your Word Processor

Think of your favorite word processing package—the one that you have mastered—as another tool for enhancing your worksheet's format. For stand-alone graphs, you will want to use 1-2-3's print features along with Allways or Wysiwyg. However, you will find a word processing package especially useful when you need to produce a report or newsletter that contains 1-2-3 data or graphs. If you have not yet selected a word processing package, you will want to consult the checklist of desirable features found on the next page.

WordPerfect 5.1 is the basis for all examples in this chapter since it is one of the most popular word processing packages available. If you are working with it, you can follow the steps detailed in this chapter to duplicate the tasks. If you are using another word processor, you will still benefit from the more general concepts and ideas regarding the use of word processors to present 1-2-3 data. You will, however, have to use your word processor's references for the specific commands to accomplish some of the tasks.

Opportunities for Combining 1-2-3 Data with Documents

You will find occasions when you want to incorporate data from a 1-2-3 file into a larger document. One of your options is to re-enter the data, using the printed output of the 1-2-3 file as a reference. However, if you are creating the document using a word processor, chances are that you have another option. This chapter discusses options

PUBLISHING 1-2-3

> ✔ **CHECKLIST**
>
> **Word Processing Features Desirable for Use with 1-2-3**
>
> ✔ Supports the release of 1-2-3 that you are using.
>
> ✔ Imports ASCII Data.
>
> ✔ Supports import with carriage return or line feed as hard or soft return.
>
> ✔ Imports a 1-2-3 range without conversion.
>
> ✔ Places 1-2-3 data into a table.
>
> ✔ Establishes a dynamic link to a 1-2-3 file that will be updated automatically or on request.
>
> ✔ Creates tabular columns automatically to contain 1-2-3's rows and columns.
>
> ✔ Displays 1-2-3 data in columnar entries.
>
> ✔ Uses 1-2-3 data to do a merge operation.
>
> ✔ Imports 1-2-3 PIC files.

for "importing" 1-2-3 data, which help you avoid re-keying information. Whether you write the desired data to an ASCIII file or import it directly, you will want to be certain that you have completed all your 1-2-3 tasks before printing to a file or saving it to a disk for direct import into 1- 2-3.

Importing data into your documents means that all of the formatting capabilities available in your word processor can be used to display your data. Depending on which ones you use, you may find your word processor and printer lend a variety of formats and type styles to your 1-2-3 data. Some word processing packages, including WordPerfect 5.1, can also be used to display the graphs produced by 1-2-3. Thus, you can have word processing documents that include 1-2-3 graphs.

Some word processing packages also have the capability of "linking" 1-2-3 data to the document. This means that you can import 1-2-3 data into a document, change some of the data values within 1-2-3, and have the new values automatically reflected within the document. This is especially useful when your 1-2-3 data is routinely updated.

You might also wish to consider the creation of "merged" documents using 1-2-3 data. For example, 1-2-3 data could include the names and addresses of people who are to receive a mass mailing. That data could be used by your word processor to create individualized letters. Depending on how your word processor works with merged documents, you may need to do some special formatting of the data to make this work. But most often, the time it takes to format the data is much less than the time consumed by typing the data in from scratch.

The following three examples provide an overview of results obtained from importing 1-2-3 data and graphs into documents. The first example illustrates what is usually the easiest method for incorporating 1-2-3 data into most word processors. However, using this method is likely to mean extensive formatting because much of the original formatting of the 1-2-3 data is lost during the transfer.

Some word processing packages provide other means for importing data that preserve some or all of the original formatting. For example, WordPerfect can reproduce the 1-2-3 data columns with tab stops, maintaining the justification of the columns as it appeared in the original spreadsheet. WordPerfect also has a Table feature that can be used to import data. WordPerfect's Table feature mimics some of the 1-2-3 spreadsheet format and will seem familiar to 1-2-3 experts. Tables can be used to import 1-2-3 data directly.

✔ CHECKLIST

Before Leaving 1-2-3

✔ Review worksheet data for use in word processing document.

✔ Check that width of rows and columns does not exceed available display width in word processor.

✔ For printing, check that you are not exceeding the maximum ASCII file line length of 240 for 1-2-3 Release 2.3 or 1000 for Release 3.

✔ Note the ranges you will work with or assign them names if possible.

✔ Use the Worksheet Column Hide command to temporarily remove unneeded columns when creating an ASCII file.

✔ If you are planning to import the data directly, save the 1-2-3 file with range names and other changes.

✔ If working with ASCII files, be certain to save them before exiting 1-2-3.

PUBLISHING 1-2-3

Adding Projected and Actual Costs to a Letter

Adding 1-2-3 data to a document can be very straight-forward. The techniques are easily followed and will be discussed in detail later in this chapter. Figure 8-1 displays a 1-2-3 spreadsheet listing the projected and actual costs for a bake sale. Granted the spreadsheet is fairly simple, but the point is that the process for importing 1-2-3 data into a document is the same whether the spreadsheet is simple or complex.

```
A13: [W22]


              A                  B          C        D        E       F
 1  BAKE SALE EXPENSES (PROJECTED & ACTUAL)
 2
 3  DESCRIPTION               PROJECTED   ACTUAL
 4  OF COSTS                   AMOUNT     AMOUNT
 5
 6  Room Rental                $50.00     $50.00
 7  Custodial Services         $75.00     $75.00
 8  Advertising                $30.00     $31.95
 9  Table And Chair Rental     $55.00     $50.00
10  Miscellaneous              $25.00     $14.95
11  ------------------------------------------
12  TOTAL                     $235.00    $221.90
13
14
15
16
17
18
19
20
BAKESALE.WK1                                                          CAPS
```

Figure 8-1: A projected and actual costs spreadsheet.

BRINGING 1-2-3 DATA INTO YOUR WORD PROCESSOR

```
                            Jan Edwards
                            1234 Main Street
                            Temperance, MI 48182
                            February 12, 1991

Beth Moeller, President
The SunnySiders Club
4321 Banton Avenue
Temperance, MI 48182

Dear Beth:

As promised, the following spreadsheet details the actual
expenditures for this year's bake sale against the projected
costs.  Notice that our expenses were actually less than
projected—a bake sale first!

BAKE SALE EXPENSES (PROJECTED & ACTUAL)

DESCRIPTION                 PROJECTED           ACTUAL
OF COSTS                    AMOUNT              AMOUNT

Room Rental                 $50.00              $50.00
Custodial Services          $75.00              $75.00
Advertising                 $30.00              $31.00
Table and Chair Rental      $55.00              $50.00
Miscellaneous               $25.00              $14.00
_____
TOTAL                       $235.00             $221.90
Kate told me today that the gross profit for the bakesale will
be somewhere between $850.00 and $900.00.  This means we
netted over $620.00 for the hospital fund—a major achievement
for our small group.

                            Sincerely,

                            Jan Edwards
```

Figure 8-2 displays a letter that contains the imported 1-2-3 spreadsheet data. While no special formatting was done to improve the letter's visual appeal, the document was produced with very little extra effort. In general, the steps used to add 1-2-3 data to a letter can be as simple as printing the 1-2-3 spreadsheet to a file and then importing the resulting ASCII file into the document. Because the data was imported and not re-keyed, the author did not have to check for typographical errors within the chart.

Producing a Newsletter

Using more advanced techniques, you can import 1-2-3 data and graphs into a document with much fancier results. Figure 8-3, shown on the next page, is a view of a bar graph created within 1-2-3. This graph and the 1-2-3 data in Figure 8-1 were both imported into the SunnySiders Club Newsletter. Figure 8-4 shows the first page of the newsletter, which was created with WordPerfect.

The 1-2-3 spreadsheet data was imported into a WordPerfect table, which in this case was used to box in the data with double and single lines. The heading of the table

PUBLISHING 1-2-3

was bolded and shaded for emphasis. The type size of the body of the table is smaller than the surrounding newsletter, making the table fit into the allotted space and giving it greater visual appeal. Similarly, the type style could have been changed to italics, bolding, etc. or a completely different font could have been selected to make the table stand out even more.

Figure 8-3:
A 1-2-3 bar graph.

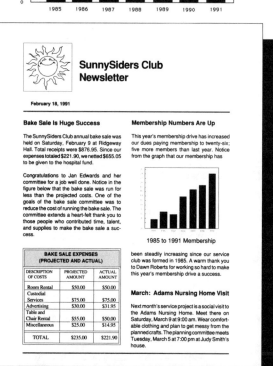

Figure 8-4: The graph was inserted into the newsletter as a WordPerfect Graphics box. Many word processing packages are capable of adding graphics to text and can either directly or indirectly import graphics from 1-2-3. The membership graph was created in 1-2-3, saved as a .PIC file, and placed into this newsletter using WordPerfect in the same manner as we did to create the sunshine graphic at the top of the newsletter.

BRINGING 1-2-3 DATA INTO YOUR WORD PROCESSOR

Creating a Financial Spreadsheet with the Addition of Graphics

When you have only 1-2-3 data or graphs to present, you will usually be able to produce attractive output using Allways or Impress. As you have seen, importing 1-2-3 data into word processing has its advantages, particularly when you are working with longer documents. However, you should also consider using a word processing package when you want to add a graphic image to the output. For example, you could add a company's logo as part of the heading on its financial spreadsheets or add other graphic images to underscore key points or to further explain the data. You could also bring in the 1-2-3 graphs as the graphic images rather than as data..

The SunnySiders Club income statement for first quarter 1991 is presented in Figure 8-5 as a 1-2-3 spreadsheet. To produce the finished statement displayed in Figure 8-6, the top part of the statement was created in the same manner as the Newsletter heading. The sunshine graphic was included and the heading was typed in as part of the normal document. Then, only the lower part of the 1-2-3 spreadsheet was imported as text. The 1-2-3 heading was not needed because it was created using a word processor. Once the data was imported the headings and totals were bolded, the subheadings were italicized, and the dividing line was added above the totals.

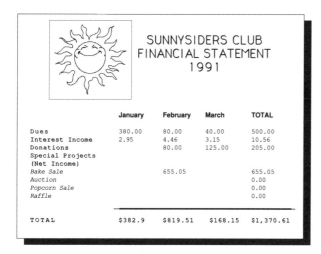

261

PUBLISHING 1-2-3

Options for Saving 1-2-3 Data for Use with a Word Processor

The previous section of this chapter suggested that there are different methods for importing 1-2-3 data into word processors. If you use a word processing package other than WordPerfect, you will need to check your manual to determine what kind of file formats it accepts. 1-2-3 can create : ASCII (sometimes called DOS, Text, or DOS Text files), WK1 or WKS (depending on what version you have), .PIC, .DIF, and .DBF files. These are the types of files you need to look for when trying to determine the formats and methods you can use for importing 1-2-3 data.

No matter what file type you use to import data, you must develop a sense of how you want the final product to look before you even get started creating the files to import. For example, you must be able to estimate how much data will fit across the printed page. There is no rigid formula you can use to make this determination. The amount of text that will fit on the page depends upon the word processor you are using, your margins, the size of the type, the type style, the size of the paper, etc. Three columns of data in a large type face may not fit across the page while 28 columns in a small type face might.

Because many spreadsheets are too large to fit on a single page, you need to imagine how your spreadsheet will look when printed. Then, as you create files for importing, you need to break them up accordingly, both across and down the spreadsheet. If the files are too wide, each line of text will word wrap down to the next line of text creating a confusing array of data. If the files are too narrow, you may have too much white space surrounding the data. You also need to consider how many rows are to be imported. Of course, you can often just break up a lengthy spreadsheet over two or more pages and add headings using your word processor.

If you are working on a spreadsheet as you go through this chapter, you will want to use ranges to specify the section of the spreadsheet to be imported. Often, you will do this by creating import files that contain a specified range, but some word processors can only import an entire file. If you can extract from your 1-2-3 worksheet only those sections that you need, you can often reduce the amount of editing required.

BRINGING 1-2-3 DATA INTO YOUR WORD PROCESSOR

Some word processors can extract a portion of a worksheet from a larger worksheet file using cell references or a named range. These ranges can later be imported. In such cases, you may not need to do much—or anything at all—to create export files from within 1-2-3. Whichever method your system uses, you should try to make sure the data being imported within the range will fit properly across the page. Although this may seem difficult at first, experience with your system and its type styles will quickly improve your skills.

Creating ASCII Files with /Print File

Most word processors will accept the ASCII file format because ASCII files are uncomplicated and a computer standard of sorts. ASCII files contain only your text, spaces and end-of-line markers. The end-of-line markers are sometimes called hard returns or carriage returns by the makers of various word processing packages. Many word processors allow you to retrieve ASCII files using the same procedures you would use to retrieve document files. Depending on your word processor, using ASCII files to import 1-2-3 data, should be as easy, or easier, than importing any other kind of file format. Unfortunately, it may not be the best method because you can lose much of the original formatting.

All versions of 1-2-3 can create ASCII files from spreadsheet data using the /Print File command. The print settings you choose are important because some settings will minimize the amount of editing you will need to do to format your data. Because 1-2-3 creates an ASCII file that mimics the output, you typically want to avoid placing headers, footers, and page breaks within the export file: Usually the locations for page breaks within the word processor will differ from those in the 1-2-3 output and you don't want extra headers, footers and blank lines to appear in a seemingly haphazard fashion. If you do want repeating headers and footers, it is usually better to create them from within the word processor anyway. Along the same lines, you can let the word processor set the page breaks for you automatically or specify them yourself. Eliminating the formatting can give you much better control of the entire process.

PUBLISHING 1-2-3

Other settings you should pay attention to are the left and right margins. Because the file you create with /Print File is supposed to be a mirror of what would otherwise be sent to the printer, a left margin greater than zero adds an equivalent number of spaces to the beginning of each line. Set the left margin to zero to eliminate these beginning spaces. Moving text to the right with margins or indents is easier than moving text to the left by removing unnecessary spaces. The right margin should be set to the maximum setting for the release of 1-2-3 that your are using. In 1-2-3, Release 2.3, the maximum is 240 and in Release 3.1 the maximum is 1,000. This will allow the ranges you specify for printing to determine the length of each line or the data will wrap naturally.

Files created with /Print File can contain more than one set of ranges within the spreadsheet. If you have a large spreadsheet from which you want to import more than one range, you have a choice of creating a separate print file for each of the ranges or including them all in one file. Your decision should be based on how comfortable you are with moving text around within the word processor and whether you have some idea beforehand about the order of the ranges appearing in the final document. If you are going to copy all of the individual ranges to one file, it is often better to print them in the order they will appear in the final document rather than moving them later. Placing all of the ranges within one file is normally faster than creating a file with /Print File for each range.

Steps for Creating an ASCII File

1. Invoke the /Print File command.

2. Enter the name of the ASCII file (1-2-3 calls it a Text file). You can either type in the name or highlight a name that already exists and press ENTER. If the file already exists, 1-2-3 asks you to specify whether you should Cancel the command or Replace the old file with a new one.

1-2-3's default extension for the ASCII file is .PRN. Some word processors automatically create their own file name extensions and refuse to use any other. If your

BRINGING 1-2-3 DATA INTO YOUR WORD PROCESSOR

word processor is one of these, you might consider naming the file with the pathname of your word processing directory instead of accepting the 1-2-3 default pathname.

Once you have named the file created with /Print File, the Print Settings dialog box is displayed. This box is the same one displayed when you use the /Print Printer command.

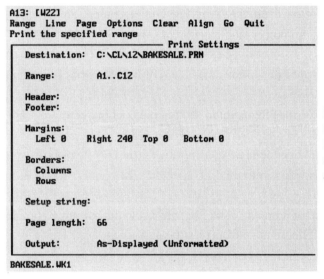

Figure 8-7 is a sample of the Print Settings box for the BAKESALE.WK1 spreadsheet used in Figure 8-1.

3. Identify the Range of the spreadsheet to be included in the Print File. If a label overlaps to another cell, make sure you include all its cells within the range. You may end up with extra columns of information that you do not want in your final document, but usually it is easier to eliminate extra text than it is to duplicate missing text. In this example, we wanted to use the entire spreadsheet and it would fit on one page, so the selected range of A1..C12 encompasses the entire spreadsheet.

Note that if any hidden columns occur within the specified range, they will not be printed to the file. You can use this feature to select the columns you want to include

PUBLISHING 1-2-3

within the ASCII file. By hiding the columns you do not want to appear using the /Worksheet Column Hide command, you eliminate them from the ASCII file.

4. Select "Options Margins None" from the /Print File menu. The None command changes the left, top and bottom margins to zero and the right margin to the maximum number of 240. With early releases you will have to change each margin setting individually.

5. Select "Other Unformatted" from the /Print File Options menu. This removes any previously defined headers, footers, and page breaks from being printed.

6. Select Quit from the /Print File Options menu to return to the /Print File menu.

7. Select Align from the /Print File menu to set the line count to zero.

8. Select Go from the /Print File menu to save the range to the file. If you only want to have one range of values saved within the file, go to step 12.

9. If you want to append another range of the spreadsheet to the bottom of the file, select Range from the /Print File menu and specify the new range.

10. If you want to add one or more blank lines to the end of the file to create some space between it and the new range, select "Line" from the /Print File menu as many times as you want blank lines.

11. Repeat steps 8 through 10 until all of the desired ranges from the spreadsheet have been added to the file.

12. Select Quit from the /Print File menu to return to the spreadsheet in Ready mode.

BRINGING 1-2-3 DATA INTO YOUR WORD PROCESSOR

Saving to a Worksheet File

Some word processors are capable of importing worksheets into their documents. 1-2-3 worksheet files will have a .WKS or WK1 extension, depending on the version you use. If your word processor can work with only one of these formats, 1-2-3 has a utility that translates files from one format to another. There are two major advantages to using worksheet files rather than ASCII files for importing 1-2-3 data. The first is that you usually do not have to create special files with special formatting to perform the import.

The second advantage of importing worksheet files instead of ASCII files is that most word processors retain more advanced formatting, usually using TABs to align columns of information instead of spaces. The reason TABs are better for imported text is that spaces can create problems with different type faces. Columns created with proportional fonts are very difficult to line up vertically because their characters vary in width. For example, the word "ill" takes up less space than the word "mom" because the letters "m" and "o" are wider than "i" and "l." Additionally, it is much easier to move columns formatted with TABs; you simply adjust the tab stops.

Some word processors allow you to import data directly from within that word processor; with others you need to first use the word processor's translation utility to convert the worksheet file into the word processor's format. WordPerfect is a word processor that can import worksheet files directly. Translation utilities are often provided by word processing companies to assist you in transferring a noncompatible file format into the word processor's format. Later in this chapter, when you work with .DIF files, you will have a chance to work with two translation utilities.

Assuming your word processor can import worksheet files, you will still have some other decisions to make. If you want the entire worksheet file imported, all you need to do is save the file as normal within 1-2-3. If your word processor is only able to import an entire worksheet file and you want to import only a range within it, you will first want to Xtract worksheet files that reflect the ranges of data to be imported. If you want columns within a range to be omitted, you should Hide the columns from

PUBLISHING 1-2-3

view before importing. If your word processor can access ranges by Range Names, you should consider naming ranges within the worksheet to simplify the process of accessing those ranges within the worksheet.

Saving Entire Worksheets for Import

To save an entire worksheet for import, you use steps already familiar to you. Perform the following steps:

1. Save the file using the /File Save command.

2. Type the name of the worksheet file or highlight the name and press ENTER.

3. If the name already exists, 1-2-3 asks you to either Cancel the command, Replace the old file with the current one, or Backup the current file with the old one.

Saving Ranges within a Worksheet for Importing

If you need to create smaller worksheets from a larger one, you will Xtract a range from the original worksheet. You could be required to do this if the file is too large to fit on one page or if you only want a part of a worksheet for your document. You will need to create a separate worksheet for each range that needs to be imported.

If you want to import a range within a worksheet and your word processor is only capable of importing entire worksheets, perform the following steps to create the worksheets to be imported:

1. Select the /File Xtract command.

2. You are then presented with two options, Formula or Values. If you choose to "Xtract the Formulas" from the larger worksheet, you need to make sure that all cell references made by the extracted formulas are themselves extracted. If you can meet this condition, then the worksheet you produce will contain the formulas for the cells that you are extracting. If the range you want to extract contains formulas whose cell

BRINGING 1-2-3 DATA INTO YOUR WORD PROCESSOR

references are not within the range, you will have to choose the Values option. The resulting worksheet will then only contain the current values of the cells where formulas resided.

3. Select the name of the file. Depending on which version of 1-2-3 you are using, an extension of .WK1 or .WKS will be assumed. You can select the name by either typing it in, accepting the default name if one appears, or highlighting a name that already exists and pressing ENTER.

4. Select the range of the worksheet to be extracted. For example, if you wanted to import everything but the main heading of the worksheet displayed in Figure 8-5, you would state the range as being A4..E15. Of course, if you had previously named this range, you could enter it by typing the name of the range.

5. If you are creating a file that already exists, you will be presented with three options. You can Cancel the command, Replace the old file with the newly extracted one, or Backup the new file with the old one.

The file is then created using the range you specified. All references are automatically adjusted to reflect any change in position within the worksheet. Sometimes you will experience difficulties with the cell references if you directly import the newly Xtracted file. Because of this, you should make the new worksheet active and save it.

6. Select /File Retrieve to make the newly created file active within 1-2-3. You can also use this time to make sure you've Xtracted the correct portion of the worksheet.

7. Select /File Save to save the file.

8. Select the name of the file. Depending on the 1-2-3 program you are using, an extension of .WK1 or .WKS will be assumed. You can select the name by either typing

PUBLISHING 1-2-3

it in, accepting the default name by pressing ENTER or highlighting a pre-existing name and pressing ENTER.

9. If the file already exists, you will need to select either the Cancel option, the Replace option which replaces the old file with the new one, or the Backup option which keeps the old file as a backup to the new one.

Hiding Columns

1-2-3 Release 2.01 and above has the capability of hiding columns from view. Many word processors will ignore columns that are hidden when the file is imported, thus making it seem as though the columns were never there.

Figure 8-8 shows a portion of a membership spreadsheet. The entire spreadsheet contains nine columns whose names are: FIRST, LAST NAME, ADDRESS, CITY, ST, ZIP, TITLE, HOURS, and DUES. HOURS refers to the number of hours each member has worked in service activities. DUES indicates whether the member has paid their dues for the year. Assume you want to create a document that contains a list of each member and their number of accumulated service hours. You could use hidden columns to hide the information you do not want included in the document before you import the file.

	A	B	C	D	E	F
1		SUNNYSIDERS MEMBERSHIP INFORMATION				
2						
3	FIRST	LAST NAME	ADDRESS	CITY	ST	ZIP
4	Nicole	Adams	9012 Hagadorn Ave.	Lambertville	MI	48144
5	Janice	Burnett	578 Madison Ave.	Temperance	MI	48182
6	Diane	Calhoun	865 Track St.	Samaria	MI	48182
7	Percy	Cameron	321 Prism Ave.	Samaria	MI	48182
8	Nathan	Curtis	126 Higgins Ave.	Lambertville	MI	48144
9	Jan	Edwards	1234 Main St.	Temperance	MI	48182
10	Janet	Edwardson	134 Main St.	Temperance	MI	48182
11	Joseph	Hamilton	1234 Carson St.	Lambertville	MI	48144
12	Marti	Harden	532 Jackson Ave.	Temperance	MI	48182
13	Emily	Hawthorne	6543 York St.	Ida	MI	48140
14	Mark	Henson	321 Secor Rd.	Lambertville	MI	48144
15	Emily	Hiram	543 Minx St.	Ida	MI	48140
16	Stephen	Johnson	145 Hawkins Rd.	Ida	MI	48140
17	Jane	Kohler	421 Banton Ave.	Temperance	MI	48182
18	Harrison	Lafferty	566 Jackman Rd.	Temperance	MI	48182
19	John	Madison	9876 Hawthorne Blvd.	Ida	MI	48140
20	Arlene	Markus	891 Adams St.	Ida	MI	48140

MEMBERS.WK1

BRINGING 1-2-3 DATA INTO YOUR WORD PROCESSOR

To create hidden columns within a spreadsheet, perform the following steps:

1. Highlight the first column to be hidden.

2. Select the /Worksheet Column Hide command.

3. Specify the column or range of columns to hide. For the spreadsheet in Figure 8-8, you could specify C3..G3. The columns immediately will disappear from view as depicted in Figure 8-9.

```
H3: "HOURS                                                              READY

           A          B          H         I      J      K      L
 1                    SUNNYSIDERS MEMBERSHIP INFORMATION
 2
 3     FIRST      LAST NAME    HOURS     DUES
 4     Nicole     Adams         34.7      Y
 5     Janice     Burnett       45.8      Y
 6     Diane      Calhoun       45.2      Y
 7     Percy      Cameron       23.5      Y
 8     Nathan     Curtis        12.4      Y
 9     Jan        Edwards       12.0      Y
10     Janet      Edwardson     65.0      Y
11     Joseph     Hamilton      34.0      Y
12     Marti      Harden        78.3      N
13     Emily      Hauthorne     13.0      Y
14     Mark       Henson        54.1      Y
15     Emily      Hiram         13.0      Y
16     Stephen    Johnson       23.9      Y
17     Jane       Kohler        23.4      Y
18     Harrison   Lafferty      45.7      Y
19     John       Madison       23.9      N
20     Arlene     Markus        65.4      Y
MEMBERS.WK1
```

Figure 8-9: The same spreadsheet as in Figure 8-8 except that columns C through G have been hidden from view.

At this point, what you do will depend on the results you want. You could create a /Print File and specify the range to be imported, you could save the entire Worksheet, or you could Xtract a portion of the worksheet. In the example, you could decide to create the chart and column headers within your word processing package and choose to exclude the Dues column. The range you would use with whichever method for importing you choose would be A4..H31.

Depending on the method you use to select the range, the hidden columns may suddenly appear with asterisks (*) next to them. Do not be concerned, the columns will disappear once the range selection has been made.

Note: To redisplay the hidden columns, you use the /Worksheet Column Display command.

Using Range Names in Worksheets to Access Parts of Files

WordPerfect is an example of a word processing package that is capable of directly accessing ranges within a worksheet. You do not need to Xtract individual ranges of a large worksheet for importing purposes. Because you do not have the worksheet in front of you, you may have difficulty identifying the range of the worksheet to be imported. Range names are used to specify a cell or range by a name. They are easier to remember and identify, but they must first be created within the 1-2-3 spreadsheet.

To create Range Names within a spreadsheet, you must:

1. Select /Range Name Create.

2. Type the name for the range. It must be fifteen characters or fewer. Range names cannot include spaces or any other symbols used for specific purposes in 1-2-3. That is, you cannot create a range name that is the same as a function name or cell address name, starts with a number, or contains only numbers.

3. Select the range to be associated with the name. As an example, you could create a range name called NAMESONLY for the spreadsheet depicted in Figure 8-8 that identifies cells A4..B31 as the range.

Saving a Graph to a .PIC File

1-2-3 creates graphic images of graphs that are in a .PIC file format. If your word processor can import graphic images, you will need to check if it accepts .PIC files.

BRINGING 1-2-3 DATA INTO YOUR WORD PROCESSOR

As with worksheet files, your word processor may import .PIC files directly or you may need to use a conversion utility to translate the .PIC file to its acceptable format.

To create a .PIC file, you must perform the following steps:

1. Create a graph. Continue viewing and modifying it until you feel that it looks good. Consider not creating titles using 1-2-3. Instead you can create them within the word processing package. Depending on the versatility of your word processor, you may also be able to create the data labels as well. If the final output of your graph will be in black and white you will want to select Graph Options B&W to obtain all the hatchmark patterns that you will need to differentiate graph ranges.

2. Select /Graph Save.

3. Type in the name of the file or highlight the name and press ENTER. 1-2-3 automatically creates the .PIC extension.

4. If the file name already exists, you must choose the Cancel or Replace the option. Cancel will abort the /Graph Save command and Replace stores the new graphic in place of the old one.

Using the Translate Utility to Create a .DIF or .DBF File

There are two other file formats for 1-2-3 worksheets that your word processor may be able to import. They are the .DIF and .DBF file formats, the first being a standard of sorts for spreadsheets and the latter for database packages such as dBase. These two formats are not created from within 1-2-3, however. You must use the Translate Utility provided by 1-2-3 to translate the WK? file to the desired format.

WordPerfect can use both .DIF and .DBF file formats. They are especially useful for creating merge files. The example in this chapter will use a .DIF file. The spreadsheet depicted in Figure 8-8 contains information that could be used to create names and addresses for merged letters. If you wanted to create a merge file using this

PUBLISHING 1-2-3

information, in WordPerfect the easiest method would be to first convert the file to a .DIF file.

1-2-3's Translate Utility can be used to translate any worksheet file. You might want to consider using 1-2-3's database capabilities to select the specific records you want and place them in an Output Range. You could then Xtract the Output Range to a worksheet file. If you do choose to create the worksheet using Xtract, no matter what the reason, you should always retrieve the Xtracted file within 1-2-3 and save it again before using the Translate Utility.

To create a .DIF file using the Translate Utility:

1. Use the /File Xtract command to Xtract the part of the file to be translated into a .DIF or .DBF file. For merge files, you will want to select a range that does not include labels and worksheet headings. Once the file has been created, use /File Retrieve to make it active and save it again using the /File Save command. For more information about Xtracting files, see the section above named "Saving Ranges Within A Worksheet For Importing."

To prepare the spreadsheet in Figure 8-8 for a WordPerfect merge file, first use /File Xtract to create a worksheet using the A4..F31 range. This eliminates all headings from the worksheet. Then use /File Retrieve to make the file active and use /File Save to save it again.

2. Exit 1-2-3 so that you are at the DOS prompt. Make your 1-2-3 directory your current directory if it is not already.

3. Type TRANS and press the ENTER key. The first screen of the Translate Utility depicted in Figure 8-10 appears on the screen. It lists the different file types this utility can translate.

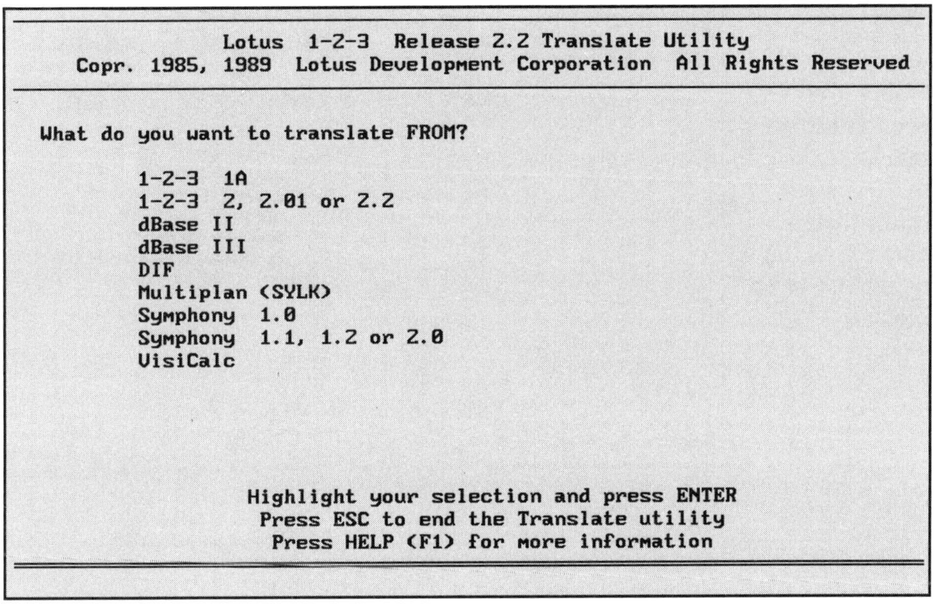

BRINGING 1-2-3 DATA INTO YOUR WORD PROCESSOR

```
            Lotus  1-2-3  Release 2.2 Translate Utility
   Copr. 1985, 1989 Lotus Development Corporation All Rights Reserved

What do you want to translate FROM?

        1-2-3  1A
        1-2-3  2, 2.01 or 2.2
        dBase II
        dBase III
        DIF
        Multiplan (SYLK)
        Symphony  1.0
        Symphony  1.1, 1.2 or 2.0
        VisiCalc




                  Highlight your selection and press ENTER
                   Press ESC to end the Translate utility
                    Press HELP (F1) for more information
```

Figure 8-10: The first screen that appears in the Translate Utility which determines the type of file being translated.

4. Highlight the version of 1-2-3 you used to create the WK? file and press ENTER to indicate the type of file that is being translated.

5. Figure 8-11 on the next page displays the second screen that appears, listing the different formats the utility can create. If you wanted to create a .DBF formatted file, you would choose one of the dBase formats. For this example, highlight the .DIF file and press ENTER.

6. A third screen appears reminding you that the Translate Utility only works on Saved files as opposed to Xtracted files. Press the ESC key to continue. Figure 8-12 displays the fourth screen of the Translate utility.

PUBLISHING 1-2-3

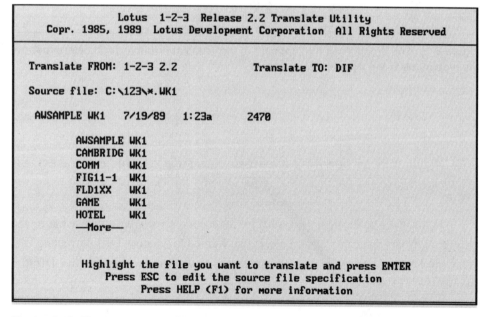

Figure 8-11: The second screen that appears in the Translate Utility that determines the type of file to be created.

Figure 8-12: The fourth screen that appears in the Translate Utility that is used to identify the name of the file to be translated.

BRINGING 1-2-3 DATA INTO YOUR WORD PROCESSOR

7. Highlight the name of the file to be translated and press ENTER to select it. If the file is not located in the current directory, press the ESC key, type in the name of the new path, and press ENTER.

8. The utility then displays the assumed name for the Target file, which is the same name as the source file with a .DIF extension. To accept the name, press ENTER. To create a new name, type it in and press ENTER. If the new file name already exists, a dialog box appears stating this and asks you to confirm that it be overwritten.

9. Select Yes in the dialog box to confirm that the translation should proceed.

10. A timing bar appears on the screen indicating the percentage of the translation that has been accomplished. When finished, press the ESC key twice and answer Yes to exit the program.

Importing Data Into A WordPerfect Document

Now that you have learned a variety of methods for creating import files, you are now ready to import them into documents. A couple of issues should be addressed at the outset because they apply to most importing of text from a foreign source. First of all, you will find that it is a good idea to do your page formatting before you import the text. Page formatting means selecting your type face, your page size, margins, spacing, and paper orientation. Your text will be formatted with the current word processing settings. It only makes sense to have that formatting be consistent within the final format of the document and, depending on the word processor, it can be hard to change the formatting later on.

If you want the formatting of the imported data to differ from that of the rest of the document, you should change the formatting at the point where the data is to be imported. The reasoning for this is similar to what we've just discussed: It can be hard to make changes afterward. For example, you may choose a base font for the document as being Courier 10 pitch but you might want the body of the worksheet data to be

A CLOSER LOOK

Importing ASCII Text

Importing ASCII text with WordPerfect is very easy. Although other options are available, the best method is to retrieve the ASCII file as if it were a document. To import ASCII text you can either use the Retrieve function or retrieve the file from the List Files screen. To use the Retrieve function:

1. Press the Retrieve (SHIFT-F10) function key

2. Type in the name of the file to be imported.

3. Press the ENTER key.

---

smaller, such as Courier 12 pitch. This will allow more chart to fit on the page and also help to make the chart stand out more from the body of the document. You would start the document in 10 pitch, change to 12 pitch at the point where the data is to appear, and then import the file. At the end of the chart you would then change the type style back to 10 pitch.

Another reason to choose your formatting before you import is that you can immediately get a feel for how the document will look. If the imported text is too wide for the current settings, you can see that and fix it immediately.

Another good habit to get into as you import text into documents is that of saving the file just before you import the text. If, after you import the text, you realize you need to make a major formatting change, it is often easier to delete the document from memory and retrieve the version saved just before the import. Then you can adjust the formatting and try again. If you do not do this, you could be left with a document that requires a lot of cleanup.

Importing ASCII Text

For most word processors, importing ASCII text is fairly simple. Often, you can use the same method you use for retrieving a normal word processing file. WordPerfect, for example, can import ASCII text with exactly the same commands used to

BRINGING 1-2-3 DATA INTO YOUR WORD PROCESSOR

import a regular document. It senses that the file is ASCII and performs the conversion immediately. For specifics on how to import ASCII text, see the "A Closer Look" on this and the opposite page.

Earlier in this chapter, we stated that, although importing ASCII files is usually easy, there are drawbacks. The letter in Figure 8-2 was created using an imported ASCII file for the chart. Because it was created using a monospaced Courier type, it looks just fine.

But look at WordPerfect's Print View Document screen of the same letter in Figure 8-13 on the following page. The only difference between this letter and the one in Figure 8-2 is that the type style was changed to a proportional font. Notice that the columns of the table no longer line up because each character's width varies. This characterizes the difficulties sometimes associated with importing ASCII files. Because the ASCII file lined up the columns according to the spaces between the columns, proportional fonts cause the columns to stagger across the page.

You would not catch this problem as you looked at the document in the normal edit screen because WordPerfect uses monospaced fonts in its edit screen. You need to use the Print View Document screen or print the document to the printer to see how the proportional type face affects the output. To fix this problem, you would need to edit the chart by delet-

A CLOSER LOOK

Importing ASCII Text Using Function List

1. Press the List (F5) function key. Type in the pathname where the file is located and press ENTER.

2. Highlight the file name to be imported.

3. Type R to retrieve the file.

4. If you are importing the file into a document, WordPerfect displays the message "Retrieve into current document? No (Yes)". To continue, you need to type a Y for yes. As the file is being imported, WordPerfect displays a "DOS Text Conversion In Progress" message to warn you that the file is not a standard WordPerfect file and that WordPerfect is converting it.

PUBLISHING 1-2-3

ing the spaces between the columns and replacing them with a tab. While this is not hard, it takes extra time because you must change each line.

Figure 8-13: The Print View Document of the same letter as in Figure 8-2 but printed with a proportional font.

```
bake sale against the projected costs. Notice that our expen
projected - a bake sale first!

BAKE SALE EXPENSES (PROJECTED & ACTUAL)

DESCRIPTION              PROJECTED          ACTUAL
OF COSTS                 AMOUNT             AMOUNT

Room Rental              $50.00             $50.00
Custodial Services       $75.00             $75.00
Advertising              $30.00             $31.95
Table And Chair Rental   $55.00             $50.00
Miscellaneous            $25.00             $14.95
----------------------------------------
TOTAL                    $235.00            $221.00

Kate told me today that the gross profit for the bakesale
$850.00 and $900.00. This means we netter over $620.00 for
```

One other point needs to be addressed in regards to proportional type styles. If the imported ASCII chart contains only numbers (no commas, dollar signs, etc.) and if each column contains the same number of digits, usually the columns will line up. Most proportional fonts make the digits the same width for purposes of lining numbers up.

Importing A .WKS Or .WK1 File

If your word processor supports the importing of worksheet files (.WKS or .WK1), you may be able to avoid some of the formatting problems created with ASCII imports. You need to use your word processor's references to determine its procedure for importing worksheets. Typically, when these files are imported, columns use tabs. Some word processors even adjust the tab stops within the document to imitate the column widths of the original worksheet. Once the import is complete, you may then go back to adjust the tab stops. Using tabs avoids the problems with columns not lining up when a proportional font is selected, although you may need to change the type of tab stop so that some numeric columns are aligned on the right side. WordPerfect uses right-aligned tabs on numeric columns when it imports a worksheet file.

BRINGING 1-2-3 DATA INTO YOUR WORD PROCESSOR

Figure 8-14 displays a portion of a letter similar to the one in Figure 8-13 using a proportional type face. The difference between the two letters is that the chart was imported using a worksheet file instead of an ASCII file. WordPerfect formats the columns using left- and right-aligned tabs. Notice that the columns now line up even with the proportional font. Also notice, that the line above the totals needs to be extended within the document because of differences in importing.

```
bake sale against the projected costs.  Notice that our expen
projected - a bake sale first!

BAKE SALE EXPENSES (PROJECTED & ACTUAL)

DESCRIPTION          PROJECTED        ACTUAL
OF COSTS             AMOUNT           AMOUNT

Room Rental                $50.00        $50.00
Custodial Services         $75.00        $75.00
Advertising                $30.00        $31.95
Table And Chair Rental     $55.00        $50.00
Miscellaneous              $25.00        $14.95
---------------------------------------------
TOTAL                     $235.00       $221.00

Kate told me today that the gross profit for the bakesale
$850.00 and $900.00.  This means we netter over $620.00 for
```

Figure 8-14: The same letter as in Figure 8-13 but using tab stops to create the columns of the chart.

A CLOSER LOOK

Using WordPerfect's Print View Document Mode

1. Press the Print (SHIFT-F7) function key.

2. Type V for View Document.

3. Change the view by typing a 1 for the 100% view (normal page size although the full page cannot appear on screen), 2 for the 200% view, 3 for Full Page (the full page is displayed in reduced size), or 4 for Facing Pages (two pages are displayed at once).

4. Use the arrow keys to move between and around the pages.

5. To leave the Print View, press either the Exit (F7) function key to return to the document or the Cancel (F1) function key to return to the Print menu.

PUBLISHING 1-2-3

Bringing Worksheet Data Files In As Text Using WordPerfect

WordPerfect requires the use of the Text In/Text Out function to import worksheet data into your document using tab-delimited columns. Within WordPerfect, you cannot import more than 20 columns of text. If you try, WordPerfect only takes the first 20 columns. To import a worksheet file into a WordPerfect document, move the cursor to the position where you want the data imported and perform the following steps:

1. Press the Text In/Text Out (CTRL-F5) function key.

2. Type 5 or s to select Spreadsheet from the menu.

3. Type 1 or I to select Spreadsheet Import from the menu.

The Spreadsheet Import screen depicted in Figure 8-15 displays on the screen.

```
Spreadsheet: Import

     1 - Filename              C:\CL\12\MEMBERS.WK1
     2 - Range                 <Spreadsheet>        A1..I95
     3 - Type                  Text
     4 - Perform Import
```

Figure 8-15: The Spreadsheet Import menu within WordPerfect.

4. Type 1 or f for the filename.

5. You can either type the name of the worksheet file to be imported or you can press the List (F5) function key to display the List screen, type the path where the file is located and press ENTER, highlight the name of the file to be imported, and type either 1 or r to retrieve the name of the file.

6. If you need to select the range of the worksheet to be imported, type a 2 or r to

BRINGING 1-2-3 DATA INTO YOUR WORD PROCESSOR

select Range. WordPerfect is flexible in that you can specify a range of a worksheet to be imported instead of first having to Xtract smaller worksheets to be imported from larger ones.

7. If you want the entire worksheet to be imported, you usually don't need to do anything. The Range that is selected by default is the entire worksheet. To select a range other than the one currently selected, you can do one of the following three things.

a. You can type in the range using the cell references and press ENTER. For example, you could type in A4..H12.

b. You can type in any range name defined for the worksheet and press ENTER.

c. You can press the List (F5) function key to display a list of the defined ranges for the spreadsheet. Figure 8-16 displays a sample screen listing the range names for the worksheet named MEMBERS.WK1. Highlight the one you want and press ENTER.

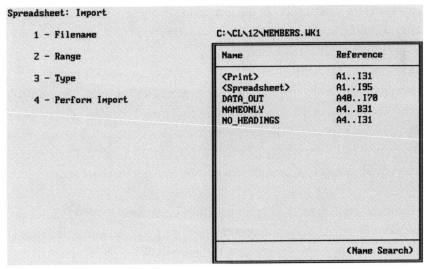

Figure 8-16: The menu of defined ranges for the specified worksheet.

PUBLISHING 1-2-3

8. Type a 3 or t for the type of import WordPerfect should perform.

9. Type 2 or e to tell WordPerfect to import the worksheet file as tabbed text.

10. Type a 4 or p to have WordPerfect import the worksheet file into the document.

WordPerfect then returns you to your document and inserts the imported text at the cursor location. WordPerfect creates line tabs to coincide with the column widths of the worksheet file. It uses left- and right-justified tabs to do this. Any center-aligned tabs from the worksheet are inserted as left justified in the document.

Bringing Worksheet Data Files In As Tables Using WordPerfect

WordPerfect has a powerful feature called Tables. In some aspects, Tables will remind you of 1-2-3 spreadsheets. WordPerfect refers to columns and rows using letters and numbers just as 1-2-3 does. It also refers to cells in much the same way as 1-2-3 does as well. Although Tables do have some math capabilities, they are very simplistic compared to 1-2-3's.

WordPerfect's Tables excel in the formatting that you can do with them. Figure 8-4 has an example of a table in the bottom left hand corner of the newsletter. Formats can be specified for cells, rows, columns, blocks of cells, and the entire table. The formatting can include justification of text horizontally and vertically, type face, type size, underlining, double underlining, shading, italics, bolding, column widths, number of decimal places, shading, types of boxing around the cells, no boxing around the cells, and many others. Whatever you place inside the cell will automatically conform to that cell's formatting. Unlike 1-2-3, two or more cells can be joined together to make one cell or one cell can be split into two or more cells.

A Table can contain up to 32 columns. If the worksheet range you are importing contains more than that, WordPerfect will import the first 32 columns. If the table you import is too wide for the paper, WordPerfect prints only the part that will fit and cuts

BRINGING 1-2-3 DATA INTO YOUR WORD PROCESSOR

off the right side of the table. You will need to make adjustments manually to make a too-large table fit onto the page.

There are three methods you can use to import a worksheet into a table. In all three cases, only the values of the worksheet are imported, none of the formulas. The first two methods produce similar results. WordPerfect defines the Table to match the imported worksheet, formatting the cells to conform to the worksheet format.

In the first method for importing, you retrieve the entire worksheet file as though it were any document file, either using the Retrieve (SHIFT-F1) function or retrieving from the List (F5) screen. WordPerfect displays the message "*Importing Spreadsheet*" as it performs the import. If the resulting table is too wide for the page, WordPerfect displays the message "Warning Table Extends Beyond Right Margin" as well.

The second method uses the same Text In/Out (CTRL-F5) function used to import a worksheet into text, which was discussed in the previous section of this chapter. The instructions for importing a worksheet into text applies for tables as well except that item 3, Type, should be set to Table. Once the table is created with the worksheet data in place, you can format it. The text contained within the formatted cells will immediately conform to the new formatting.

The third method for retrieving a worksheet into a table requires more knowledge of WordPerfect tables. Briefly, you must first define the table within WordPerfect by using the Columns/Table (ALT-F7) function key and selecting Tables and then Create. Type the number of columns and press ENTER and then type the number of rows and press ENTER. The table is then created and you are placed within the table in Table Edit mode, depicted in Figure 8-17 on the following page. At this point you can use the menu at the bottom of the screen to do any formatting you want for the table.

PUBLISHING 1-2-3

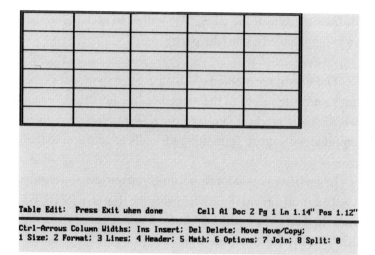

Figure 8-17: A newly created table in Table Edit mode.

Once you have finished the formatting of the table, press the Exit (F7) function key to leave table edit mode. Use the tab or SHIFT-tab keys within the table to quickly move around the cells of the table. Locate the cursor within the top-leftmost cell where the imported worksheet is to be placed. Normally this will be cell A1 because you will want the entire table to be filled with the worksheet. Use either of the two previously discussed methods for importing worksheets into tables. WordPerfect performs the import differently because the cursor is located within a table already. It assumes that instead of it creating and defining a new table, it should import the values into the one already defined.

Occasionally, you will receive a warning "Replace previous contents of table with spreadsheet? No (Yes)" to warn you that any data stored in cells of the current table may be overwritten by the importing worksheet. Type a "y" to continue the import. The imported data is then placed into the table, with the contents of each cell conforming to the formatting of the existing table. If you have done no formatting, all cells are left justified regardless of the justification of the worksheets cells because that is the default justification of table cells. If the worksheet is larger than the table, WordPerfect fits as much as it can into the table and ignores the rest.

BRINGING 1-2-3 DATA INTO YOUR WORD PROCESSOR

Editing The Formatting of Tables After Importing

Once you have imported the worksheet into a table, you might decide to change its formatting. The quickest method for editing a table is to place the cursor somewhere inside of it and press the Columns/Table (ALT-F7) function key. This places you back in Table Edit mode for this table. You can then use any of the formatting functions at the bottom of the screen to adjust the appearance of the table. For example, you can adjust the width of a column by placing the highlight within the column and then use the CTRL-LEFT ARROW key to decrease the width and CTRL-RIGHT ARROW to increase the width. It is important to note here, that you cannot alter the contents of a cell within Table Edit mode. To edit the contents of cells, you must first us the Exit (F7) function key to return to normal document editing and then change the contents of the cell.

Creating a Formatted Document with Imported Data

You are now ready to format an entire document that includes imported 1-2-3 worksheet data. This example does not contain a lot of text, but the techniques used would be the same for longer documents.

Figure 8-18: A display of the finished document with imported worksheet file as the chart. It is shown now to help you visualize the result so that you might understand some of the steps taken to create it.

PUBLISHING 1-2-3

One of the factors you should consider immediately as you look over the finished product is that the worksheet file contains seven fairly wide columns. Since the space available across the page will probably be a concern, you should initially consider how wide your margins are and the size of the type you will use. For this document, we decided to go with 0.6-inch left and right margins to help make room for the worksheet. We also decided to attempt to use the same size type in the chart as in the main body of the document but, when charts don't fit across the page, remember you can reduce the type size.

The following steps outline the general procedures you could use with a word processor to produce the document displayed in Figure 8-18:

1. Create the formatting for the document. a. Change the left and right margin settings so that they are approximately 0.6 inches.

   b. Choose the font to be used for the main body of the document. Skip this step if your word processor requires manually selecting each type face whenever you require a change in type size.

2. Create the heading for the document.

   a. Choose a font that is larger than the font for the main body of the text.

   b. Turn on bolding of text.

   c. Horizontally center **SUNNYSIDERS CLUB** on one line, press ENTER, and horizontally center **MEMBERSHIP INFORMATION**.

   d. Turn off bolding and return the font size to the size for the main document.

   e. Press ENTER twice to move down the page.

BRINGING 1-2-3 DATA INTO YOUR WORD PROCESSOR

3. Type the main body of the document.

a. Type **Below are listed the members and affiliated members of the SunnySiders Club, their addresses and number of accumulated service hours for the year.** This is the main body of the text. (Remember, the length of text for this example is very short but the same techniques can be used for very long documents as well.)

b. Press ENTER twice to move the cursor to the location where the chart is to be imported.

4. Import the chart.

a. Save the current document before you import the chart.

b. Use the method your system requires to import worksheets.

The original worksheet, an example of which can be seen in Figure 8-8, contains nine columns. You only want seven columns of information. You also want to eliminate the first two rows of the worksheet which contain the headings. If your system can import a range of a worksheet directly, you only need to do an import. If your system cannot, you must first create the import file using either the /Print File command or the /File Xtract command discussed in the previous section.

c. After the import, you will discover that there is not quite enough room to have the worksheet display across the page without word wrapping. See Figure 8-19 on page 37 for an example of the word wrapping being done to the chart. Exit the document without saving it and retrieve the version you saved before the import.

d. Move to the bottom of the document.

e. Change the font to a smaller one.

PUBLISHING 1-2-3

Some of you might wonder why you go through the extra steps of exiting the document, retrieving the previous version, etc. You may not need to go through all those steps depending on your word processor. You could just assign a smaller font to the chart and everything would look fine. This will most often work when you are importing ASCII files. However, if you are importing other types of files, your word processor may be inserting formatting codes into your document. WordPerfect, for example, inserts new tab stops which would not work well with a smaller font. It is often easier to just start over than it is to modify the formatting that is already there.

f. Import the worksheet again. This time it fits.

5. Continue typing the main body of the document.

a. Move to the end of the document.

b. Change back to the main font size.

c. Type ENTER twice for space between the chart and the document.

d. Type **Please notify Janice Williams if you find that any of this information is inaccurate.**

6. Format the chart.

a. Add a blank line between the column headings and first line of the chart by moving the cursor to the N in Nicole. Press ENTER.

b. You may want to move the columns horizontally. If you imported an ASCII file, this is done by adding or deleting spaces to each line. If you imported some other formatted file, you may still use spaces or you may be able to adjust by changing tab stops or other formatting capabilities.

c. Bold the line of column headings.

d. Use spaces to center the headings over the columns.

e. Add lines above and below the columns headings and at the end of the chart to add some visual interest. If your word processor does not support some sort of graphic line, use the underscore key to create the top and bottom line by turning on underlining and pressing the space bar to create a line of underscored blanks. To create the middle line, reformat the column headers so they are underlined.

7. Finish the job.

a. Preview the document (if you cannot preview a document, print it).

b. Make any corrections.

c. Print the document.

d. Save the document.

```
                                 SUNNYSIDERS CLUB
                              MEMBERSHIP INFORMATION


Below are listed the members and affiliated members of the SunnySiders Club, th
number of accumulated service hours for the year.


FIRST               LAST NAME           ADDRESS                          CITY
TITLE                           HOURS
Nicole              Adams               9012 Hagadorn Ave.               Lambertvil
Janice              Burnett             578 Madison Ave.                 Temperance
Diane               Calhoun             865 Track St.                    Samaria
Percy               Cameron             321 Prism Ave.                   Samaria
Nathan              Curtis              126 Higgins Ave.                 Lambertvil
Jan                 Edwards             1234 Main St.                    Temperance
Vice-President                                                   12.0
Janet               Edwardson           134 Main St.                     Temperance
Joseph              Hamilton            1234 Carson St.                  Lambertvil
Marti               Harden              532 Jackson Ave.                 Temperance
Emily               Hawthorne           6543 York St.                    Ida
Mark                Henson              321 Secor Rd.                    Lambertvil
Emily               Hiram               543 Minx St.                     Ida
C:\CL\12\INFO                                      Doc 1 Pg 1 Ln 3" Pos 0.7"
```

Figure 8-19: Example of an imported worksheet that is too wide for the page. Notice that some of the lines of the worksheet have word-wrapped to a second line.

PUBLISHING 1-2-3

Formatting a Document with Imported Data

To produce the document displayed in Figure 8-18 with WordPerfect 5.1:

1. To create the initial formatting for the document: a. Press the Format (SHIFT-F8) function key, select Line Margins, and type .6, ENTER, .6 and ENTER to set the margins.

b. Press ENTER to return to the Format menu, select Document and Initial Base Font, highlight the font and size (the example used was Dutch Roman 12 point), type Select, and press ENTER twice to return to the document.

2. To create the heading for the document:

a. Increase the size of the heading by pressing the Font (CTRL-F8) function key, type Size Large.

b. Press the Bold (F6) function key.

c. Press the Center (SHIFT-F6) function key to center the text, type **SUNNYSIDERS CLUB** and press ENTER. Create the second line by pressing the Center (SHIFT-F6) function key and typing **MEMBERSHIP INFORMATION**.

d. Stop bolding by pressing the Bold (F6) function key and return to the normal font by pressing the Font (SHIFT-F8) function key and selecting Normal.

e. Press ENTER twice to move down the page.

BRINGING 1-2-3 DATA INTO YOUR WORD PROCESSOR

3. To produce the main body of the document:

a. Type: **Below are listed the members and affiliated members of the SunnySiders Club, their addresses and number of accumulated service hours for the year.**

b. Press ENTER twice to move to the location where the chart is to be imported.

4. To import the chart:

a. Save the document by pressing the Save (F10) function key, typing a name for the document and pressing ENTER.

b. Import the range from a spreadsheet file by pressing the Text In/Out (CTRL-F5) function key, and selecting **S**preadsheet **I**mport. Select **F**ilename, type the name of the file not forgetting to use the WK? extension, and press ENTER. Select **R**ange, type A3..H31 for the range, and press ENTER. Select import type by selecting **T**ype **T**ext. Have WordPerfect import the document by selecting **P**erform Import.

c. You discover that the chart does not fit across the page using the current font (See Figure 8-19). Exit the document without saving it by pressing the Exit (F7) key, type **N**o to the saving file query and **N**o to the exit query. Retrieve the previously saved version of the document by pressing the Retrieve (SHIFT-F10) function key, typing the name you gave the document in step a, and pressing ENTER.

d. Move to the bottom of the document by pressing HOME, HOME, and then DOWN ARROW.

e. Change the font size to small by pressing the Font (CTRL-F8) function key and selecting **S**ize **S**mall.

PUBLISHING 1-2-3

f. Re-import the worksheet by pressing the Text In/Out (CTRL-F5) function key, and selecting **S**preadsheet **I**mport. Since WordPerfect retained the previous selections within this menu, just press **P**erform Import.

5. To continue the main body of the document:

a. Press HOME HOME DOWN ARROW to move to the end of the document.

b. Because step a moves you past the [small] code for determining font size, you can omit this step in WordPerfect.

c. Press ENTER twice to give you some space between the chart and the main body of the text.

d. Type **Please notify Janice Williams if you find that any of this information is inaccurate.**

6. To format the chart:

a. Use the ARROW keys to place the cursor on the N in Nicole.

Press ENTER to add a blank line between the column headings and the body of the chart.

b. To bold the line of column headings, press the UP ARROW twice so that the cursor rests on the F of FIRST. Press the Block (ALT-F4 or F12) function key, the END key to block the entire line, and the Bold (F6) function key.

c. In this example, the columns are lined up nicely. If you need to adjust the tab stops, move the cursor just to the right of the current [TabSet] code, press the Format (SHIFT-F8) function key, and select Line Tab Set. For further information about setting Tabs, see the WordPerfect manual.

BRINGING 1-2-3 DATA INTO YOUR WORD PROCESSOR

d. To center the column headings, turn on Reveal Codes by pressing the Reveal Codes (ALT-F3 or F11) function key. Reveal Codes needs to be turned on so that you can see the exact location of the cursor, whether it is on a letter or a code. See Figure 8-20 for a look at the document with Reveal Codes turned on. Press CTRL-LEFT ARROW twice to highlight the T in TITLE. Press the SPACEBAR four times to add four spaces between the [tab] code and TITLE. ZIP has a right-aligned tab governing it. To move ZIP to the left, use the LEFT ARROW keys to highlight the [tab] code just to the right of the P in ZIP. Press the SPACEBAR twice to move ZIP to the left. Move CITY and ADDRESS to the RIGHT by moving the cursor to the beginning letter of each word (using CTRL-LEFT ARROW) and pressing ENTER four times each. Press the Reveal Codes (ALT-F3 or F11) function key to turn off Reveal Codes.

```
hours for the year.

DRESS              CITY           ST    ZIP      TITLE           HOURS

12 Hagadorn Ave.   Lambertville   MI    48144                    34.7
8 Madison Ave.     Temperance     MI    48182                    45.8
5 Track St.        Samaria        MI    48182                    45.2
1 Prism Ave.       Samaria        MI    48182                    23.5
6 Higgins Ave.     Lambertville   MI    48144                    12.4
34 Main St.        Temperance     MI    48182    Vice-President  12.0
4 Main St.         Temperance     MI    48182                    65.0
C:\CL\12\TEST                                     Doc 2 Pg 1 Ln 2.22" Pos 6.56"
                      ▲▲          ▲     ▲   ▲▲        ▲▲         ↵
[HRt]
[SMALL][Tab Set:Abs: 1.41",1.46",2.66",2.7",4.28",4.33",5.37",5.42",5.77",5.82",
6.33",6.37",7.11",7.16",7.89",7.94"][BOLD]FIRST[RGT TAB][TAB]LAST NAME[RGT TAB][
TAB]ADDRESS[RGT TAB][TAB]CITY[RGT TAB][TAB]ST[RGT TAB][TAB][RGT TAB]ZIP[TAB]
TITLE[RGT TAB][TAB][RGT TAB]HOURS[TAB][bold][HRt]
[HRt]
Nicole[RGT TAB][TAB]Adams[RGT TAB][TAB]9012 Hagadorn Ave.[RGT TAB][TAB]Lambertvi
lle[RGT TAB][TAB]MI[RGT TAB][TAB][RGT TAB]48144 [TAB][RGT TAB][TAB][RGT TAB]34.7
 [TAB][HRt]
Janice[RGT TAB][TAB]Burnett[RGT TAB][TAB]578 Madison Ave.[RGT TAB][TAB]Temperanc

Press Reveal Codes to restore screen
```

Figure 8-20: Using Reveal Codes to help center text above the columns.

PUBLISHING 1-2-3

e. Use WordPerfect's Graphics Line function to create the lines. Move to the beginning of the current line by pressing HOME HOME and then LEFT ARROW. Create the graphic line by pressing the Graphics (ALT-F9) function key, selecting Line Horizontal. If desired, change the width of the line by selecting Width of Line, typing .02 and ENTER three times. WordPerfect's graphics lines do not appear in the document edit screen. To see them you must use the Print View Document screen. Preview the appearance of the line by pressing the Print (SHIFT-F7) function key and selecting View Document. You will note that the line is still too close to the headers. Press the Exit (F7) function key to return to the document and press ENTER to add another blank line.

Create the other two graphics lines using the steps presented in the previous paragraph. To create the line below the header, you must first move the cursor to the N on Nicole. To create the bottom line, move to the blank line below the chart. You may want to add or delete a blank line above or below the graphic lines depending on your own preferences.

7. To finish the document:

a. Use the Print View Document screen to preview the document by pressing the Print (SHIFT-F7) function key and selecting View Document.

b. Return to the edit screen to make any corrections by pressing the Exit (F7) function key. Continue steps a and b until the document is as you want it.

c. Once the document is formatted to your satisfaction, print it by pressing the Print (SHIFT-F7) function key and selecting **F**ull.

d. Save the document by pressing the Save (F10) function key, ENTER to accept the current name, and Yes to confirm the Replace document query.

BRINGING 1-2-3 DATA INTO YOUR WORD PROCESSOR

Using The Landscape Option To Increase The Width Of The Page

As in the document created in the above section, you will often have difficulty fitting a chart within the margins of a page because it is too wide. There are methods you can use to increase the amount of chart that will fit. The above example used two methods: selecting a smaller font and using narrower margins. Other methods for solving this problem include printing on larger sheets of paper or turning the paper sideways. Of course, these two methods are dependent on your printer's paper handling abilities.

Turning the paper so that it prints sideways is referred to as either changing the orientation of the paper or printing in landscape mode. Figure 8-21 is an example of the previous document printed using a standard sheet of paper in landscape mode. Because of the change in orientation, the body of the chart fit using the same font size as the body of the text. Because the length of the chart now has become the critical issue, the centered heading of the document was changed to fit on one line instead of two. Making this change kept the entire document on one page using the one size font.

SUNNYSIDERS CLUB MEMBERSHIP INFORMATION

Below are listed the members and affiliated members of the SunnySiders Club, their addresses and number of accumulated service hours for the year.

FIRST	LAST NAME	ADDRESS	CITY	ZIP	TITLE	HOURS
Nicole	Adams	9012 Hagadorn Ave.	Lambertville	48144		34.7
Janice	Burnett	578 Madison Ave.	Temperance	48182		45.8
Percy	Cameron	321 Prism Ave.	Samaria	48182		23.5
Nathan	Curtis	126 Higgins Ave.	Lambertville	48144		12.4
Jan	Edwards	1234 Main St.	Temperance	48182	Vice-President	12.0
Janet	Edwardson	134 Main St.	Temperance	48182		65.0
Joseph	Hamilton	1234 Carson St.	Lambertville	48144		34.0
Marti	Harden	532 Jackson Ave.	Temperance	48182		78.3
Emily	Hawthorne	6543 York St.	Ida	48140		13.0
Stephen	Johnson	145 Hawkins Rd.	Ida	48140		23.9
Jane	Kohler	421 Banton Ave.	Temperance	48182		23.4
Harrison	Lafferty	566 Jackman Rd.	Temperance	48182		45.7
John	Madison	9876 Hawthorne Dr.	Ida	48140		23.9
Arlene	Markus	891 Adams St.	Ida	48140		65.4
Beth	Moeller	4321 Banton Ave.	Temperance	48182	President	43.0
Mary	Randolph	4321 Gingham Ave.	Samaria	48182		23.8
Kate	Robertson	5678 Jackman Rd.	Temperance	48182	Treasurer	45.7
Judy	Smith	148 Sterns Rd.	Lambertville	48144		34.9
Janice	Williams	1234 Sterns Rd.	Lambertville	48144	Secretary	34.9
Carol	Wilson	137 Carlson St.	Lambertville	48144		32.1

Please notify Janice Williams if you find that any of this information is inaccurate.

Figure 8-21: The finished document printed in landscape mode.

A CLOSER LOOK

Changing Page Size or Orientation within WordPerfect

1. Within the document edit screen, make sure the cursor is located where the new page size is to begin. This will normally be at the beginning of the document or at the very beginning of a page.

2. Press the Format (SHIFT-F8) function key and select Page Paper Size.

3. Using the UP and DOWN arrow keys, highlight the appropriate paper size and orientation type.

4. Press s to Select.

5. Press the Exit (F7) function key to return to the edit screen.

If your printer is capable, you could also use larger sizes of paper, including legal size, in the landscape orientation. This would allow for even more room for wider charts. Figure 8-21: A document created using landscape printing.

Linking Spreadsheet Data to a Document

Some word processors can "Link" imported spreadsheet data with their original spreadsheet files, automatically updating the document with any changes made in the spreadsheet data. This means that you can import 1-2-3 data into a document, later change the data within 1-2-3, and have the new values automatically reflected within the document. This is especially useful for documents that are routinely used to present 1-2-3 data that is constantly being changed. You can produce documents that automatically reflect the latest version of a spreadsheet, never having to worry if the latest version of the data is present.

Considerations For Linking Files

Word processors that support linked files usually have elements in common. Usually the document files are updated against the spreadsheet at one of two times, either whenever the document file is retrieved into memory or as a result of a command by the user. Some word processors can perform the update using either method, leaving it to your discretion.

BRINGING 1-2-3 DATA INTO YOUR WORD PROCESSOR

All word processors require the name and location of the spreadsheet file. Some require that the spreadsheet file already exist before you define the link, while others only require that the file exist when you use the link.

You may be limited to the types or number of import files you can use with linking. Your word processor may be able to import a variety of formats of text as discussed earlier in this chapter, but may be limited to which ones it can link. Usually these limits are WK1 and WKS files.

If you change the document's imported spreadsheet data by adding/deleting text or formats, these changes will disappear after the update. This is because the update is usually done by deleting the old imported information and performing an import all over again. Therefore, you will need to be careful with any formatting that you want done to affect the spreadsheet. It is usually possible to affect the entire spreadsheet by having the format affect the entire area of the linked file and it is ususally impossible to have formatting affect only part of a spreadsheet. If you need special formatting done to sections of a linked file, most word processors contain a macro or style feature that can be used to quickly reformat the text after each update.

Usually the link changes are not made unless the document is retrieved into memory. For example, most word processors allow you to print a file without retrieving it. If you change spreadsheet data within 1-2-3, save and quit the file; you must enter your word processor and retrieve the file before the document can reflect the changes to the spreadsheet. You normally cannot enter your word processor and print the document without retrieving it and still expect the new data to be reflected in the output.

Linking With WordPerfect

WordPerfect has spreadsheet linking capabilities for both text and table imports. You are limited to using worksheet (WK?) files, although you are still able to designate ranges within the worksheet files. You cannot link a spreadsheet file that is imported

PUBLISHING 1-2-3

into a previously existing table, however. WordPerfect has to be the one that creates the table.

Updating the links can be specified as either being done when the file is retrieved, on command, or both. Any formatting done within a linked area of the document will disappear when an update is done. This formatting includes the changes made to a Table, including the modification of column width.

To create a link within WordPerfect:

1. Press the Text In/Out (CTRL-F5) function key and select Spreadsheet Create Link.

The Spreadsheet Create Link menu appears. This menu is identical in appearance and function to the Spreadsheet Import menu in Figure 8-15 except for the title of the menu. The Filename, Range, Type, and Perform Import selections all work the same and produce similar results. The one difference is that the imported spreadsheet data will be linked and the edit screen will appear as in Figure 8-22 with link boxes indicating the beginning and ending of the linked text.

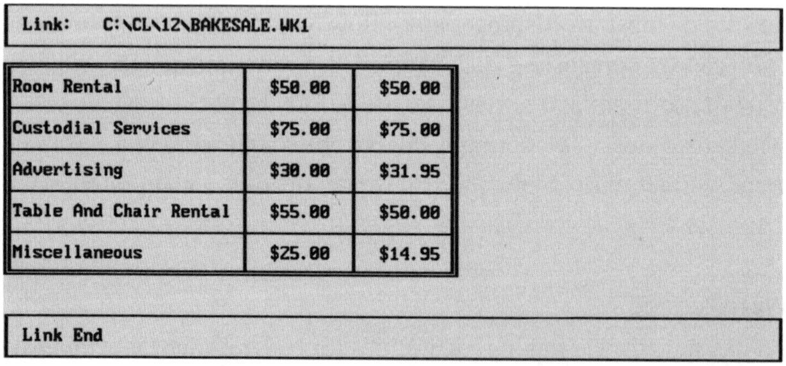

Link:	C:\CL\12\BAKESALE.WK1	
Room Rental	$50.00	$50.00
Custodial Services	$75.00	$75.00
Advertising	$30.00	$31.95
Table And Chair Rental	$55.00	$50.00
Miscellaneous	$25.00	$14.95

| Link End | | |

Figure 8-22: WordPerfect edit screen with a linked spreadsheet file imported into a table.

BRINGING 1-2-3 DATA INTO YOUR WORD PROCESSOR

2. Using the Filename, Range and Type menu items, designate the file to be linked, its range, and whether it is to be imported as text or a Table.

3. Select Perform Link to have WordPerfect import the file. Figure 8-22: WordPerfect edit screen with a linked spreadsheet file imported into a Table.

The boxed areas marking the beginning and ending of the link are not printed to the printer, they just display in the edit screen. WordPerfect does allow you to remove the codes from the screen, using the Link Options menu. To use the Link Options menu, press the Text In/Out (CTRL-F5) function key and select Spreadsheet Link Options. The menu displayed in Figure 8-23 appears on the screen.

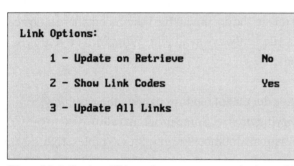

Figure 8-23: The Spreadsheet Link Options menu.

Update on Retrieve: This is where you designate whether WordPerfect should automatically update all linked import files when the document file is retrieved into memory.

Show Link Codes: This option can remove the boxed link codes from the screen.
Update All Links: This option is the command used to update all linked import files within the document at your discretion.

Occasionally, you will want to make some editing changes to a linked file or want to update just one file. You can do this using the Edit Link menu. First of all, you must make sure the cursor is located after the link you want to edit. When you invoke this command, WordPerfect searches backwards from the cursor position to the first linked file it finds. If it finds none, it returns to the original cursor position and moves forward. If only one linked file exists, the cursor's position is irrelevant; but you should develop the habit of always moving the cursor just after the link to be edited to avoid any mistakes.

PUBLISHING 1-2-3

To use the Edit Link menu, press the Text In/Out (CTRL-F5) function key and select Spreadsheet Edit Link. Again, the resulting menu looks similar to Figure 8-15 except for the title of the menu. All options work similarly except that the Perform Link option only updates the affected linked file.

Bringing 1-2-3 .PIC Files into Your Documents

Most word processing packages that can produce and accept graphic files will be able to somehow accept 1-2-3 .PIC files. If it cannot do so directly, there is probably a conversion utility provided with the program to make the 1-2-3 .PIC file conform to the word processor's standards. Some packages reference the graphic file to their documents, which means that the graphic file's location needs to be identified and maintained for the graphic to print with the document. Some packages import the graphic into the document, which means the document file is larger but there is no need to make sure the original graphic file is always available. WordPerfect gives you a choice between these two methods.

In general, adding a graphic to a document requires naming the graphic, defining the location on the page and specifying its size. Some programs allow you to provide captions. Some allow you to automatically number the graphics as tables, figures, etc. Some programs allow you to place different borders around the graphic or to shade them.

Using .PIC Files In WordPerfect

WordPerfect has all of the above described options. Altogether it uses five types of "Graphic Boxes" to hold graphics, only four of the types being commonly used for this purpose. These graphic boxes are **F**igure, **T**able Box, Text **B**ox, and **U**ser Box. They are all identical in what they can do with .PIC files; the only differences being the default settings for their appearance. Each of them are maintained within WordPerfect as separate families of graphics, so that their numbering and referencing can be segregated. In other words, Figures are numbered separately from Table Boxes, etc. This is done because WordPerfect can generate separate listings of Figures, Table Boxes, etc.

BRINGING 1-2-3 DATA INTO YOUR WORD PROCESSOR

The following example will use a Figure box, but everything discussed applies to the other three as well. Figure 8-3 displays the 1-2-3 graph that is going to be imported into a WordPerfect Figure box. It was saved within 1-2-3 using the /Graph Save command, creating a file with a .PIC extension.

Importing graphic images into WordPerfect can be separated into two sections. The first defines how the box looks using Options and the second is the creating or editing of the graphic within the box using Create and Edit. To define how the Figure box is to look, press the Graphics (ALT-F9) function key and select Figure Options.

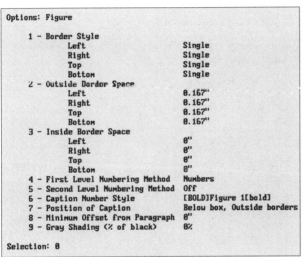

Figure 8-24: The Options Figure Box in WordPerfect.

Border Style: Each side, or outside border of the box, may have no lines at all, single, double, dashed, dotted, thick or extra thick lines.

Outside Border Space: These settings maintain a distance from the outside of the box to the surrounding text of the document.

Inside Border Space: These settings maintain a distance from the border of the box to the graphic (or text) inside.

First Level Numbering Method: Boxes can be numbered using arabic numbers, letters, Roman numerals, or they can remain unnumbered.

Second Level Numbering Method: Used to number in the format 1-1, 1-2, 1-3, etc. The same options apply.

Caption Number Style: If you use a caption and want it to be something other than the default, you can change it.

Position Of Caption: A caption can be placed above or below the graphic, inside or outside of the box.

Minimum Offset from Paragraph: If a graphic is to move with the paragraph within which it is defined, this tells WordPerfect how far up within the paragraph you want it to be placed.

Gray Shading (% of black): If you want the background of the graphic to be shaded, you can indicate the percent of shading.

PUBLISHING 1-2-3

To produce the options for the 1-2-3 graphic: 1. Press the Graphics (ALT-F9) function key and select FigureOptions.

2. Change the border style so that the right and bottom are thick by selecting **B**order Style, ENTER to accept Single, **T**hick, ENTER, and **T**hick.

3. Press ENTER to return to the document screen. Nothing appears in the normal edit screen. If you use Reveal Codes (ALT-F3 or F11), you will see an [Fig Opt] code.

When you create or edit a graphic by using the Graphics Figure Create or Edit function, the menu in Figure 8-25 appears on the screen.

Figure 8-25: The Figure Definition screen.

```
Definition: Figure

  1 - Filename
  2 - Contents           Empty
  3 - Caption
  4 - Anchor Type        Paragraph
  5 - Vertical Position  0"
  6 - Horizontal Position Right
  7 - Size               3.25" wide x 3.25" (high)
  8 - Wrap Text Around Box Yes
  9 - Edit
```

Filename: Can be imported into the document as either a graphic or text file.

Contents: Tells WordPerfect what kind of file to expect. WordPerfect can decide what goes here based on the Filename. Choices include: graphic, graphic on disk, text, or equation. Graphic on Disk keeps the graphic from being saved with the document.

Caption: Describes the graphic.

Anchor Type: One option used to determine the location of the graphic on the page. Other options are Paragraph, Page, or Character. Depending on your choice here, the Vertical and Horizontal Positions options change. Graphic locations can be linked to the paragraph in which the graphic is defined, anchored to a specific part of a page, or treated like a character.

Vertical and Horizontal Positions: Determines the location of the graphic based upon its Anchor Type.

Size: The dimensions of the graphic box. These can be set by you, one dimension can be set by you and the other be automatically generated, or both dimensions can automatically be generated.

BRINGING 1-2-3 DATA INTO YOUR WORD PROCESSOR

Wrap Text Around Box: You can have the text wrap around the box or you can have the text print over the graphic box as though the graphic were not there.

Edit: The Edit options differ depending on the Contents of the box. If the contents are text, this is where you can enter or edit the text. If the contents are graphic, the graphics editor (see Figure 8-26) appears. Within the graphics editor you can move, increase or decrease the size, rotate, create a mirror image, or reverse the black and white of the graphic image.

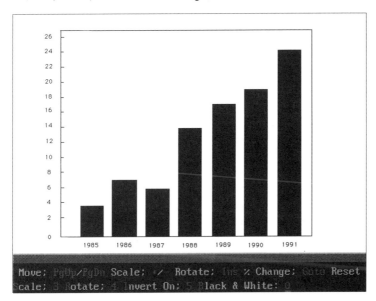

Figure 8-26: The edit graphic screen within WordPerfect

To create the 1-2-3 graphic: 1. Press the Graphics (ALT-F9) function key and select Figure Create.

2. Select Filename, type the name of the .PIC file, and press ENTER.

3. Place the graphic in the top left hand corner of the page by selecting Anchor Type Page. Press ENTER to accept zero as the default for the Number of pages to skip query. Vertical Position changes to Top as you change the Anchor type, which means it can now remain as it is. Select Horizontal Position Margins Left to move the graphic to the left margin.

PUBLISHING 1-2-3

4. Select Edit to view the graphic (Figure 8-26). Make the graphic larger within the box by pressing the PGUP key twice.

5. Press the Exit (F7) function key twice to return to the edit screen.

Since graphics are not displayed within the WordPerfect edit screen, all that displays is the top of a box numbered FIG 1. As you add text to the document, the box will fill in and the text will wrap around it (See Figure 8-27).

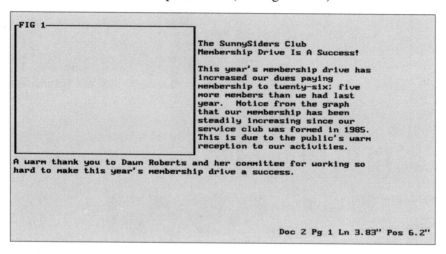

Figure 8-27: The edit screen which contains a Figure box.

To view how the graphic looks in the document, you can either use the Print View Document screen or print it. To view it, press the Print (SHIFT-F7) function key and select View Document. Figure 8-28 displays the View Document screen of the same text as in Figure 8-27. Press the Exit (F7) function key to return to the edit screen.

BRINGING 1-2-3 DATA INTO YOUR WORD PROCESSOR

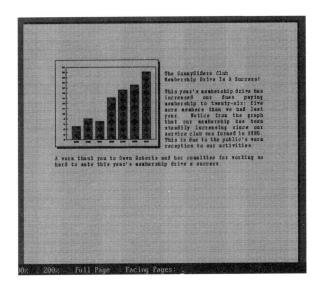

Figure 8-28: The View Document screen of the document in Figure 8-27.

If you want to change how the graphic looks, you need to consider the change you want to make. If the change has to do with the options, you will need to move the cursor to the right of the [Fig Opt] code and select Graphics Figure Options. After you make the changes you will notice there are two [Fig Opt] codes (using Reveal Codes). The first is the original and the second is the one you just created. It is a good idea to check your changes using Print View Document and if you like them you can delete the first [Fig Opt] code. If you do not like them, delete the second code and you will have your original selections back.

If the changes you want to make have to do with the definition of the graphic, use the Graphics Figure Edit command. The screen will ask you which Figure you want to edit. Type the number and press ENTER. You will be returned to the Figure Definition screen displayed in Figure 8-25.

PUBLISHING 1-2-3

Using Names and Addresses in a 1-2-3 Database to Create a Mail Merge List

Word processing merges are procedures where a master file of data, usually called the "Secondary File," is used to create individualized documents for each record. A document that includes data from the secondary file is produced for each its records. The repetitive portion of the document (the part that remains the same from document to document) is created using a file called the "Primary File". The primary and secondary files are "merged" together to produce an individualized document for each record of the secondary file.

The typical example of a merge is the boilerplate letter, where the body of the letter is the primary file and the file of names and addresses is the secondary file. Different word processors use different procedures for merges, although the concepts of primary and secondary files usually remain the same. The differences have to do with how these concepts are implemented.

Creating A WordPerfect Secondary Merge File From A 1-2-3 .DIF File

WordPerfect's secondary files are normally created using the End Field and Merge Codes functions. However, for this example you will be learning how to create a secondary file from a 1-2-3 data file. Figure 8-29 is an example of a WordPerfect secondary merge file. Each record of the file ends with an {END RECORD} code, and each field within each record ends with an {END FIELD} code. If this data already exists in a 1-2-3 file, WordPerfect includes a convert utility that can convert the data from a .DIF file to a mail merge file. Earlier in this chapter, you learned how to create a .DIF file using 1-2-3's Transfer Utility. Now you will learn how to create a secondary using WordPerfect's Convert Utility.

To convert a .DIF to a merge file:

1. At the DOS prompt, type cd \wp51 to change to the WordPerfect directory.

BRINGING 1-2-3 DATA INTO YOUR WORD PROCESSOR

2. Type convert "source file" "target file" where the source file is the name of the .DIF file to be converted and target file is the name of the new WordPerfect merge file.

3. Select option A - Spreadsheet DIF to WordPerfect Secondary Merge from the Convert Utility menu. The conversion is done immediately. When you retrieve the resulting document, it will be in the form of a secondary merge.

```
Nicole{END FIELD}
Adams{END FIELD}
9012 Hagadorn Ave.{END FIELD}
Lambertville{END FIELD}
MI{END FIELD}
48144{END FIELD}
{END RECORD}
Janice{END FIELD}
Burnett{END FIELD}
578 Madison Ave.{END FIELD}
Temperance{END FIELD}
MI{END FIELD}
48182{END FIELD}
{END RECORD}
Diane{END FIELD}
Calhoun{END FIELD}
865 Track St.{END FIELD}
Samaria{END FIELD}
MI{END FIELD}
48182{END FIELD}
{END RECORD}
Percy{END FIELD}
Cameron{END FIELD}
321 Prism Ave.{END FIELD}
Field: 1                                    Doc 1 Pg 1 Ln 1" Pos 1"
```

Figure 8-29: Example of a WordPerfect secondary merge document.

PUBLISHING 1-2-3

Creating The Primary Merge File

Creating the primary merge file is almost as simple as creating a normal document. The only difference is that you need to insert some codes inside the document to tell WordPerfect where the data is to be placed. Notice in Figure 8-29 that each record contains the same number of fields and the fields are each in the same order. In this example, Field 1 is always the first name, Field 2 is always the last name, Field 3 the street address, etc. You will need this information to create a primary file similar to the one displayed in Figure 8-30.

```
                    SunnySiders Club
                   4321 Banton Avenue
                   Temperance, MI 48182

                     March 28, 1991


{FIELD}1~ {FIELD}2~
{FIELD}3~
{FIELD}4~, {FIELD}5~  {FIELD}6~

Dear {FIELD}1~:

      The April meeting of the SunnySiders Club has been moved to
the Rec Center on Hagadorn Avenue.  It is still scheduled for April
12 at 7:00 pm.

Sincerely,



Beth Moeller
President
C:\CL\12\SUNNY.PRI                              Doc 1 Pg 1 Ln 1" Pos 1"
```

Figure 8-30: The primary merge file.

To create the letter, type the beginning of the letter as you normally would. At the point where you would normally type the inside address, you will insert some codes instead. To insert the primary merge codes:

1. Place the cursor at the position where you would want the inside address to start.

BRINGING 1-2-3 DATA INTO YOUR WORD PROCESSOR

2. Press the Merge Codes (SHIFT-F9) function key. 3. Select Field and type a 1 and press ENTER to indicate that field number one of the secondary merge file should be placed at this location. Remember, this is the first name of the addressee.

4. Because you want a space to come between the first and last names, press the SPACEBAR.

5. Press the Merge Codes (SHIFT-F9) function key. 6. Select Field and type a 2 and press ENTER to indicate that field number two (last name) of the secondary merge file should be placed at this location.

7. Press the ENTER key to move to the next line where the street address should be placed. Repeat steps 5 and 6 except type a 3 to indicate the street address field is to be placed here.

8. To move to the city/state/zip code line, press ENTER. Follow the same steps outlined above for each of the next three fields, using Figure 8-30 as your guide. Place a comma and a space immediately after Field 4 and two spaces after Field 5 for proper spacing.

9. Press the ENTER key twice to move to the salutation. Type Dear and SPACEBAR. Insert Field 1 followed by a colon (:).

10. Continue the letter as normal.

11. When you are finished, save and exit the document.

PUBLISHING 1-2-3

Performing The Merge

Once these steps are completed, all that is left is to tell WordPerfect to create the letters. To perform the merge:

1. At an empty edit screen, press the Merge/Sort (CTRL-F9) function key and select Merge.

2. When prompted, type the filename of the primary file and press ENTER. This is the file you just saved.

3. When prompted, type the filename of the secondary file and press ENTER. This is the file you converted from the 1-2-3 .DIF file.

4. WordPerfect will tell you that it is merging. Once it is finished, the letters will appear in the edit screen. There should be one letter for each record of the secondary file. Figure 8-31 displays the first letter of the newly created file of letters. Each succeeding page has the same letter with a different inside address and salutation.

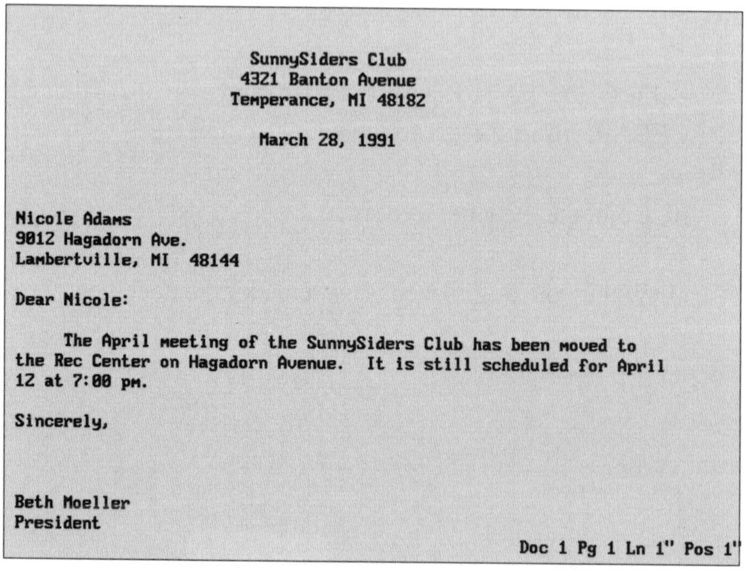

Figure 8-31: Merged data.

```
                    SunnySiders Club
                    4321 Banton Avenue
                    Temperance, MI 48182

                    March 28, 1991

Nicole Adams
9012 Hagadorn Ave.
Lambertville, MI  48144

Dear Nicole:

     The April meeting of the SunnySiders Club has been moved to
the Rec Center on Hagadorn Avenue.  It is still scheduled for April
12 at 7:00 pm.

Sincerely,


Beth Moeller
President
                                      Doc 1 Pg 1 Ln 1" Pos 1"
```

312

BRINGING 1-2-3 DATA INTO YOUR WORD PROCESSOR

Using 1-2-3's Database Features To Select Records To Be Merged

Once you understand the concepts of merging, you should look at 1-2-3's database capabilities. You can use them to select specific records for merging based on the contents of one or more cells for each record. For example, you could select only those records whose ZIP is a specific number or those people that have not paid their dues. You can Extract the selected records to the Output Range and then Xtract the data within the Output Range to a worksheet for conversion to a .DIF file.

CHAPTER 9

Using Other Graphics Products to Enhance 1-2-3 Output

The addition of the Allways and Wysiwyg add-ins to 1-2-3's basic features provide significant enhancements to the 1-2-3 output that you can create. There are new types of graphs to explore, the ability to print both text and graphics on the same page, and easy access to all the features that your printer supports, including multiple fonts and landscape mode.

It may seem like there is no need for further enhancements and, in many cases, the output is perfectly adequate to meet the needs of the business user. But there are those who will want further enhancements or who have existing graphics products that they would like to try out with 1-2-3.

Almost every graph or charting product in widespread use supports both 1-2-3 worksheet file access as well as the ability to read 1-2-3 graph (.PIC) files and can enhance them further. Thus, you will not need to reenter or to modify your 1-2-3 data when using such packages. Although it is not possible to fully explore any graphics product thoroughly in one chapter, you will have the opportunity to take a look at a few of the features offered by the leading packages. The examples for each product highlight a feature in which the particular product excels, although you will find that there is considerable overlap between the products presented. Just because a particular feature, such as slide-show capability was not presented for a product does not mean that the product does not have that feature. In the case of slide-show capability, they all do. Rather, our approach lets you learn a little about each of the products while also giving you an opportunity to look at some of the features common to the majority of graphics products. Although the packages offer many similar features there are differences in implementations, functionality, and ease of use. You have to make an assessment based on the tasks that you think that you will need to perform. You can use the checklist, "Selecting A Graphics Package" for some idea of what features to look for.

We will begin this chapter with an overview of some of the generic features that a graphics product can provide to enhance 1-2-3 worksheets. From there you will have an opportunity to look at sample graphs created in 1-2-3 and altered with one of the products. You will see that you can add company logos, use the graph as part of a slide show, add clip art images to enhance the interest level, or view a gallery of options before making a selection. Although the purpose of these examples is not to provide a tutorial in the use of the various packages, the "Closer Look" boxes provide keystroke summaries that you can use to create similar examples if you have the graphics products we discuss. However, you will find this chapter of interest even if you use other graphics products since it will provide some ideas for changes that you can make to 1-2-3 output with your package.

Exploring Graphics Products

Most popular graphics products are stand-alone packages that provide a full set of presentation capabilities. There are other add-in products specifically designed to enhance 1-2-3 graphs.

The graphics packages with full features provide everything you need to create outstanding presentations. Although these packages can provide significant enhancements to 1-2-3 graphs, they also allow you to create other charts, maps, diagrams, and

USING OTHER GRAPHICS PRODUCTS TO ENHANCE 1-2-3 OUTPUT

drawings. These packages provide professionally drawn clip art images in a variety of categories that will add interest to your presentations. Drawing features allow you to create some of your own images and you may also find support for scanning images and drawings into the package. Slide-show type features allow you to organize a number of graphs, drawings or other images into a presentation on your screen. Special effects, such as wipes and fades, and the ability to keep notes on your presentation are some of the finer details these packages can handle for you. Most packages also provide a portfolio of pre-defined graph types that make it easy to create a graph. The popular packages also support a variety of fonts and output devices. At a minimum, each of the packages discussed in this section provides support for these features. You will find that their ability to enhance 1-2-3 graphs is but one way to use their features. Although we will focus on how to use these packages with 1-2-3, you will be using only a fraction of their capability if you restrict your use of them to enhancing 1-2-3 graphs.

The add-in packages discussed in this chapter are not full presentation packages. As add-ins to 1-2-3, they serve only to enhance 1-2-3 graphs. Their limited scope of features keeps the price of these packages well below that of the full-scale packages. And they are easier to learn than full-scale packages. Because their features are more limited and their menus are almost identical to 1-2-3's, you will find that the discussion of these packages is much more detailed than the discussion of the stand-alone packages.

Using Harvard Graphics

Harvard Graphics is one of the most popular graphics products sold today. It is easy to use with options selectable from a series of menus. Release 2.3 of Harvard Graphics includes a variety of new features, such as a slide-show feature—formerly marketed as an add-in, and drawing features through the DrawPartner add-in, which also now ships with the product.

PUBLISHING 1-2-3

✔CHECKLIST

Selecting a Graphics Package

Your choice of graphics packages will depend on what you want to accomplish. To create freehand drawings, you might focus on one set of packages; but, if ease-of-use is your primary criteria, you will look at other packages. Consider the following features before making your decision.

CHART TYPES
✔ Creates all the basic chart types needed.
✔ Creates templates for all charts.
✔ Changes the chart's color palette.

TEXT CHARTS
✔ Creates all types of text charts, such as bullet, list, two-column and three-column.
✔ Allows customization of the font size, style, and color of text charts.
✔ Checks spelling of text entries.

DRAWING FEATURES
✔ Provides a full set of drawing tools.
✔ Allows you to select and work with one section of an image.
✔ Erases a single line in an image.

CLIP ART
✔ Provides useful images.
✔ Quality of the images meet expectations.
✔ Imports clip art from other sources.

PRESENTATION CAPABILITIES
✔ Supports creation of slide shows.
✔ Supports both text and graphics portions of the presentation.
✔ Stores notes for slides.

DEVICE SUPPORT
✔ Supports your printer or plotter.
✔ Interfaces with popular film recorders.
✔ Slide services can use image format.

INTERFACE CAPABILITIES
✔ Uses graphic images created with 1-2-3 and other software you have.
✔ Accesses ranges of 1-2-3 data and displays them as a graph without first creating a 1-2-3 graph.
✔ Reads data directly (rather than requiring it be converted).
✔ Exports graphics into your desktop publishing or word processing program.

USING OTHER GRAPHICS PRODUCTS TO ENHANCE 1-2-3 OUTPUT

Using Chart Galleries

Harvard Graphics provides a set of easy-to-use chart galleries that allow you to choose a customized graph type from a series of graphic examples rather than a descriptive menu list. You can choose from the following gallery options each of which provides a graphic illustration of as many as nine graphs of the selected type. The options are: text charts, pie charts, bar charts, line charts, area charts, high/low/close/open organization charts, horizontal bar charts, and combination charts.

Harvard Graphics provides eleven pre-defined and four customizable palettes that allow you to preview the galleries with different palettes in effect.

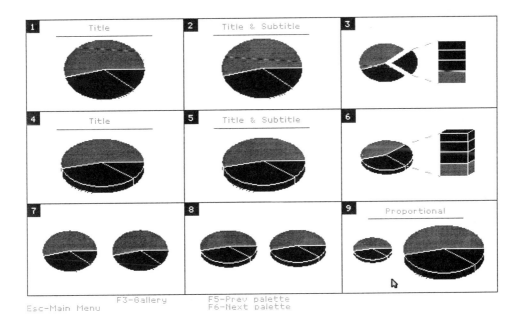

Figure 9-1: The pie chart options that you can select for 1-2-3 data from within Harvard Graphics. You can use the keyboard or make your selection with a quick mouse click after deciding on the best format.

PUBLISHING 1-2-3

Harvard Graphics Slide-show Features

Harvard Graphics 2.3 includes several utilities solely for the creation of slide shows. The ScreenShow utility allows you to sequentially display a list of slides on your screen. You can create practice cards that outline the comments you want to make when a slide is displayed on the screen.

Enhancing 1-2-3 Data

Harvard Graphics imports 1-2-3 data and graphs from Lotus .WKS or .WK1 files. If you choose to import the graph you must specify a named graph on a worksheet rather than a .PIC file. The graph that is imported closely resembles the graph that you viewed on your 1-2-3 screen. You can enhance it with Draw Partner or add it to a

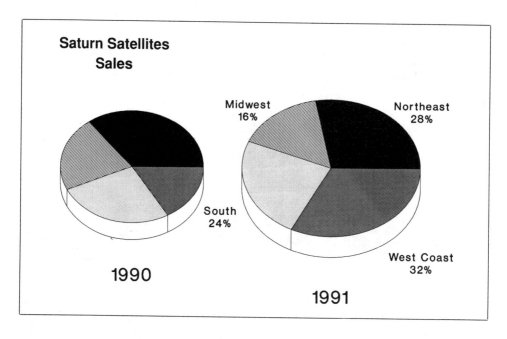

Figure 9-2: A proportional pie chart used to show the percentage sales for each region in 1991. This graph also shows the dramatic growth in sales between 1990 and 1991 based on the size of the two pie charts. Since proportional pie charts are not an option in 1-2-3, you would need to show this data with line or bar charts in 1-2-3.

USING OTHER GRAPHICS PRODUCTS TO ENHANCE 1-2-3 OUTPUT

Harvard Graphics slide show. If you choose to import the data from a 1-2-3 worksheet, all the data values, titles and legends will be imported, but data labels will not. To import the data without it being in that particular graph type, you must select Import data only.

Using Lotus Freelance

Lotus Freelance is one of two graphics products that Lotus markets. Freelance is a full-featured graphics product that can be used to enhance 1-2-3 graphs, create new graphs, add clip art and some drawings, and create presentations. It can also be used to create production graphs each month if you link to 1-2-3 worksheet files from Freelance.

Creating a Template or Backdrop

A consistent appearance can be created for all the screens in a presentation by creating a drawing that serves as a backdrop for all the screens in your presentation. Figure 9-3 (on the following page) shows the backdrop developed for a presentation for Igloos, Inc. Both clip art, a drawing, and text are part of this screen. When the presentation is created with the Portfolio features of the package all that is needed is one entry to make this part of every chart and graph in the presentation. Freelance also provides the ability to create an chart in the presentation without this backdrop.

Creating Text Charts

Freelance provides several different types of text charts from which to choose as well as organization charts and the ability to create flow charts or other

---

A CLOSER LOOK

A Proportional Pie Chart with Harvard

After creating and saving the spreadsheet data in 1-2-3, save the file and start Harvard Graphics. Next, follow these steps:

• Select Create new chart then select From gallery.

•Select Pie then Proportional.

•Escape to the main menu then select Import/Export and import the Lotus data

•Enter the ranges for the desired data then press F2 Draw.

PUBLISHING 1-2-3

Figure 9-3 (above): The backdrop for a presentation. **Figure 9-4 (below):** Embellishments have been added from clip art for the first slide in the group.

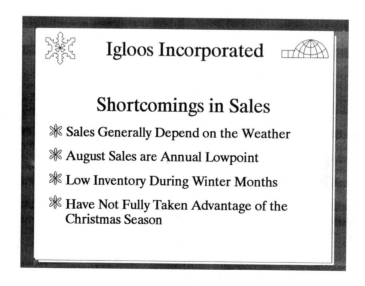

USING OTHER GRAPHICS PRODUCTS TO ENHANCE 1-2-3 OUTPUT

diagrams. You can choose the desired text chart style for a gallery of options. You can use a backdrop for these charts as well as text. The bullet chart shown in Figure 9-4 has the bullets replaced with clip art snowflakes and is shown with a backdrop.

Using the Features of GrandView

Text charts are even easier to create with Freelance 4.0 since the product now comes with a limited version of GrandView. GrandView only requires an additional 20K of incremental memory over Freelance and must always be run with Freelance. GrandView's outlining capabilities make it easy to organize the information for charts. The spell-checking features of GrandView insure that your charts are error free. A direct hot-key connection allows you to create a stack of text charts quickly from the GrandView outline that you created.

Creating a Presentation

The individual components of a presentation are created with Grandview and/or Charts & Drawing. They are combined on the portfolio screen and may be used with a backdrop for the presentation. As many as 100 screens can be placed in a portfolio. You can use linking features to have these charts automatically updated with the new 1-2-3 data. The Portfolio can be used to create a Screen Show. Special effects such as wipes and fades can be used to tailor the progression of the display shown on the computer monitor. Screen Shows can be created on a system without Freelance as long as it has DOS.

Enhancing 1-2-3 Materials

Although you can create a macro from within 1-2-3 and display a series of graphs as a slide show, you are limited to graphs alone. You can use a full-featured graphics package such as Freelance to create not only a show of 1-2-3 graphs but other screens as well. You can combine the techniques just discussed to make a presentation as described further in "A Closer Look at the Freelance Igloo Presentation," which follows. You might add a company logo to graph screens, use text screens, and add introductory or closing screens.

PUBLISHING 1-2-3

As an example, initially three 1-2-3 graphs were created in 1-2-3. Two 1-2-3 graphs of these were created as line graphs and one graph was created as a pie graph. Although these graphs convey the data that is the main point of the presentation, they lack flair that might increase the interest of the audience. The graphs can be modified with the addition of a drawing backdrop, text, and lines and built into a presentation that includes additional screen and professional transition effect between them.

The snowflake screen for Igloos, Inc. shown in Figure 9-5 might be a good introductory screen. You might use a graph with a backdrop shown in Figure 9-3 and follow it with text charts shown in Figure 9-6 and 9-7. The graph screens might be modified with a backdrop as in Figure 9-7, 9-8, and 9-9. A total of six screens are now part of the presentation. They are much more appealing than the three simple graphs created in 1-2-3 and may help your audience obtain more information from the presentation.

Figure 9-5: An appropriate introductory screen for the presentation.

USING OTHER GRAPHICS PRODUCTS TO ENHANCE 1-2-3 OUTPUT

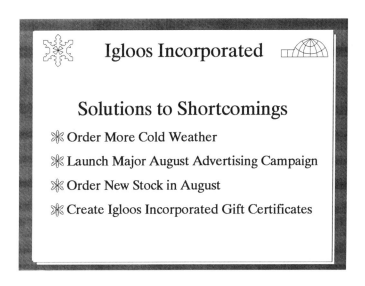

Figures 9-6 (above) and 9-7 (below) build upon the backdrop in Figure 9-5.

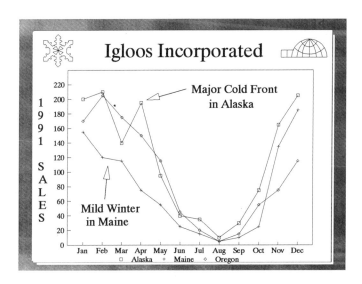

PUBLISHING 1-2-3

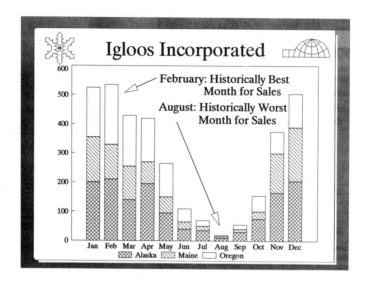

Figures 9-8 and 9-9 complete the presentation.

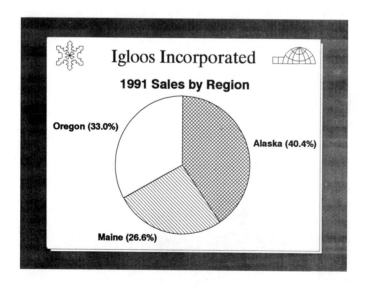

USING OTHER GRAPHICS PRODUCTS TO ENHANCE 1-2-3 OUTPUT

A CLOSER LOOK

The Freelance Igloo Presentation

After creating and saving graphs in Lotus, you would perform the following tasks in Freelance:
- Select Charts and Drawings.
- Go to the second page of a blank screen, then add the desired clip art with File Retrieve. The snowflake was one of the seasons selections.
- Determine the letter for the desired piece of clip art.
- Go to page 1 and press ALT and the letter of your selection.
- Position the cursor and press ENTER to add the clip art to the desired location.
- Add Line and Add Bow were used repeatedly to create the igloo.
- Add Text was used to add "Igloos Incorporated."
- Save this work to use it as a backdrop for other graph screens.
- Use View Clear to blank the current page.
- Add snowflakes from the Seasons clip art along with text to create the initial presentation screen.
- Save this drawing screen initial screen.
- Use File/Import/Pic and specify the Lotus 1-2-3 graph.
- Use Modify and Add to make additions and enhancements to the line charts created with Lotus. Each chart was then saved.
- To create the text charts, after clearing the view Chart, select New Text with a location of Full Page.
- Add headings and specify the number of lines needed.
- Select a bullet style and enter text body.
- Delete bullets and replace with snowflake clip art sized appropriately.
- After saving each graph, drawing, and chart, select Quit Yes, then select Portfolio.
- Enter the name of the drawing to be used as a backdrop. You should also

PUBLISHING 1-2-3

A CLOSER LOOK

indicate on the initial screen that you do not wish to use the backdrop.
- Select Print Options and check to insure that the device is the screen, orientation is horizontal, options are read from the saved file.
- Select Screen Show settings and check to insure that output mode is set to save screen file, the screen file path is as desired, and overwrite screen file is set to Yes. Also change the show list file name and set create show list file and overwrite show list file to Yes.
- Print the Screen Show to a file with Print Go.
- Select Quit Yes then select Screen show and retrieve the screen show.
- Use Edit List and edit effect, direction, speed, and time to meet your needs.

Using DrawPerfect

DrawPerfect, made by WordPerfect Corp., is one of the newest graphics product offerings. For WordPerfect users it may be the product of choice since it has significant keystroke compatibility with WordPerfect 5.1, the leading word processing package. Commands such as retrieve, save, exit, and fonts are identical with the same requests in WordPerfect making new DrawPerfect users feel as though they are instantly familiar with at least some package features. Even the codes for features such as underlining, hard carriage returns, boldface, and tab are exactly the same as the codes for these features in WordPerfect. After only a few minutes of use, there is some feeling of familiarity because the products share some elements.

If you use the WordPerfect Shell 3.0 that is shipped with DrawPerfect you will find that it is easy to transfer images between WordPerfect 5.1 and DrawPerfect 1.0 or 1.1. This will further extend your ability to enhance 1-2-3 data and graphics and transfer 1-2-3 data between the packages.

Objects in DrawPerfect

DrawPerfect supports the use of four different types of objects: figures, charts, text, and drawings.

USING OTHER GRAPHICS PRODUCTS TO ENHANCE 1-2-3 OUTPUT

Figures can be any type of object including text, a geometric shape, a scanned image, or a chart. It can be retrieved as a figure or a file. When retrieved as a figure, the entire figure is treated as one object. When the same data is retrieved as a file, it is made up of a series of objects with each separately selectable. DrawPerfect provides more than 500 figures that you can add to 1-2-3 graphs. The quality of these clip art images is excellent.

Charts are either graphs or text charts. You can import your 1-2-3 data and display it in a WordPerfect chart anywhere on a page. The types of graph charts supported are pie, bar, stacked bar, scatter, HiLo, area, and mixed which is a combination of two or more charts. Twenty-four text and graph templates can speed up the creation of your chart.

DrawPerfect supplies nine drawing objects that you can use for enhancing a 1-2-3 graph. These are lines, boxes, arrows, polygons, arcs, circles, ellipses, and rounded boxes. You can use colors and patterns to fill any of these objects. Using a mouse, you can even draw freehand.

Text can be inserted into a 1-2-3 graph in locations where 1-2-3 does not normally support labels. DrawPerfect's full selection of 30 differents fonts in a wide variety of styles and sizes is available for these additions.

Other DrawPerfect Features

DrawPerfect provides support for creating a graphics show. Overlays and special backgrounds are some of the options available. The disk that you create with the Presentation feature does not require that you have DrawPerfect in the computer that runs the show.

A trends feature allows you to compute a regression analysis on your data. Linear, logarithmic, exponential, power, and moving average trend lines are available for displaying the results.

PUBLISHING 1-2-3

A CLOSER LOOK

Bob's Stock Chart with DrawPerfect

You can bring the HLCO chart created in 1-2-3 into DrawPerfect. You can also import the worksheet data directly without creating a graph first and all you will need to do is to save the worksheet data. Launch DrawPerfect and follow these steps:

1. Select Draw/Chart/HiLo.

2. Double click the mouse for a full screen chart.

3. Import and clear all the existing data.

4. Enter range of data and perform the import, then make desired changes. Exit and save. Select a diamond tool and drag a box for the clip art to the desired place. Retrieve the clip art and place it in the appropriate spot.

Enhancing 1-2-3 Graphs

1-2-3 graph enhancements can be made by bringing a .PIC file image into WordPerfect or by importing spreadsheet data. The first graph example is created by importing the spreadsheet data. The second is created by retrieving the .PIC file image. The import procedure for the spreadsheet data allows you to edit the data. You can also set up a link to the spreadsheet file to cause DrawPerfect to import new data every time the spreadsheet file is updated. Once the data is imported, you can choose any type of graph that you want.

Figure 9-10 shows a 1-2-3 bar graph designed to show deer population by county. Although the numbers are correctly represented on the graph, there is little to draw the reader's attention to the output. The graph data was imported into DrawPerfect and the figure of a deer from DrawPerfect's figures was used to fill each of the bars. This more interesting graph is shown in Figure 9-11.

Figure 9-12 shows a chart created by retrieving an HLCO chart created with 1-2-3 Release 2.3 and saved as a .PIC file with Graph Save. A figure of the bull was added to this chart along with an arrow and some text. "A Closer Look: Bob's Stock Chart," summarizes the steps used to create the chart. Similar steps are used for the deer chart shown earlier.

USING OTHER GRAPHICS PRODUCTS TO ENHANCE 1-2-3 OUTPUT

Figure 9-10 (above): A bar graph that shows deer population by county. Figure 9-11: When imported into DrawPerfect, the information is much more eye-catching.

Deer Population
Population by County

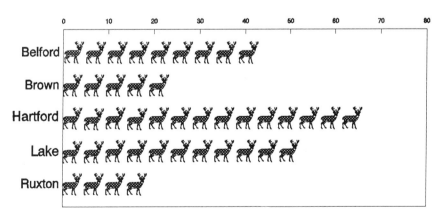

PUBLISHING 1-2-3

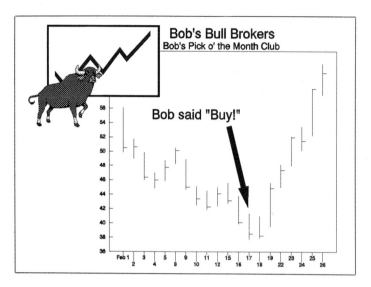

Figure 9-12: This chart was first retrieved as an HLCO chart, then saved as a .PIC file. Later graphics were added.

Using CorelDRAW

CorelDRAW is the only one of the products covered that requires Windows to run. It has the most extensive collection of clip art images of any of the offerings. It is also the cadillac package if you plan to use drawing features. Its CorelTRACE utility does an excellent job of converting bitmapped images from a scanner or other source into vector-based images that cam be scaled to new sizes without distortion.

Using Text Creatively

CorelDRAW provides well over 100 textures that can be used to fill text letters if you have a Postscript printer. These range from bars and stars to cracks and the appearance of a mesh covering.

CorelDRAW can repeat objects or rotate them allowing you to create some interesting text effects. Figure 9-13 shows ROTATE entered once but it was then transformed with Rotate and Skew. The original entry was retained as it was rotated 45 degrees until a fill circle was achieved.

USING OTHER GRAPHICS PRODUCTS TO ENHANCE 1-2-3 OUTPUT

Figures 9-13 (top) and 9-14 demonstrate some of CorelDRAW's special effects.

The WAVES text in Figure 9-14 was created with the Effect menu of CorelDRAW as an envelope was created for the text and the desired shape was selected and modified.

There are many other options in CorelDRAW which can then be used to change plain text into a creative logo that can be added to a 1-2-3 chart.

PUBLISHING 1-2-3

Figure 9-15 (top): An unmodified clip art image retrieved from CorelDRAW's large libary of images. **Figure 9-16:** You can modify images, deleting or adding objects.

USING OTHER GRAPHICS PRODUCTS TO ENHANCE 1-2-3 OUTPUT

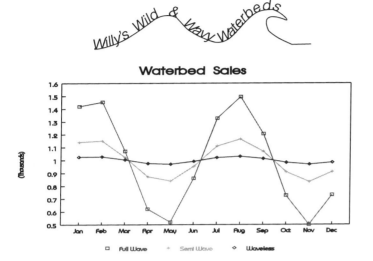

Figure 9-17: Adding simple line art to a graph.

A CLOSER LOOK

Willy's Wild & Wavy with CorelDRAW

After creating the line chart in 1-2-3 and saving it as a .PIC file, perform the following tasks:

1. Start CorelDRAW and select File import Lotus .PIC followed by the name of your .PIC file.
2. Enlarge the graph by selecting and dragging handles to the appropriate size.
3. Select Arrange Ungroup.
4. Select text where fonts will change. The font was changed for all X and Y axis labels with Edit and Edit text.
5. Draw a line or curve for the logo text at the top of the graph.
6. Add the desired text.
7. Select the text and curve then select Shift select.
8. Select Arrange and Fit text to path.

PUBLISHING 1-2-3

Modifying Clip Art

CorelDRAW comes with over 750 clip art images. These images can be used as they are or they can be modified after ungrouping to delete or add objects. Figure 9-15 (following) shows a picture of an unmodified devil woman retrieved from the clip art. This was retrieved with the Mosaic utility provided with CorelDRAW. After Mosaic expands the file and places you in the CorelDRAW screen you can make modifications after ungrouping the object. After a few deletions and one addition, the modified file looks like Figure 9-16. You might use your modified clip art image in a logo or other 1-2-3 graph enhancements. It is much quicker to modify an existing image than draw one from the beginning.

Modifying a 1-2-3 Graph

Figure 9-17 shows a 1-2-3 graph that was imported into CorelDRAW as a .PIC file. The graph was enlarged and ungrouped. The fonts were changed and a logo was added at the top. Bahama Light is the font that was chosen for the illustrated graph.

Using 1-2-3 Add-ins to Enhance 1-2-3 Graphs

There are a number of products that function as add-ins to 1-2-3 for the enhancement of graphics. You will have to decide on which release of 1-2-3 you are interested in using before beginning your search for add-ins. This is because add-ins that work with Release 2.2 are not necessarily available for Release 3 products. Most Release 2.2 add-ins are compatible with Release 2.3. Assuming that their features are not incorporated into Release 2.3 you can continue to use them. The two add-in graphics products discussed in this section are 2D-Graphics and 3D-Graphics. Both are marketed by Intex.

All 1-2-3 add-ins must be attached before you can use them. The procedure for attaching an add-in is to press ALT-F10, select Attach, then select the name of the desired .ADN file representing the add-in. You can assign the add-in to a key combination of ALT-F7, ALT-F8, or ALT-F9. If you make this assignment you will be able to invoke the add-in's features by pressing the combination key. If you choose no-key you will need to press ALT-F10 then select Invoke. You can both auto-attach

USING OTHER GRAPHICS PRODUCTS TO ENHANCE 1-2-3 OUTPUT

and auto-invoke any add-in. Although it is unlikely that you will want to auto-invoke a graphics add-in you might want to automatically attach it with Worksheet Global Default Other Add-in Setup.

Using 2D-Graphics

Intex offers 2D-Graphics as an add-in to 1-2-3 that offers a number of new two-dimensional graphic offerings. New graph types, additional data ranges, and other customization options provide for distinguishing graphs.

Working With Different Types of Graphs

The 2D-Graphics add-in allows you to create the following graph types: line, bar, stacked bar, XY, pie, filled line, radial, circle, and hi-low-close-open. In addition, mixed graph consisting of bar, stacked bar, and filled lines can be combined with lines for some of the ranges.

Since the first five graph types match the graph types available under 1-2-3 Release 2.2, it may not seem as though there are many new options yet there is support for additional data ranges and scaling options. Even though you can create these graph types in 1-2-3, you cannot use the twelve potential data ranges allowed by 2D-Graphics since 1-2-3 limits you to six data ranges.

Selecting a Mode

The Mode command in 2D-Graphics is one of the few menu options that do not have a direct correlation with the 1-2-3 graph menu. These options allow you to create a mixed graph or a graph with a second Y-axis. When you select Mode you can choose from the default single Y-axis or dual Y-axes where the second Y-axis is called a W-axis and allows you to show data ranges with incompatible scaling. Other Mode options include Line which allows you to show selected data ranges as a line. Both allows you to show selected data ranges as a line on the W-axis. Use the Select command to define which ranges you want to affect.

PUBLISHING 1-2-3

Compatibility with 1-2-3

The 2D menu is almost identical to the 1-2-3 graph menu. If you know how to select a graph type under 1-2-3, you will know without reading any documentation exactly what you need to do to choose one under 2D-Graphics. You can choose graph ranges of A through F just as with 1-2-3 or you can select G..L to choose another six data ranges.

To save the settings you choose with 2D-Graphics you only need to save the worksheet file. A file with the same name as the worksheet but with a .2DP extension is created for you. Another way to create this settings file is to select Name Create from the 2D-Graphics menu. When you select Save for the 2D-Graphics menu, the effect is the same as from 1-2-3 since a .PIC file for later printing of the graph is created.

Using 2D-Graphics with 1-2-3 Data

At first glance the chart in Figure 9-18 on the following page looks like a graph that you could create with a selection of stacked bar from the 1-2-3 Graph Type menu. Upon closer examination, you will see that there are eight different data ranges shown in the graph. Since 1-2-3 is limited to an A through F range there is no way to show more than six. With 2D-Graphics, after assigning the A through F ranges, G..L is selected and a G and H range is assigned. This allows you to see the sales from each of the eight products yet still be able to read the total for all vegetable sales. It would not be possible to show this on a single 1-2-3 graph. Your only choice would be to combine beets, radishes, and carrots into root crops and show the total for this designation rather than the three separate vegetable entries shown. Of course, you could create another grouping of your own choice, such as salad vegetables or red vegetables, but would always be restricted by the limit of six separate ranges.

Using 3D-Graphics

Most of the 1-2-3 graphs that you have seen have been flat representations of your data. With 1-2-3 Release 2.3 and 3 there is a capability for adding three dimensionality to bar graphs. With 3D-Graphics you view the graph at an angle with an additional axis used to add dimensionality. The X-axis remains the same but the Y-axis seems to go

USING OTHER GRAPHICS PRODUCTS TO ENHANCE 1-2-3 OUTPUT

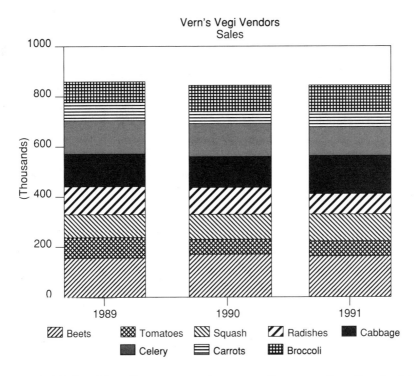

Figure 9-18: 2D-Graphics allows you to show more than more than the six data ranges that are the uppermost limit in 1-2-3.

into the screen with the additional Z-axis taking the place of a second Y-axis as it goes up the screen.

The 3D-Graphics menu is not as close to 1-2-3's graph menu as is 2D-Graphics' menu. All the data must be stored in one rectangular area and is chosen as the A-range. The options X and Y allow you to specify data labels for the X- and Y-data ranges. The Display option allows you to change rotation, axis and contours.

Selecting a Graph Type

The graph types that 3D-Graphics supports are surface—for scientific or engineering applications, lines, bar, joined bar, and financial bar. One restriction that 3D-Graphics has on 1-2-3 is that all of the data for any graph type must be in an adjacent

PUBLISHING 1-2-3

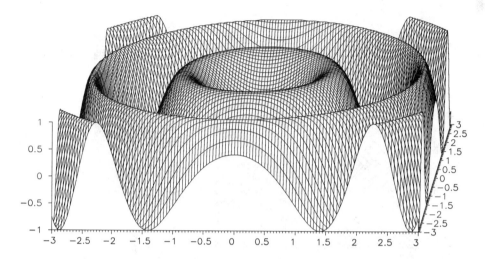

Figure 9-19 (above) might be excellent for diplaying temperatures, but this surface chart format will probably not be useful for business presentations. Figure 9-20 (below) also shows contours but is much more illustrative of spreadsheet data.

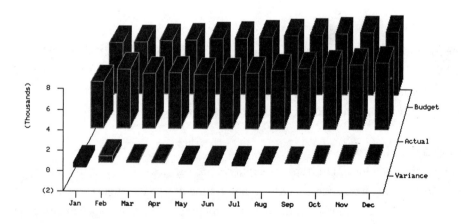

USING OTHER GRAPHICS PRODUCTS TO ENHANCE 1-2-3 OUTPUT

range in the worksheet. It must be copied or rearranged before it can be used with 3D-Graphics if it is located in several non-adjacent ranges.

Some of the graph types that you can create are quite unique when compared to 1-2-3's basic graph types. A surface chart displays contours and is excellent for charting a mathematical function or looking at surface temperatures. These charts are quite unusual in appearance if you do standard business charting since they might look something like Figure 9-19. Bar graphs are three-dimensional and are either filled or unfilled. Joined bars are connected at the top to show the connecting slopes between bars. The line graph looks like the joined top surfaces of a bar graph without the lower part of each bar. Financial bar graphs allow you to create graphs where negative values are shown descending from the origin plane. Figure 9-20 shows a financial chart created with 3D-Graphics.

The Z-Scale

In addition to the X- and Y-axis and options for scaling and changing these axes, you will have a Z-axis on three-dimensional graphs. You can set the format for this scale. You can also select automatic or manual scaling for this axis. If you choose manual you can specify the upper and lower scale limits.

Other Enhancements

You can set the number of contours for a surface chart between 1 and 15. Each number will correspond to a color when plotted even if you view the graph on a color monitor. Three is the default for this setting.

You can set both the width and depth of bars in a 3D graph. Any number between 0 and 10 is acceptable. A width and depth of 5 creates bars that look like cubes. A width of 10 and a depth of 1 produces a bar which is long but flat. A width of 1 and a depth of 10 creates tall, thin bars. A width and depth of 0 creates a vertical line.

All 3D-Graphics graphs can be rotated 90, 180, or 270 degrees. You can also change your view of the graph. With a low viewpoint the maximum height contrast

PUBLISHING 1-2-3

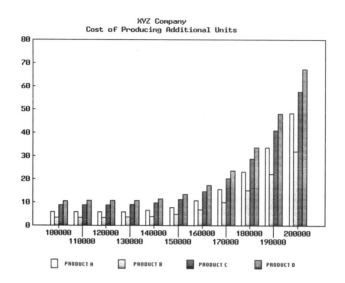

Figure 9-21(above): A standard bar chart created with 1-2-3. The same data is shown in 3D in Figure 9-22.

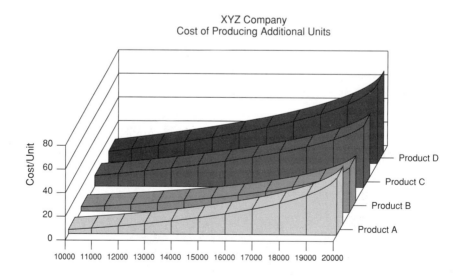

USING OTHER GRAPHICS PRODUCTS TO ENHANCE 1-2-3 OUTPUT

on a bar or surface chart is shown. A selection of High for viewpoint lets you see the maximum amount of the bar or surface chart. The Axis option allows you to turn off the display of graph grids to the left and back of the chart.

Using 3D-Graphics Options Instead of 1-2-3

Figure 9-21 shows a standard bar chart created with 1-2-3. It is designed to show the cost of producing additional units for products A through D. The same data is shown in Figure 9-22. This new chart makes it much easier to distinguish the data for the different products. This chart is a joined bar chart created as a horizontal chart. Other selections are Display Axis Yes.

If you have never enhanced a 1-2-3 graph in another package you will be surprised at how quickly you can make significant enhancements. A few extra minutes of work can make the difference between a mediocre and an impressive presentation.

APPENDIX A
LICS Codes

LICS (Lotus International Character Set) codes are used to create special characters that are not options on your keyboard when you are using 1-2-3 Release 1A, 2.01, 2.2 or 2.3. These include lines, boxes, and foreign characters. The code that represents each character is unique.

There are several ways to enter the LICS codes into a worksheet cell. You can enter the characters represented by 32 through 127 directly from the keyboard by typing a character on the keyboard since these numbers correspond to the keyboard options. The COMPOSE (ALT-F1) key sequence offers another way to enter these codes for LICS codes where compose sequences are available. To enter a character with these codes press ALT-F1 and type both entries in the compose sequence column. For example to create a British pound symbol, you would press ALT-F1 and type l then =. The @CHAR function can be used to enter any LICS character. To enter the LICS character for LICS code 201 you would type @CHAR(201).

You will need to check whether your monitor and printer support the LICS codes that you want to use. If you choose the Xsymbol font available in Release 2.3, the characters will look completely different. The Xsymbol column in the table which follows shows how these codes should appear with the Xsymbol font.

PUBLISHING 1-2-3

Character	Description	Compose Sequence	LICS Code	Xsymbol Font Character
	Space		32	
!	Exclamation point		33	♣
"	Double quotes		34	♦
#	Pound sign	++	35	♥
$	Dollar sign		36	♥
%	Percent		37	♣
&	Ampersand		38	♛
'	Close quote		39	♞
(	Open parenthesis		40	♣
)	Close parenthesis		41	♦
*	Asterisk		42	♥
+	Plus sign		43	♠
,	Comma		44	①
−	Minus sign		45	②
.	Period		46	③
/	Slash		47	④
0	Zero		48	⑤
1	One		49	⑥
2	Two		50	⑦
3	Three		51	⑧
4	Four		52	⑨
5	Five		53	⑩
6	Six		54	❶
7	Seven		55	❷
8	Eight		56	❸
9	Nine		57	❹
:	Colon		58	❺
;	Semicolon		59	❻
<	Less than		60	❼
=	Equal sign		61	❽
>	Greater than		62	❾
?	Question mark		63	❿
@	At sign	aa or AA	64	①
A	A, uppercase		65	②
B	B, uppercase		66	③
C	C, uppercase		67	④
D	D, uppercase		68	⑤
E	E, uppercase		69	⑥
F	F, uppercase		70	⑦
G	G, uppercase		71	⑧
H	H, uppercase		72	⑨
I	I, uppercase		73	⑩
J	J, uppercase		74	❶
K	K, uppercase		75	❷
L	L, uppercase		76	❸

† Indicates a character where the order of the compose characters is important

Character	Description	Compose Sequence	LICS Code	Xsymbol Font Character
M	M, uppercase		77	❹
N	N, uppercase		78	❺
O	O, uppercase		79	❻
P	P, uppercase		80	❼
Q	Q, uppercase		81	❽
R	R, uppercase		82	❾
S	S, uppercase		83	❿
T	T, uppercase		84	→
U	U, uppercase		85	→
V	V, uppercase		86	↔
W	W, uppercase		87	↕
X	X, uppercase		88	↘
Y	Y, uppercase		89	→
Z	Z, uppercase		90	↗
[	Open bracket	((	91	→
\	Backslash	//	92	→
]	Close bracket	))	93	→
	Caret	vv	94	
	Underscore		95	⇒
⁒†	Open single quote		96	⇒
a	a, lowercase		97	➡
b	b, lowercase		98	➢
c	c, lowercase		99	➣
d	d, lowercase		100	➤
e	e, lowercase		101	➡
f	f, lowercase		102	➟
g	g, lowercase		103	❥
h	h, lowercase		104	➡
i	i, lowercase		105	⇨
j	j, lowercase		106	⇨
k	k, lowercase		107	⇐
l	l, lowercase		108	⇐
m	m, lowercase		109	⇩
n	n, lowercase		110	⇨
o	o, lowercase		111	⇨
p	p, lowercase		112	
q	q, lowercase		113	⇨
r	r, lowercase		114	↻
s	s, lowercase		115	➳
t	t, lowercase		116	↘
u	u, lowercase		117	➳
v	v, lowercase		118	↗
w	w, lowercase		119	↘
x	x, lowercase		120	➳
y	y, lowercase		121	↗

† Indicates a character where the order of the compose characters is important

PUBLISHING 1-2-3

Character	Description	Compose Sequence	LICS Code	Xsymbol Font Character
z	z, lowercase		122	→
{	Open brace	(–	123	↔
|	Bar	^/	124	▶▶
}	Close brace	–)	125	▶▶
~	Tilde	– –	126	⇒
⌂	Delete		127	
`	Grave accent, uppercase	'(space) †	128	
´	Acute accent, uppercase	'(space) †	129	
ˆ	Circumflex accent, uppercase	^(space) †	130	
¨	Umlaut accent, uppercase	"(space) †	131	
˜	Tilde accent, uppercase	~(space) †	132	
■	Not Used		133	
■	Not Used		134	
■	Not Used		135	
■	Not Used		136	
■	Not Used		137	
■	Not Used		138	
■	Not Used		139	
■	Not Used		140	
■	Not Used		141	
■	Not Used		142	
■	Not Used		143	
`	Grave accent, lowercase	(space)' †	144	
´	Acute accent, lowercase	(space)' †	145	
ˆ	Circumflex accent, lowercase	(space)^ †	146	
¨	Umlaut accent, lowercase	(space)" †	147	
˜	Tilde accent, lowercase	(space)~ †	148	
ı	i without dot (lowercase)	i(space)	149	
¯	Ordinal indicator	_(space)	150	
▲	Begin attribute	ba	151	
▼	End attribute	ea †	152	
■	Not Used		153	
•	Hard space (display only)	(space)(space)	154	
←	Merge character (display only)	mg	155	
■	Not Used		156	
■	Not Used		157	
■	Not Used		158	
■	Not Used		159	
ƒ	Guilder	ff	160	
¡	Exclamation point, inverted	!!	161	
¢	Cent sign	c| c/ C| or C/	162	
£	British pound sterling symbol	L=l= L– or l–	163	
„	Low double quotes, opening	"^	164	
¥	Yen sign	Y= y= Y– or y–	165	
Pt	Peseta sign	PT Pt or pt †	166	

† Indicates a character where the order of the compose characters is important

LICS CODES

Character	Description	Compose Sequence	LICS Code	Xsymbol Font Character
§	Section symbol	SO so So or S0	167	
¤	International currency sign	XO or xo	168	
©	Copyright symbol	CO C0 co or c0	169	
ª	Feminine ordinal indicator	a_ or A_	170	
«	Left angle quotes	<<	171	
Δ	Delta	dd or DD	172	
π	Pi	PI pi or Pi †	173	
≥	Greater−than−or−equals sign	>= †	174	
÷	Division sign	:−	175	
°	Degree symbol	^0	176	
±	Plus or minus sign	+−	177	
²	Two superscript	^2	178	
³	Three superscript	^3	179	
„	Low double quotes, closing	"v	180	
μ	Greek mu, lowercase	/u †	181	
¶	Paragraph symbol	!P or !p	182	
•	Center dot	^.	183	
™	Trademark symbol	TM Tm or tm †	184	
¹	One superscript	^1	185	
º	Masculine ordinal indicator	o_ or O_	186	
»	Right angle quotes	>>	187	
¼	One quarter	14 †	188	
½	One half	12 †	189	
≤	Less−than−or−equals sign	=< †	190	
¿	Question mark inverted	??	191	
À	A grave, uppercase	A'	192	
Á	A acute, uppercase	A'	193	
Â	A circumflex, uppercase	A^	194	
Ã	A tilde, uppercase	A~	195	
Ä	A umlaut, uppercase	A"	196	
Å	A ring, uppercase	A*	197	
Æ	AE diphthong, uppercase	AE †	198	
Ç	C cedilla, uppercase	C,	199	
È	E grave, uppercase	E'	200	
É	E acute, uppercase	E'	201	
Ê	E circumflex, uppercase	E^	202	
Ë	E umlaut, uppercase	E"	203	
Ì	I grave, uppercase	I'	204	
Í	I acute, uppercase	I'	205	
Î	I circumflex, uppercase	I^	206	
Ï	I umlaut, uppercase	I"	207	
Ð	Icelandic eth, uppercase	D−	208	
Ñ	N tilde, uppercase	N~	209	
Ò	O grave, uppercase	O'	210	
Ó	O acute, uppercase	O'	211	

† Indicates a character where the order of the compose characters is important

PUBLISHING 1-2-3

Character	Description	Compose Sequence	LICS Code	Xsymbol Font Character
Ô	O circumflex, uppercase	O^	212	
Õ	O tilde, uppercase	O~	213	
Ö	O umlaut, uppercase	O"	214	
Œ	OE ligature, uppercase	OE †	215	
Ø	O slash, uppercase	O/	216	
Ù	U grave, uppercase	U'	217	
Ú	U acute, uppercase	U'	218	
Û	U circumflex, uppercase	U^	219	
Ü	U umlaut, uppercase	U"	220	
Ÿ	Y umlaut, uppercase	Y"	221	
Þ	Icelandic thorn, uppercase	P_	222	
ß	German sharp, lowercase or Beta	ss	223	
à	a grave, lowercase	a'	224	
á	a acute, lowercase	a'	225	
â	a circumflex, lowercase	a^	226	
ã	a tilde, lowercase	a~	227	
ä	a umlaut, lowercase	a"	228	
å	a ring, lowercase	a*	229	
æ	ae diphthong, lowercase	ae †	230	
ç	c cedilla, lowercase	c,	231	
è	e grave, lowercase	e'	232	
é	e acute, lowercase	e'	233	
ê	e circumflex, lowercase	e^	234	
ë	e umlaut, lowercase	e"	235	
ì	i grave, lowercase	i'	236	
í	i acute, lowercase	i'	237	
î	i circumflex, lowercase	i^	238	
ï	i umlaut, lowercase	i"	239	
ð	Icelandic eth, lowercase	d-	240	
ñ	n tilde, lowercase	n~	241	
ò	o grave, lowercase	o'	242	
ó	o acute, lowercase	o'	243	
ô	o circumflex, lowercase	o^	244	
õ	o tilde, lowercase	o~	245	
ö	o umlaut, lowercase	o"	246	
œ	oe dipthong, lowercase	oe †	247	
ø	o slash, lowercase	o/	248	
ù	u grave, lowercase	u'	249	
ú	u acute, lowercase	u'	250	
û	u circumflex, lowercase	u^	251	
ü	u umlaut, lowercase	u"	252	
ÿ	y umlaut, lowercase	y"	253	
þ	Icelandic thorn, lowercase	p-	254	
■	Not Used		255	

† Indicates a character where the order of the compose characters is important

APPENDIX B
LMBCS Codes

LMBCS (Lotus Multibyte Character Set) codes are used to create special characters that are not options on your keyboard when you are using 1-2-3 Release 3 or 3.1. These characters include lines, boxes, and foreign characters. The code that represents each character is unique. There are a number of groups of LMBCS codes with each group containing 255 codes. LMBCS codes provide a more extensive set of options than LICS codes but are only available in the Release 3 product line.

There are several ways to enter the LMBCS codes into a worksheet cell. You can enter the characters in group 0 represented by 32 through 127 directly from the keyboard by typing a character on the keyboard since these numbers correspond to the keyboard options. The COMPOSE (ALT-F1) key sequence offers another way to enter these codes for LMBCS codes where compose sequences are available. To enter a character with these codes press ALT-F1 and type both entries in the compose sequence column. For example to create a British pound symbol, you would press ALT-F1 and type l then =. You can use the extended compose sequence by pressing ALT- F1 twice then typing the group number followed by the code number for the symbol that you want. The ALT key offers another option. To use the ALT key, press ALT then type the code number from the numeric keypad. The @CHAR function can be used to enter any LMBCS character. To enter the character for LMBCS code 201 you would type @CHAR(201).

You will need to check to see if your monitor and printer support the LMBCS codes that you want to use. If you choose the Xsymbol font available in Release 3.1, the characters will look completely different than when the default font is used. The Xsymbol column in the table which follows shows how these codes should appear with the Xsymbol font.

PUBLISHING 1-2-3

Character	Description	Compose Sequence	LMBCS Code	Xsymbol Font Character	Extended Compose Sequence
	Space		32		0−032
!	Exclamation point		33	♣	0−033
"	Double quotes		34	♦	0−034
#	Pound sign	+ +	35	♥	0−035
$	Dollar sign		36	♥	0−036
%	Percent		37	♠	0−037
&	Ampersand		38	☙	0−038
'	Close quote		39	❧	0−039
(	Open parenthesis		40	♣	0−040
)	Close parenthesis		41	♦	0−041
*	Asterisk		42	♥	0−042
+	Plus sign		43	♠	0−043
,	Comma		44	①	0−044
−	Minus sign		45	②	0−045
.	Period		46	③	0−046
/	Slash		47	④	0−047
0	Zero		48	⑤	0−048
1	One		49	⑥	0−049
2	Two		50	⑦	0−050
3	Three		51	⑧	0−051
4	Four		52	⑨	0−052
5	Five		53	⑩	0−053
6	Six		54	❶	0−054
7	Seven		55	❷	0−055
8	Eight		56	❸	0−056
9	Nine		57	❹	0−057
:	Colon		58	❺	0−058
;	Semicolon		59	❻	0−059
<	Less than		60	❼	0−060
=	Equal sign		61	❽	0−061
>	Greater than		62	❾	0−062
?	Question mark		63	❿	0−063
@	At sign	aa or AA	64	①	0−064
A	A, uppercase		65	②	0−065
B	B, uppercase		66	③	0−066
C	C, uppercase		67	④	0−067
D	D, uppercase		68	⑤	0−068
E	E, uppercase		69	⑥	0−069
F	F, uppercase		70	⑦	0−070
G	G, uppercase		71	⑧	0−071
H	H, uppercase		72	⑨	0−072
I	I, uppercase		73	⑩	0−073
J	J, uppercase		74	❶	0−074
K	K, uppercase		75	❷	0−075
L	L, uppercase		76	❸	0−076

† Indicates a character where the order of the compose characters is important

LMBCS CODES

Character	Description	Compose Sequence	LMBCS Code	Xsymbol Font Character	Extended Compose Sequence
M	M, uppercase		77	④	0–077
N	N, uppercase		78	⑤	0–078
O	O, uppercase		79	⑥	0–079
P	P, uppercase		80	⑦	0–080
Q	Q, uppercase		81	⑧	0–081
R	R, uppercase		82	⑨	0–082
S	S, uppercase		83	⑩	0–083
T	T, uppercase		84	→	0–084
U	U, uppercase		85	→	0–085
V	V, uppercase		86	↔	0–086
W	W, uppercase		87	↕	0–087
X	X, uppercase		88	↘	0–088
Y	Y, uppercase		89	→	0–089
Z	Z, uppercase		90	↗	0–090
[	Open bracket	((	91	→	0–091
\	Backslash	//	92	→	0–092
]	Close bracket	))	93	→	0–093
	Caret	vv	94		0–094
	Underscore		95	⇒	0–095
⁻†	Open single quote		96	⇒	0–096
a	a, lowercase		97	⇒	0–097
b	b, lowercase		98	➢	0–098
c	c, lowercase		99	➢	0–099
d	d, lowercase		100	➢	0–100
e	e, lowercase		101	➡	0–101
f	f, lowercase		102	➡	0–102
g	g, lowercase		103	▸	0–103
h	h, lowercase		104	➡	0–104
i	i, lowercase		105	⇨	0–105
j	j, lowercase		106	⇨	0–106
k	k, lowercase		107	⇌	0–107
l	l, lowercase		108	⇦	0–108
m	m, lowercase		109	⇨	0–109
n	n, lowercase		110	⇨	0–110
o	o, lowercase		111	⇨	0–111
p	p, lowercase		112		0–112
q	q, lowercase		113	⇨	0–113
r	r, lowercase		114	⤴	0–114
s	s, lowercase		115	➤	0–115
t	t, lowercase		116	↘	0–116
u	u, lowercase		117	➤	0–117
v	v, lowercase		118	↗	0–118
w	w, lowercase		119	↘	0–119
x	x, lowercase		120	➤	0–120
y	y, lowercase		121	↗	0–121

† Indicates a character where the order of the compose characters is important

PUBLISHING 1-2-3

Character	Description	Compose Sequence	LMBCS Code	Xsymbol Font Character	Extended Compose Sequence
z	z, lowercase		122	→	0-122
{	Open brace	(-	123	↔	0-123
|	Bar	^/	124	⇉	0-124
}	Close brace	-)	125	⇛	0-125
~	Tilde	--	126	⇒	0-126
⌂	Delete		127		0-127
Ç	C cedilla, uppercase	C,	128		0-128
ü	u umlaut, lowercase	u"	129		0-129
é	e acute, lowercase	e'	130		0-130
â	a circumflex, lowercase	a^	131		0-131
ä	a umlaut, lowercase	a"	132		0-132
à	a grave, lowercase	a'	133		0-133
å	a ring, lowercase	a*	134		0-134
ç	c cedilla, lowercase	c,	135		0-135
ê	e circumflex, lowercase	e^	136		0-136
ë	e umlaut, lowercase	e"	137		0-137
è	e grave, lowercase	e'	138		0-138
ï	i umlaut, lowercase	i"	139		0-139
î	i circumflex, lowercase	i^	140		0-140
ì	i grave, lowercase	i'	141		0-141
Ä	A umlaut, uppercase	A"	142		0-142
Å	A ring, uppercase	A*	143		0-143
É	E acute, uppercase	E'	144		0-144
æ	ae diphthong, lowercase	ae †	145		0-145
Æ	AE diphthong, uppercase	AE †	146		0-146
ô	o circumflex, lowercase	o^	147		0-147
ö	o umlaut, lowercase	o"	148		0-148
ò	o grave, lowercase	o'	149		0-149
û	u circumflex, lowercase	u^	150		0-150
ù	u grave, lowercase	u'	151		0-151
ÿ	y umlaut, lowercase	y"	152		0-152
Ö	O umlaut, uppercase	O"	153		0-153
Ü	U umlaut, uppercase	U"	154		0-154
ø	o slash, lowercase	o/	155		0-155
£	British pound sterling symbol	L=l=L- or l-	156		0-156
Ø	O slash, uppercase	O/	157		0-157
×	Multiplication sign	xx or XX	158		0-158
ƒ	Guilder	ff	159		0-159
á	a acute, lowercase	a'	160		0-160
í	i acute, lowercase	i'	161		0-161
ó	o acute, lowercase	o'	162		0-162
ú	u acute, lowercase	u'	163		0-163
ñ	n tilde, lowercase	n~	164		0-164
Ñ	N tilde, uppercase	N~	165		0-165
ª	Feminine ordinal indicator	a_ or A_	166		0-166

† Indicates a character where the order of the compose characters is important

LMBCS CODES

Character	Description	Compose Sequence	LMBCS Code	Xsymbol Font Character	Extended Compose Sequence
º	Masculine ordinal indicator	o_ or O_	167		0-167
¿	Question mark inverted	??	168		0-168
®	Registered trademark symbol	RO or ro	169		0-169
¬	End of line symbol/Logical NOT	-]	170		0-170
½	One half	12 †	171		0-171
¼	One quarter	14 †	172		0-172
¡	Exclamation point, inverted	!!	173		0-173
«	Left angle quotes	<<	174		0-174
»	Right angle quotes	>>	175		0-175
░	Solid fill character, light		176		0-176
▓	Solid fill character, medium		177		0-177
▒	Solid fill character, heavy		178		0-178
│	Center vertical box bar		179		0-179
┤	Right box side		180		0-180
Á	A acute, uppercase	A'	181		0-181
Â	A circumflex, uppercase	A^	182		0-182
À	A grave, uppercase	A`	183		0-183
©	Copyright symbol	CO C0 co or c0	184		0-184
╣	Right box side, double		185		0-185
║	Center vertical box bar double		186		0-186
╗	Upper right box corner double		187		0-187
╝	Lower right box corner double		188		0-188
¢	Cent sign	c| c/ C| or C/	189		0-189
¥	Yen sign	Y= y= Y- or y-	190		0-190
┐	Upper right box corner		191		0-191
┘	Lower right box corner		192		0-192
┴	Lower box side		193		0-193
┬	Upper box side		194		0-194
├	Left box side		195		0-195
─	Center horizontal box bar		196		0-196
┼	Center box intersection		197		0-197
ã	a tilde, lowercase	a~	198		0-198
Ã	A tilde, uppercase	A~	199		0-199
╚	Lower left box corner, double		200		0-200
╔	Upper left box corner, double		201		0-201
╩	Lower box side, double		202		0-202
╦	Upper box side, double		203		0-203
╠	Left box side, double		204		0-204
═	Center horizontal box bar double		205		0-205
╬	Center box intersection, double		206		0-206
¤	International currency sign	XO or xo	207		0-207
ð	Icelandic eth, lowercase	d-	208		0-208
Ð	Icelandic eth, uppercase	D-	209		0-209
Ê	E circumflex, uppercase	E^	210		0-210
Ë	E umlaut, uppercase	E"	211		0-211

† Indicates a character where the order of the compose characters is important

PUBLISHING 1-2-3

Character	Description	Compose Sequence	LMBCS Code	Xsymbol Font Character	Extended Compose Sequence
È	E grave, uppercase	E'	212		0-212
ı	i without dot (lowercase)	i (space)	213		0-213
Í	I acute, uppercase	I'	214		0-214
Î	I circumflex, uppercase	I^	215		0-215
Ï	I umlaut, uppercase	I"	216		0-216
┘	Lower right box corner		217		0-217
┌	Upper left box corner		218		0-218
■	Solid fill character		219		0-219
▄	Solid fill character, lower half		220		0-220
¦	Vertical line, broken	/ (space)	221		0-221
Ì	I grave, uppercase	I'	222		0-222
▀	Solid fill character, upper half		223		0-223
Ó	O acute, uppercase	O'	224		0-224
ß	German sharp, lowercase	ss	225		0-225
Ô	O circumflex, uppercase	O^	226		0-226
Ò	O grave, uppercase	O'	227		0-227
õ	o tilde, lowercase	o ~	228		0-228
Õ	O tilde, uppercase	O ~	229		0-229
µ	Greek mu, lowercase	/u †	230		0-230
þ	Icelandic thorn, lowercase	p-	231		0-231
Þ	Icelandic thorn, uppercase	P-	232		0-232
Ú	U acute, uppercase	U'	233		0-233
Û	U circumflex, uppercase	U^	234		0-234
Ù	U grave, uppercase	U'	235		0-235
ý	y acute, lowercase	y'	236		0-236
Ý	Y acute, uppercase	Y'	237		0-237
‾	Overline character	^ _	238		0-238
´	Acute accent		239		0-239
-	Hyphenation symbol	- =	240		0-240
±	Plus or minus sign	+-	241		0-241
═	Double underscore	_ _ or ==	242		0-242
¾	Three quarters sign	34 †	243		0-243
¶	Paragraph symbol	!p or !P	244		0-244
§	Section symbol	SO S0 so or s0	245		0-245
÷	Division sign	:-	246		0-246
¸	Cedilla accent	, ,	247		0-247
°	Degree symbol	^0	248		0-248
¨	Umlaut accent		249		0-249
•	Center dot	^.	250		0-250
¹	One superscript	^1	251		0-251
³	Three superscript	^3	252		0-252
²	Two superscript	^2	253		0-253
■	Square bullet		254		0-254
	Null		255		0-255
Not Used	Null		256		1-000

† Indicates a character where the order of the compose characters is important

LMBCS CODES

Character	Description	Compose Sequence	LMBCS Code	Xsymbol Font Character	Extended Compose Sequence
☺	Smiling face		257		1-001
☻	Smiling face, reversed		258		1-002
♥	Heart suit symbol		259		1-003
♦	Diamond suit symbol		260		1-004
♣	Club suit symbol		261		1-005
♠	Spade suit symbol		262		1-006
•	Bullet		263		1-007
◘	Bullet, reversed		264		1-008
○	Open circle		265		1-009
◙	Open circle, reversed		266		1-010
♂	Male symbol		267		1-011
♀	Female symbol		268		1-012
♪	Musical note		269		1-013
♫	Double musical note		270		1-014
☼	Sun symbol		271		1-015
►	Forward arrow indicator		272		1-016
◄	Back arrow indicator		273		1-017
↕	Up-down arrow		274		1-018
‼	Double exclamation points		275		1-019
¶	Paragraph symbol		276		1-020
§	Section symbol		277		1-021
▬	Solid horizontal rectangle		278		1-022
↨	Up-down arrow, perpendicular		279		1-023
↑	Up arrow		280		1-024
↓	Down Arrow		281		1-025
→	Right arrow		282		1-026
←	Left arrow	mg †	283		1-027
⌐	Right angle symbol		284		1-028
↔	Left-right symbol		285		1-029
▲	Solid triangle	ba †	286		1-030
▼	Solid triangle inverted	ea †	287		1-031
¨	Umlaut accent, uppercase	" (space) †	288		1-032
~	Tilde accent, uppercase	~ (space) †	289		1-033
°	Ring accent, uppercase		290		1-034
^	Circumflex accent, uppercase	^ (space) †	291		1-035
`	Grave accent, uppercase	` (space) †	292		1-036
´	Acute accent, uppercase	' (space) †	293		1-037
"	High double quotes, opening	" ^	294		1-038
'	High single quote, straight		295		1-039
…	Ellipsis		296		1-040
–	En mark		297		1-041
—	Em mark		298		1-042
Not Used	Null		299		1-043
Not Used	Null		300		1-044
Not Used	Null		301		1-045

† Indicates a character where the order of the compose characters is important

PUBLISHING 1-2-3

Character	Description	Compose Sequence	LMBCS Code	Xsymbol Font Character	Extended Compose Sequence
‹	Left angle parenthesis		302		1−046
›	Right angle parenthesis		303		1−047
¨	Umlaut accent, lowercase	(space)" †	304		1−048
~	Tilde accent, lowercase	(space)~ †	305		1−049
°	Ring accent, lowercase		306		1−050
^	Circumflex accent, lowercase	(space)^ †	307		1−051
`	Grave accent, lowercase	(space)` †	308		1−052
´	Acute accent, lowercase	(space)' †	309		1−053
„	Low double quotes, closing	"v	310		1−054
‚	Low single quote, closing		311		1−055
"	High double quotes, closing		312		1−056
—	Underscore, heavy	_ (space) †	313		1−057
Not Used	Null		314		1−058
Not Used	Null		315		1−059
Not Used	Null		316		1−060
Not Used	Null		317		1−061
Not Used	Null		318		1−062
Not Used	Null		319		1−063
Œ	OE ligature, uppercase	OE †	320		1−064
œ	oe ligature, lowercase	oe †	321		1−065
Ÿ	Y umlaut, uppercase	Y"	322		1−066
Not Used	Null		323		1−067
Not Used	Null		324		1−068
Not Used	Null		325		1−069
╞	Left box side, double joins single		326		1−070
╟	Left box side, single joins double		327		1−071
▌	Solid fill character, left half		328		1−072
▐	Solid fill character, right half		329		1−073
Not Used	Null		330		1−074
Not Used	Null		331		1−075
Not Used	Null		332		1−076
Not Used	Null		333		1−077
Not Used	Null		334		1−078
Not Used	Null		335		1−079
╧	Lower box side, double joins single		336		1−080
╤	Upper box side, single joins double		337		1−081
╥	Upper box side, double joins single		338		1−082
╙	Lower single left double box corner		339		1−083
╘	Lower double left single box corner		340		1−084
╒	Upper double left single box corner		341		1−085
╓	Upper single left double box corner		342		1−086
╫	Center box intersection, vertical double		343		1−087
╪	Center box intersection, horizontal double		344		1−088
╡	Right box side, double joins single		345		1−089
╢	Right box side, single joins double		346		1−090

† Indicates a character where the order of the compose characters is important

LMBCS CODES

Character	Description	Compose Sequence	LMBCS Code	Xsymbol Font Character	Extended Compose Sequence
╖	Upper single right double box corner		347		1−091
╕	Upper double right single box corner		348		1−092
╜	Lower single right double box corner		349		1−093
╛	Lower double right single box corner		350		1−094
╧	Lower box side, single joins double		351		1−095
ij	ij ligature lowercase	ij †	352		1−096
IJ	IJ ligature, uppercase	IJ †	353		1−097
fi	fi ligature, lowercase	fi †	354		1−098
fl	fl ligature, lowercase	fl †	355		1−099
ń	n comma, lowercase	' n	356		1−100
ŀ	l bullet, lowercase	l .	357		1−101
Ŀ	L bullet, uppercase	L .	358		1−102
Not Used	Null		359		1−103
Not Used	Null		360		1−104
Not Used	Null		361		1−105
Not Used	Null		362		1−106
Not Used	Null		363		1−107
Not Used	Null		364		1−108
Not Used	Null		365		1−109
Not Used	Null		366		1−110
Not Used	Null		367		1−111
†	Single dagger symbol		368		1−112
‡	Double dagger symbol		369		1−113
Not Used	Null		370		1−114
Not Used	Null		371		1−115
Not Used	Null		372		1−116
Not Used	Null		373		1−117
™	Trademark symbol	TM Tm or tm †	374		1−118
ℓ	Liter symbol	lr †	375		1−119
Not Used	Null		376		1−120
Not Used	Null		377		1−121
Not Used	Null		378		1−122
Not Used	Null		379		1−123
Kr	Krone sign	KR Kr or kr †	380		1−124
⌐	Start of line symbol	−[	381		1−125
£	Lira sign	LI Li or li †	382		1−126
Pt	Peseta sign	PT Pt or pt †	383		1−127

LMBCS codes from 384 and 511 create the same characters as LMBCS codes with numbers between 128 and 255. These characters are created with the extended compose keys by typing 1− and the code number between 384 and 511.

† Indicates a character where the order of the compose characters is important

APPENDIX C
Vendor Contacts

1-2-3
Freelance
Lotus Development Corp.
  55 Cambridge Parkway
  Cambridge, MA 02142
  (617)577-8500

2D Graphics
3D Graphics
JetSet
Intex Solutions, Inc.
  1616 Highland Avenue
  Needham, MA 02194
  (617)449-6222

CorelDRAW
Corel Systems Corp.
  1600 Carling Ave.
  Ottawa, Ontario K1Z 8R7
  (613)728-8200

DrawPerfect
WordPerfect
WordPerfect Corp.
  1555 Technology Way
  Orem, UT 84057
  (801)225-5000

Harvard Graphics
Software Publishing
  1901 Landings Drive
  Mountain View, CA 94043
  (415) 962-8910

P.D. Queue
Sideways
Funk Software
  222 Third Street
  Cambridge, MA 02142-9909
  (617)497-6339

Index

A

Adding a Footer   110
  /Print Printer Options Footer   110
  special symbols   110
Adding a page break   119
Advancing to a new page   119
Allways   203
  activating   205
  attaching   205
    /Worksheet Global Default Other Add-In Cancel   205
    /Worksheet Global Default Other Add-In Set   205
    /Worksheet Global Update   205
  borders   216
    /Layout Borders Top or Left   216
    /Print Options Borders Columns or Rows   216
  boxes   226
  color   224
    /Display Colors   226
    /Format Color   226
  column width   232
    /Worksheet Column Set-Width   232
  exiting   206
  footers   214
  graphs   232
    adding   233
    deleting   233
    settings   234
    /Display Graphs No.   235
    /Display Mode Graphics   235
    /Display Mode Text.   235
    /Graph Add   233
    /Graph Fonts-Directory   236
    /Graph Options B&W   238
    /Graph Remove   233
    /Graph Save   232
    /Graph Settings   233, 235
    /Graph Settings PIC-File   234
    /Graph Settings Range   234
    F10 (GRAPH)   235
  headers   214
    /Layout Titles. *See Allways: Footers*
    /Layout Titles Clear. *See Allways: Footers*
    /Print Settings First. *See Allways: Footers*
  installing   203
  line spacing
    /Worksheet Row Auto   217
    /Worksheet Row Set-Height   216
  lines   226
    /Layout Options Line-Weight   227
  page breaks   216
    Worksheet Page Column   *216*
    Worksheet Page Row   *216*
  page orientation   212
  printing   207
    /Display Zoom   208
    /Print Configuration   207
    /Print File   207
    /Print Go   207
    /Print Range Clear   *207*
    /Print Range Set   207
    /Print Settings   211
    setting margins   210
    setting the page size   209
  shading   228
    /Format Shade   228
    /Format Shade Clear   228
  spacing   216
  text ranges   230
    /Range Justify   230

PUBLISHING 1-2-3

/Special Justify 230
type 218
   /Format Font 219
   /Print Configurations Cartridge 221
   accelerator keys 224
   font 224
   points 220
   type style 223
   /Format Bold Clear 223
   /Format Bold Set 223
   /Format Reset 223
   /Format Underline Clear 223
   /Format Underline Double 223
   /Format Underline Single 223

B

Bitstream fonts 242
Borders 105
   adding borders to your printout 106
   eliminate borders 107
   Print Printer Clear Borders 107

C

Changing alignment 95
   changing the alignment of existing label entries 96
   range label 95
   Worksheet Global Label-Prefix 95, 96
   alignment characters 95
   default alignment 95
Changing the appearance of data 97
   default format 98
   using range format 97
   general format 98
Changing the margins 119
   compressed print 119
   enlarged print 119
   Print Printer Options Margins 119
Changing the way data is presented 133
   1-way 135
      1-way table 135
      2-way table 135
      3-way table 136

   changing the column width 138
   copy 133
   data sort 142
      first or primary sort key 142
      secondary sort key 142
   data tables 134
   move 133
   Range Trans 141
      change the orientation of existing entries 141
   Worksheet Column Hide 138
Checklist for model construction 95
Color 184
   :Display Colors Shadow command 187
   drop shadow 187
   :Format Color 184
   :Format Lines, 185
   :Format Lines Shadow 187
   formatting sequences 185
   Wysiwyg display, colors 185
   Wysiwyg display, defaults 185
   :Display Colors 185
Combining 1-2-3 data with documents 255
CorelDRAW 332
Creating ASCII files 263
   /Print File 264
   /Print File Options 266
   ASCII 263
Creating special characters 112
   adding boxes 118
   ALT key 112
   ALT-F1 (COMPOSE) 112
   compose key sequence 112
   using @CHAR 117
   @REPEAT 114
   repeating label indicator 112
   @CHAR function 112

D

Data query 128
   copy record to another cell 128
   recording criteria 128
   Database statistical functions 130
      @DAVG 131

INDEX

@DSUM 131
@DMAX, 131
@DSTD 131
@DTOTAL 131
@DMIN 131
@DVAR 131
@DCOUNT 131
exception report 128
extracting a subset of records 128
locate a subset of records 128
output area 128
output area 130
recording criteria 128
selectively computing statistics 131
Design elements 32
   arrows 32
   borders 32
   boxes 32
   captions 32
   color 32
   graphic images 32
   graphs 32
   headers and footers 32
   labels 32
   line spacing 32
   lines 32
   page breaks 32
   page layout 32
   page orientation 32
   shading 32
   tabs 32
   type size 32
   type style 32
   typeface 32
   weight, or the thickness of the characters 32
   white space 32
Differences in 1-2-3 releases 92
   1-2-3 release 1A 92
   1-2-3 release 2.2 92
   1-2-3 release 2.3 92
   1-2-3 release 2/2.01 92
   1-2-3 release 3 93
   1-2-3 release 3.1 93
Disks 68

DrawPerfect 328

F

Film recorders *88*
Format lines 186
   adding boxes 186
   adding lines 186
Formatting options 99
   changing the global format 101
   formatting a range of values 102
   imbedding setup strings 102
   setting the global label alignment 102
   using the group command in release 3.1 102

G

General format 98
Graphics
   :Display Mode Graphics 197
   moving 194
Graphics adapters 62. *See also Monitors*
Graphics packages 315
   2D-Graphics 338
   3D-Graphics 338
   Chart Galleries 319
   CorelDRAW 332
   DrawPerfect 328
   Harvard Graphics 317
   Lotus Freelance 321
   selecting a graphics package 318
Graphs 56, 190
   :Display Mode Graphics 197
   :Display Mode Text 196
   :Graph Add 192
   :Graph Compute 193
   :Graph Remove 193
   :Graph Settings Display 196
   :Graph Settings Graph 195
   :Graph Settings Opaque 195
   :Graph Settings Range 194
   :Graph Settings Sync 193
   adding a graphic to a worksheet 193
   adding graphics to a worksheet 191
   creating a graphic with Wysiwyg 197

PUBLISHING 1-2-3

deleting   233
graph types   60
   area   60
   bar   60
   HLCO   60
   line   60
   mixed   60
   pie   60
   stacked bar   60
   XY   60
   100%   60
graphics update   193
Metafile   191, 198
printing worksheets and graphs   190
remove a graphic   193
setting text mode   196
Wysiwyg, graphs   190

H

Harvard Graphics   317
   clip art   320
      modifying clip art   320
      enhancing 1-2-3 data   320
Headers   109
   # and @   110
   creating a header   110
      Select Print Printer Options Header   110
   current page number   110
   current system date   110
   split vertical bar   110
Hewlett-Packard LaserJet printers   77, 83
   adding printer commands to a spreadsheet   79
   printer control codes with menu selections   83
   Hewlett-Packard LaserJet printer commands   78
   using the printing menu on the printer control panel   83
Hiding columns   270
   /Worksheet Column Hide   271

I

Importing ASCII text   278
   using Function List   279
Importing into WordPerfect   277
   as Tables   284
   formatting imported data   277, 292
   importing a .WKS or .WK1 file   280
Inserting rows and columns   120

J

JetSet   247

L

Labeling data   122
   Range Justify   122, 124
   Range Justify   125
Labels   54
Line spacing   174
   row heights   174
   :Worksheet Row Auto   174
   :Worksheet Row Set-Height   174
Linking spreadsheet data to a document   298
Lotus Freelance
   presentations with 1-2-3 data   323
   templates   321

M

Macros   148
   Macro Recorder   152
   perform repetitive tasks   148
   Range Name Create   152
Mail merge list, creating   308
   creating a secondary merge file   308
   inserting primary merge codes   310
   performing the merge   312
   using 1-2-3's database features to select records to be merged   313
Memory   67
   DOS   67
   expanded memory   67
   extended memory   67

INDEX

RAM 67
Monitors 62
    8514/A 65
    CGA 65
    EGA 65
    Hercules 65
    MCGA 65
    MDA 65
    VGA 65

N

Naming cells 124
    Range Name Label 124
    Entering names from the keyboard 126
    Range Name Create 126
    Range Name Table 126

O

Orientation 170
    :Print Layout Borders 172
    :Print Layout Titles 171
    footers 171
    headers 171
    layout borders 172
    print layout titles 171
    Worksheet Page Row 173

P

P.D.Queue 244
Page breaks 173
    :Print Layout Compression 173
    Worksheet Page Column 173
    Worksheet Page Row 173
Page layout options with Wysiwyg 161
    print 161
    :Display Zoom 165
Page layout libraries 170
    :Print Layout Library Save 170
    page layout defaults 170
        :Print Layout Default Restore 170
        :Print Layout Default Update 170
        :Print Layout Library Retrieve 170
    :Print Settings Begin 166

:Display Mode B&W 165
:Display Options Frame 165
:Print Layout Compression Automatic 166
:Print Layout Compression Manual 166
End 166
margins 163
page size 163
preview printed data 163
print dialog boxes 162
Page layouts
    :Print Layout Library Save 170
    page layout defaults 170
Page orientation 143
    landscape mode 143
        Print Printer Options Advanced Layout Orientation 143
    portrait mode 143
Pixels 64
Plotters 88
Print Printer Page 119
Printers 70
    capabilities 70
    printer considerations 70
    printer types 70
Printing in Wysiwyg 157
    :Display Mode B&W 165
    :Display Options Frame 165
    :Display Options Page-Breaks 158
    :Display Zoom 165
    :Print Background 158
    :Print Config (or Configuration) Printer 159
    :Print File 158
    :Print Go 158
    :Print Layout Compression Automatic 166
    :Print Layout Compression Manual 166
    :Print Range 158
    :Print Range Clear 158
    :Print Range Set 157
    :Print Settings Begin 166
    :Print Settings End 166
    format indicator 160
    margins 163
    page layout options with Wysiwyg 161
    page size 163

PUBLISHING 1-2-3

preview printed data   163
Print   161
   print dialog boxes   162
   :Display Options Page-Breaks   158
Providing summaries   21

R

Range names in worksheets to access parts of files   272
   /Range Name Create   272
Reasonableness   8, 12
   appropriate level of detail   12
   completeness   16
   Cconveying your message   8
   correct size   17
   design objectives   8
   different interpretation   11
   enhance message's impact   12
   highlighting problems   15
   holding the readers' interest   12
   making a plan   9
   management summary presentation   14
   message clear   11
   misinterpretation   12
   multiple views   17
   organizing information   21
      appropriate spacing   21
      providing summaries   21
   presenting understandable data   19
   readable information   16
   report distribution schedule   13
   review end products   12
   reviewing the final product   11
   showing exceptions   15
   understandable data
      graphs   19
      footnotes   19
   varying presentation method   23
Reveal Codes   295

S

Saving 1-2-3 data for use with a word processor   262
Saving a graph to a .PIC file   272
   /Graph Save   273
Saving entire worksheets for import   268
   /File Save   268
Saving ranges within a worksheet for importing   268
   /File Xtract   268
   /File Retrieve   269
Saving to a worksheet file   267
Separating data   112
   dividing lines   112
   Lotus International Character Set (LICS)   112
   Lotus Multibyte Character Set (LMBCS)   112
Setting alignment   42
Shading   187
   :Display Color Text   188
   :Format Shade   187
Sideways   241

T

25 Cartridges in One   242
2D-Graphics   338
3D-Graphics   338
Text ranges   188
   editing   189
   editing   190
   aligning   189
   text in a worksheet   188
   text to include in a worksheet   188
   :Range Justify   189
   reformatting   189
   :Text Align   189
   :Text Edit   189
   :Text Reformat   189
   :Text Set   189
Type
   /Format Font   *219*
Typeface   175
   :Format Font   176
   :Format Font Replace   176

INDEX

add formats to cell entries   180
boldfacing   179
change the font   176
fonts, default   178
fonts, libraries   178
fonts, replacing   176
formatting sequences   180
italicizing   179
point sizes   179
text ranges, formatting   181
underlining   179
Xsymbol   181

U

Using graphs to convey your message   144
   creating a graph
      options legends   147
   choosing a type   144
      35mm slides   146
      basic graph types   144
      HLCO graph   145
      release 2.3 adds HLCO   144
      bar, stacked bar, line, pie, and XY   144
   creating a graph manually   147
      Graph Name Create   147
      Graph Type   147
      Options Titles   147
      Quit   147
Using the translate utility to create a .DIF or .DBF file   273
   /File Xtract   274
Using titles   107
   adding titles   108, 109
   eliminate all titles   108
   temporarily duplicate these rows and columns   109
   Worksheet Global Titles Clear   108
Using white space   119
   white space around your information   119
   top and left margin   119

W

Weight, or the thickness of the characters   32

White space information   119
   top/left margin   119
Word processing   features desirable for use with 1-2-3 data   256
WordPerfect, use with   277
   bringing .PIC files in   302
   Graphics Line function   296
   Figure box option   303
   Figure definition screen   304
   Landscape option   297
   linking with   299
   Print View Document   279
   Spreadsheet Create Link   300
   Spreadsheet: Import   282
   Table Edit mode   286
   Text In/Text Out   282
   using .PIC files in   302
   word wrapping   289
Worksheet insert   120
Wysiwyg graphics
   sizing   194
Wysiwyg formatting sequences   183
Wysiwyg   155
   :Print File   158
   :Print Range Set   157
   activating the Wysiwyg menu   157
   attaching Wysiwyg   156
   automatically attach Wysiwyg   156
   format indicator   160
   formatting indicators   157
   What-You-See-Is What-You-Get   155
Wysiwyg formatting commands   183
Wysiwyg graphics   199
   :Graph Edit   197
   :Special Import Graphs   200
   add objects   199
   adding objects   201
   changing graphic   195
   graphics editing window   197
   moving   194
   resize text   199
   setting graphics mode   197
   transferring   199

M&T BOOKS

A Library of Technical References from M&T Books

NetWare User's Guide
by Edward Liebing

Endorsed by Novell, this book informs NetWare users of the services and utilities available, and how to effectively put them to use. Contained is a complete task-oriented reference that introduces users to NetWare and guides them through the basics of NetWare menu-driven utilities and command line utilities. Each utility is illustrated, thus providing a visual frame of reference. You will find general information about the utilities, then specific procedures to perform the task in mind. Utilities discussed include NetWare v2.1 through v2.15. For advanced users, a workstation troubleshooting section is included, describing the errors that occur. Two appendixes, describing briefly the services available in each NetWare menu or command line utility are also included.

Book only   **Item #071-0**   **$24.95**

Blueprint of a LAN
by Craig Chaiken

Blueprint of a LAN provides a hands-on introduction to microcomputer networks. For programmers, numerous valuable programming techniques are detailed. Network administrators will learn how to build and install LAN communication cables, configure and troubleshoot network hardware and software, and provide continuing support to users. Included are a very inexpensive zero-slot, star topology network, remote printer and file sharing, remote command execution, electronic mail, parallel processing support, high-level language support, and more. Also contained is the complete Intel 8086 assembly language source code that will help you build an inexpensive to install, local area network. An optional disk containing all source code is available.

Book & Disk (MS-DOS)   **Item #066-4**   **$39.95**
Book only   **Item #052-4**   **$29.95**

M&T BOOKS

NetWare for Macintosh User's Guide
by Kelley J. P. Lindberg

NetWare for Macintosh User's Guide is the definitive reference to using Novell's NetWare on Macintosh computers. Whether a novice or advanced user, this comprehensive text provides the information readers need to get the most from their NetWare network. It includes an overview of network operations and detailed explanations of all NetWare for Macintosh menu and command line utilities. Detailed tutorials cover such tasks as logging in, working with directories and files, and printing over a network. Advanced users will benefit from the information on managing workstation environments and troubleshooting.

Book only   **Item #126-1**   **$29.95**

NetWare 386 User's Guide
by Christine Milligan

NetWare 386 User's Guide is a complete guide to using and understanding Novell's NetWare 386. It is an excellent reference for 386. Detailed tutorials cover tasks such as logging in, working with directories and files, and printing over a network. Complete explanations of the basic concepts underlying NetWare 386, along with a summary of the differences between NetWare 286 and 386, are included. Advanced users will benefit from the information on managing workstation environments and the troubleshooting index that fully examines NetWare 386 error messages.

Book only   **Item #101-6**   **$29.95**

1-800-533-4372 (in CA 1-800-356-2002)

M&T BOOKS

The NetWare Manual Makers
Complete Kits for Creating Customized NetWare Manuals

Developed to meet the tremendous demand for customized manuals, The NetWare Manual Makers enables the NetWare supervisor and administrator to create network training manuals specific to their individual sites. Administrators simply fill in the blanks on the template provided on disk and print the file to create customized manuals and command cards. Included are general "how-to" information on using a network, as well as fill-in-the-blank sections that help administrators explain and document procedures unique to a particular site. The disk files are provided in WordPerfect and ASCII formats. The WordPerfect file creates a manual that looks exactly like the one in the book. The ASCII file can be imported into any desktop publishing or word processing software.

The NetWare 286 Manual Maker
The Complete Kit for Creating Customized NetWare 286 Manuals
by Christine Milligan

Book/Disk   Item #119-9 $49.95

The NetWare 386 Manual Maker
The Complete Kit for Creating Customized NetWare 386 Manuals
by Christine Milligan

Book/Disk   Item #120-2 $49.95

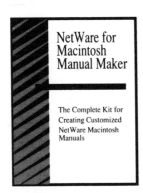

The NetWare for Macintosh Manual Maker
The Complete Kit for Creating Customized NetWare for Macintosh Manuals
by Kelley J. P. Lindberg

Book/Disk   Item #130-X $49.95

1-800-533-4372 (in CA 1-800-356-2002)

M&T BOOKS

Running WordPerfect on Netware
by Greg McMurdie and Joni Taylor

Written by NetWare and WordPerfect experts, the book contains practical information for both system administrators and network WordPerfect users. Administrators will learn how to install, maintain, and troubleshoot WordPerfect on the network. Users will find answers to everyday questions such as how to print over the network, how to handle error messages, and how to use WordPerfect's tutorial on NetWare.

Book only	Item #145-8	$29.95

Graphics Programming in C
by Roger T. Stevens

All the information you need to program graphics in C, including source code, is presented. You'll find complete discussions of ROM BIOS, VGA, EGA, and CGA inherent capabilities, methods of displaying points on a screen; improved, faster algorithms for drawing and filling lines, rectangles, rounded polygons, ovals, circles, and arcs; graphic cursors; and much more! Both Turbo C and Microsoft C are supported.

Book/Disk (MS-DOS)	Item #019-4	$36.95
Book only	Item #018-4	$26.95

Object-Oriented Programming for Presentation Manager
by William G. Wong

Written for programmers and developers interested in OS/2 Presentation Manager (PM), as well as DOS programmers who are just beginning to explore Object-Oriented Programming and PM. Topics include a thorough overview of Presentation Manager and Object-Oriented Programming, Object-Oriented Programming languages and techniques, developing Presentation Manager applications using C and OOP techniques, and more.

Book/Disk (MS-DOS)	Item #079-6	$39.95
Book only	Item #074-5	$29.95

1-800-533-4372 (in CA 1-800-356-2002)

M&T BOOKS

Fractal Programming in C
by Roger T. Stevens

If you are a programmer wanting to learn more about fractals, this book is for you. Learn how to create pictures that have both beauty and an underlying mathematical meaning. Included are over 50 black and white pictures and 32 full color fractals. All source code to reproduce these pictures is provided on disk in MS-DOS format and requires an IBM PC or clone with an EGA or VGA card, a color monitor, and a Turbo C, Quick C, or Microsoft C compiler.

Book/Disk (MS-DOS)	Item #038-9	$36.95
Book only	Item #037-0	$26.95

Fractal Programming in Turbo Pascal
by Roger T. Stevens

This book equips Turbo pascal programmers with the tools needed to program dynamic fractal curves. It is a reference that gives full attention to developing the reader's understanding of various fractal curves. More than 100 black and white and 32 full color fractals are illustrated throughout the book. All source code to reproduce the fractals is available on disk in MS/PC-DOS format. Requires a PC or clone with EGA or VGA, color monitor, and Turbo Pascal 4.0 or better.

Book/Disk (MS-DOS)	Item #107-5	$39.95
Book	Item #106-7	$29.95

Programming the 8514/A
by Jake Richter and Bud Smith

Written for programmers who want to develop software for the 8514/A, this complete reference includes information on both the 8514/A register and adapter Interface. Topics include an introduction to the 8514/A and its architecture, a discussion on programming to the applications interface specification, a complete section on programming the hardware, and more. A sample source code and programs are available on the optional disk in MS-DOS format.

Book/Disk (MS-DOS)	Item #103-2	$39.95
Book only	Item #086-9	$29.95

1-800-533-4372 (in CA 1-800-356-2002)

M&T BOOKS

C++ Techniques and Applications
by Scott Robert Ladd

This book guides the professional programmer into the practical use of the C++ programming language—an object-oriented enhancement of the popular C programming language. The book contains three major sections. Part One introduces programmers to the syntax and general usage of C++ features; Part Two covers object-oriented programming goals and techniques; and Part Three focuses on the creation of applications.

Book/Disk (MS-DOS)	Item #076-1	$39.95
Book only	Item #075-3	$29.95

Fractal Programming and Ray Tracing with C++
by Roger T. Stevens

Finally, a book for C and C++ programmers who want to create complex and intriguing graphic designs. By the author of three best-selling graphics books, this new title thoroughly explains ray tracing, discussing how rays are traced, how objects are used to create ray-traced images, and how to create ray tracing programs. A complete ray tracing program, along with all of the source code is included. Contains 16 pages of full-color graphics.

Book/Disk (MS-DOS)	Item 118-0	$39.95
Book only	Item 134-2	$29.95

Advanced Fractal Programming in C
by Roger T. Stevens

Programmers who enjoyed our best-selling *Fractal Programming in C* can move on to the next level of fractal programming with this book. Included are how-to instructions for creating many different types of fractal curves, including source code. Contains 16 pages of full-color fractals. All the source code to generate the fractals is available on an optional disk in MS/PC-DOS format.

Book/Disk (MS-DOS)	Item #097-4	$39.95
Book only	Item #096-6	$29.95

1-800-533-4372 (in CA 1-800-356-2002)

M&T BOOKS

Advanced Graphics Programming in Turbo Pascal
by Roger T. Stevens and Christopher D. Watkins

This new book is must reading for Turbo Pascal programmers who want to create impressive graphic designs on IBM PC's and compatibles. There's 16 pages of full color graphic displays along with the source code to create these dramatic pictures. Complete explanations are provided on how to tailor the graphics to suit the programmer's needs. Covered are algorithms for creating complex 2-D shapes including lines, circles and squares; how to create advanced 3-D shapes, wire-frame graphics, and solid images; numerous tips and techniques for varying pixel intensities to give the appearance or roundness to an object; and more.

Book/Disk (MS-DOS)	Item #132-6	$39.95
Book only	Item #131-8	$29.95

Advanced Graphics Programming in C and C++
by Roger T. Stevens

This book is for all C and C++ programmers who want to create impressive graphic designs on thier IBM PC or compatible. Though in-depth discussions and numerous sample programs, readers will learn how to create advanced 3-D shapes, wire-frame graphics, solid images, and more. All source code is available on disk in MS/PC-DOS format. Contains 16 pages of full color graphics.

Book/Disk (MS-DOS)	Item #173-3	$39.95
Book only	Item #171-7	$29.95

Graphics Programming with Microsoft C 6.0
by Mark Mallet

Written for all C programmrs, this book explores graphics programming with Microsoft C 6.0, including full coverage of Microsoft C's built-in graphics libraries. Sample programs will help readers learn the techniques needed to create spectacular graphic designs, including 3-D figures, solid images, and more. All source code in book is available on disk in MS/PC-DOS format. Includes 16 pages of full-color graphics.

Book/Disk (MS-DOS)	Item #167-9	$39.95
Book only	Item #165-2	$29.95

1-800-533-4372 (in CA 1-800-356-2002)

M&T BOOKS

The Verbum Book of PostScript Illustration
by Michael Gosney, Linnea Dayton, and Janet Ashford

This is the premier instruction book for designers, illustrators and desktop publishers using Postscript. Each chapter highlights the talents of top illustrators who demonstrate the electronic artmaking process. The artist's narrative keys readers in on the conceptual vision, providing valuable insight into the creative thought processes that go into a real-world PostScript illustration project.

Book only   Item #089-3 $29.95

Object-Oriented Turbo Pascal
by Alex Lane

This comprehensive reference explains OOP techniques as they apply to Turbo Pascal 5.5, and teaches programmers how to use objects in Turbo Pascal programs. Extensive explanations familiarize readers with essential OOP concepts, including objects—the focus of OOP, inheritance and methods. Readers will also learn how to apply objects to artificial intelligence, database, and graphics applications. All source code is available on disk in MS/PC-DOS format.

Book/Disk (MS-DOS)   Item #109-1 $36.95
Book only   Item #087-7 $26.95

The Tao of Objects:
A Beginner's Guide to Object-Oriented Programming
by Gary Entsminger and Bruce Eckel

The Tao of Objects is clearly written, user-friendly guide to object-oriented programming (OOP). Easy-to-understand discussions detail OOP techniques teaching programmers teaching programmers who are new to OOP where and how to use them. Useful programming examples in C++ and Turbo Pascal illustrate the concepts discussed in real-life applications.

Book only   Item #155-5 $26.95

1-800-533-4372 (in CA 1-800-356-2002)

M&T BOOKS

Using QuarkXPress
by Tim Meehan

Written in an enjoyable, easy-to-read style, this book addresses the needs of both beginning and intermediate users. It includes numerous illustrations and screen shots that guide readers through comprehensive explanations of QuarkXPress, its potential and real-world applications. Using QuarkXPress contains comprehensive explanations of the concepts, practices, and uses of QuarkXPress with sample assignments of increasing complexity that give readers actual hands-on experience using the program.

Book/Disk	Item #129-6	$34.95
Book only	Item #128-8	$24.95

An OPEN LOOK at UNIX
A Developer's Guide to X
by John David Miller

This is the book that explores the look and feel of the OPEN LOOK graphical user interface, discussing its basic philiosophy, environment, and user-interface elements. It includes a detailed summary of the X Window System, introduces readers to object-oriented programming, and shows how to develop commercial-grade X applications. Dozens of OPEN LOOK program examples are presented, along with nearly 13,000 lines of C code. All source code is available on disk in 1.2 MB UNIX cpio format.

Book/Disk	Item #058-3	$39.95
Book only	Item #057-5	$29.95

Turbo C++ by Example
by Alex Lane

Turbo C++ by Example includes numerous code examples that teach C programmers new to C++ how to skillfully program with Borland's powerful Turbo C++. Detailed are key features of Turbo C++ with code examples. Includes both Turbo Debugger and Tools 2.0—a collection of tools used to design and debug Turbo C++ programs, and Turbo Profiler. All listings available on disk in MS/PC-DOS format.

Book/Disk (MS-DOS)	Item #141-5	$36.95
Book only	Item #123-7	$26.95

1-800-533-4372 (in CA 1-800-356-2002)

M&T BOOKS

FoxPro: A Developer's Guide
Application Programming Techniques
by Pat Adams and Jordan Powell

Picking up where the FoxPro manual leaves off, this book shows programmers how to master the exceptional power of FoxPro. Useful tips and techniques, along with FoxPro's features, commands, and functions are all covered. Special attention is given to networking issues. Contains discussions on running FoxPro applications on both PCs and Macs that are on the same network. All source code is available on disk in MS/PC-DOS format.

Book/Disk (MS-DOS)	Item #084-2	$39.95
Book only	Item #083-4	$29.95

SQL and Relational Basics
by Fabian Pascal

SQL and Relational Basics was written to help PC users apply sound and general objectives to evaluating, selecting, and using database management systems. Misconceptions about relational data management and SQL are addressed and corrected. The book concentrates on the practical objectives of the relational approach as they pertain to the micro environment. Users will be able to design and correctly implement relational databases and applications, and work around product deficiencies to minimize future maintenance.

Book only:	Item #063-X	$28.95

A Small C Compiler, Second Edition
by James Hendrix

This is a solid resource for all programmers who want to learn to program in C. It thoroughly explains Small C's structure, syntax, and features. It succinctly covers the theory of compiler operation and design, discussing Small C's compatibility with C, explaining how to modify the compiler to generate new versions of itself, and more. A full-working Small C compiler, plus all the source code and files are provided on disk in MS/PC-DOS format.

Book/Disk (MS-DOS)	Item #124-5	$29.95

1-800-533-4372 (in CA 1-800-356-2002)

M&T BOOKS

The One Minute Memory Manager
Every PC user's Guide to Faster More Efficient Computing
by Phillip Robinson

Readers will learn why memory is important, how and when to install more, and how to wring the most out of their memory. Clear, concise instructions teach users how to manage their computer's memory to multiply its speed and ability to run programs simultaneously. Tips and techniques also show users how to conserve memory when working with popular software programs.

| Book only: | Item #102-4 | $24.95 |

Windows 3.0: A Developer's Guide
Jeffrey M. Richter

This example-packed guide is for all experienced C programmers developing applications for Windows 3.0. This book describes every feature, function, and components of the Windows Application Programming Interface, teaching programmers how to take full advantage of its many capabilities. Diagrams and source code examples are used to demonstrate advanced topics, including window subclassing, dynamic memory mamagement, and software installation techniques.

| Book/Disk (MS-DOS) | Item #164-4 | $39.95 |
| Book | Item #162-8 | $29.95 |

Windows 3.0 By Example
by Michael Hearst

Here is a hands-on guide to Windows 3.0. Written for all users new to Windows, this book provides thorough, easy-to-follow explanations of every Windows 3.0 feature and function. Numerous exercises and helpful practice sessions help readers further develop their understanding of Windows 3.0

| Book only | Item #180-6 | $26.95 |

1-800-533-4372 (in CA 1-800-356-2002)

M&T BOOKS

The Verbum Book of Digital Typography
by Michael Gosney, Linnea Dayton, and Jason Levine

The Verbum Book of Digital Typography combines information on good design principles with effective typography techniques, showing designers, illustrators, and desk-top publishers how to create attractive printed materials that communicate effectively. Each chapter highlights the talents of professional type designers as they step readers through interesting real-like projects. Readers will learn how to develop letterforms and typefaces, modify type outlines, and create special effects.

Book only   **Item #092-3**   **$29.95**

The Verbum Book of Electronic Design
by Michael Gosney and Linnea Dayton

This particular volume introduces designers, illustrators, and desktop publishers to the electronic page layout medium and various application programs, such as PageMaker, QuarkXPress, Design Studio, and Ventura Publishing. Each chapter highlights the talents of a top designer who guides readers through the thinking as well as the "mousing" that leads to the creation of various projects. These projects range in complexity from a trifold black and white brochure to a catalog produced with QuarkXPress. More than 100 illustrations, with 32 pages in full-color, are included.

Book only   **Item #088-5**   **$29.95**

The Verbum Book of Digital Painting
by Michael Gosney, Linnea Dayton, and Paul Goethel

Contained herein are a series of entertaining projects that teach readers how to create compelling designs using the myriad of graphics tools available in commercial painting programs. Presented by professional designers, these projects range from a simple greeting card to a complex street scene. This book also includes portfolios of paintings created by the featured artists, plus an extensive gallery of works from other accomplished artists and 64 pages of full-color paintings.

Book only   **Item #090-7**   **$29.95**

1-800-533-4372 (in CA 1-800-356-2002)

M&T BOOKS

ORDER FORM

To Order: Return this form with your payment to M&T books, 501 Galveston Drive, Redwood City, CA 94063 or **call toll-free 1-800-533-4372 (in California, call 1-800-356-2002).**

ITEM #	DESCRIPTION	DISK	PRICE

Subtotal

CA residents add sales tax ___%

Add $3.50 per item for shipping and handling

TOTAL

Charge my:
- ☐ Visa
- ☐ MasterCard
- ☐ AmExpress

☐ **Check enclosed, payable to M&T Books.**

CARD NO. _____

SIGNATURE _____ EXP. DATE _____

NAME _____

ADDRESS _____

CITY _____

STATE _____ ZIP _____

M&T GUARANTEE: If your are not satisfied with your order for any reason, return it to us within 25 days of receipt for a full refund. Note: Refunds on disks apply only when returned with book within guarantee period. Disks damaged in transit or defective will be promptly replaced, but cannot be exchanged for a disk from a different title.